Five Approaches
of Literary Criticism

An Arrangement of Contemporary Critical Essays

WILBUR S. SCOTT

COLLIER BOOKS

A Division of Macmillan Publishing Co., Inc.

NEW YORK

COLLIER MACMILLAN PUBLISHERS

LONDON

Macmillan Publishing Co., Inc.
866 Third Avenue, New York, N.Y. 10022
Collier-Macmillan Canada Ltd.
First Collier Books Edition 1962
Seventh Printing 1974

Five Approaches of Literary Criticism *was published in a hardcover*
edition by Macmillan Publishing Co., Inc.

PRINTED IN THE UNITED STATES OF AMERICA

Acknowledgments

Burke, Kenneth: "The Poetic Process" from *Counter-Statement,*
1931, is reprinted with the permission of Mr. Burke.

Caudwell, Christopher: "George Bernard Shaw: A Study of the
Bourgeois Superman" from *Studies in a Dying Culture,* 1938, is
reprinted with the permission of Dodd, Mead & Co., and of The
Bodley Head, Ltd.

Eliot. T. S.: "Religion and Literature" from *Essays Ancient and
Modern,* 1936, is reprinted with the permission of Harcourt,
Brace & World, Inc., and of Faber & Faber, Ltd.

Fiedler, Leslie: "Come back to the Raft Ag'in, Huck Honey" from
An End of Innocence, 1952, is reprinted with the permission of
Mr. Fiedler.

Fuller, Edmund: "The New Compassion in the American Novel"
from *Man in Modern Fiction,* 1957, is reprinted with the permission of Mr. Fuller and of Random House, Inc.

Gorer, Geoffrey: "Myth in Jane Austen" from *American Imago,*
1941, is reprinted with the permission of George B. Wilbur,
Managing Editor.

Heilman, Robert: *"The Turn of the Screw* as Poem" from *The University of Kansas City Review* XIV, No. 4, (Summer, 1948), is reprinted with the permission of *The University of Kansas City Review* and of Mr. Heilman.

Krutch, Joseph: "The Tragic Fallacy" from *The Modern Temper,* 1929, is reprinted with the permission of Harcourt, Brace & World, Inc.

Lesser, Simon O.: "The Image of the Father" from *Partisan Review* XXII, No. 3 (Summer, 1955), is reprinted with the permission of Mr. Lesser and of *Partisan Review.* The article, somewhat expanded, is part of Mr. Lesser's *Fiction and the Unconscious,* 1957.

Murray, Gilbert: "Hamlet and Orestes" from *The Classical Tradition in Poetry,* 1927, is reprinted with the permission of The President and Fellows of Harvard College (Harvard University Press).

Olson, Elder: "Sailing to Byzantium: Prolegomena to a Poetics of the Lyric" from *The University of Kansas City Review* VIII, No. 3 (Spring, 1942), is reprinted with the permission of Mr. Olson and of *The University of Kansas City Review.*

Orwell, George: "Rudyard Kipling" from *Dickens, Dali and Others,* 1946, is reprinted with the permission of Martin Secker & Warburg Ltd., and Harcourt, Brace & World, Inc.

Smith, James: "As You Like It" from *Scrutiny* IX., No. 1 (1940-41) is reprinted with the permission of Mr. Smith.

To my parents

Wilbur Stewart and Gertrude Haven Scott

Contents

Argument

FIRST, IT SEEMS ADVISABLE to insist that the title of this book is deliberate: the organizational principle of the selection has to do with critical *approaches* rather than with critics. Without this distinction, the reader would rightly be outraged at the omission of essays by such writers as I. A. Richards, Lionel Trilling, Sir Herbert Read, Yvor Winters, and many others. But my choice has been determined chiefly by the desire to find clear examples, whoever the authors, of each of the five categories of modern criticism—Moral, Psychological, Sociological, Formalistic, and Archetypal.

It may seem that my arrangement represents too tidy a schematism. I should be forced to admit the validity of this charge, if I had proposed these five approaches as absolutely comprehensive. No; there are many good critical pieces which defy the compulsion to pigeonhole; and it is equally foolish to suppose that any critic deserving of continued attention will stay within the confines of a single approach. On the contrary, he is likely to employ that method—or better, those methods in combination—which best suit his knowledge, his particular critical sensitivities, and the work of art before him.

But I do maintain that, very broadly speaking, most of the critical efforts of our time lend themselves to the categories I have used here. For instance, Irving Babbitt, T. S. Eliot (in his later development) and Edmund Fuller have chosen to consider literature for its moral applications to humanity. Although this has always been of concern to critics and aestheticians (for example, Plato and Sir Philip Sidney), the twentieth century impulse to make this relationship reflects concern with the abandonment of Victorian values, and with the replacement of faith in some traditional code, by faith in science.

While the Humanists are trying to break away from the limitations of science, another group has been happy to use the terms and insights of a new science, Psychology, as a means of interpreting literature. Thus Kenneth Burke has studied the poetic process as the poet's discovery of symbols to express his emotions, and as the arrangement of them to communicate his experience; Geoffrey Gorer has psychoanalyzed the author of *Pride and Prejudice;* Simon Lesser has examined the unconscious drives of two characters in modern fiction.

Another field developed in our time, Sociology, has modified the traditional historical research of scholars. By considering a work of art emphatically as a consequence of the social milieu, or as affecting it, a critical school has introduced a new tone of literary judgment. Joseph Wood Krutch relates the failure of modern tragedy to the quality of our modern temper, and George Orwell shows relationships between the art of Kipling and the intellectual atmosphere of his time. In the twenties and thirties especially, literary judgment was bound up with political and economic values. Caudwell's essay on Shaw is one of the best examples of the Marxist approach.

The most influential group has consisted of critics like James Smith, Olson, and Brooks, who have eschewed the relationship between art and aspects of society, history, or personal biography. They have concentrated on the structure, the *form* of literary pieces, examining with such scrupulosity as to seem scientific in their analyses.

A still more recent critical approach might be called archetypal. Its concern is with some human or social pattern unrelated to particular time, yet to be found in particular works of literature, as if the unconscious mind of the human race were partially the author. Gilbert Murray shows that both *Hamlet* and the Orestes story are instances of some basic plot of the son-mother relationship. Heilman treats *The Turn of the Screw* as a variant of the tale of the Garden of Eden. And Fiedler finds in *The Adventures of Huckleberry Finn* a surprising cultural pattern of the United States.

There are two other approaches unrepresented here, however. One concerns itself with the particular literary tradition behind the work of art; noting, for example, the place of Shakespeare's sonnets within the sonnet tradition; or the effect of the Petrarchan tradition upon the poems of Donne, and of these upon later writers. Such studies (characteristically the work of scholars with a leaning toward literary history rather than evaluation) are of great interest and value; but I agree with a general tendency to make a separation between them and essays in criticism.

A second approach also unrepresented is the impressionistic. Everyone has impressions in the face of literary experience, and many are compelled to record them. Their value depends, of course, upon the taste, knowledge, and writing ability of the critic. But by the very nature of the "type," such essays are either beyond grouping, or they fall into one or another of the categories used here.

In my teaching experience, I have concluded that the student who knows he has things to say about a work of literature, but has no direction by which to shape his perceptions, finds his problem solved by taking on the discipline and organization of one of the five approaches used here. If he does not wish to try his own hand at practical criticism, he will, I believe, find that his study of these essays and their groupings will unravel what often seems the maze of contemporary criticism.

In the introductions, I have tried to touch on three elements of each approach (though not necessarily in this order): its origins and development, its nature, and its limitations. My purpose has not been to write a scholarly treatise about each type, but, of course, I have aimed at accuracy. With each introduction, there is a bibliography. Once again, the intention was not to be comprehensive, but rather to suggest books and articles that further define the particular approach; that further illustrate the application of the approach; or that quarrel with the kind. With such references, the reader can go considerably further into each of the methods, according to his interests. Aside from the critical pieces themselves, the books which will be of greatest guidance, as they have been to me, are the following: Wellek and Warren,

Theory of Literature, 1942; Stanley Hyman, *The Armed Vision*, 1948; Charles Glicksburg, *American Literary Criticism, 1900-1950*, 1951; William Van O'Connor, *An Age of Criticism, 1900-1950*, 1952; Floyd Stovall, editor, *The Development of American Literary Criticism*, 1955; David Daiches, *Critical Approaches to Literature*, 1956; J. P. Pritchard, *Criticism in America*, 1956; W. Y. Tindall, *Forces in Modern British Literature, 1885-1956* (Vintage Books edition), 1956; and Wimsatt and Brooks, *Literary Criticism, A Short History*, 1957.

* * *

I want to acknowledge the aid of my wife, Ann Elizabeth Scott, and my friend, Edward L. Hubler. Their interest and help were of considerable importance to me; I thank them both, heartily.

Garden City, N. Y., 1961

Five Approaches of Literary Criticism

The Background

IN THE EARLY YEARS of this century, literary criticism was dominated by academicians: W. C. Brownell, George Woodberry, and George Santayana in America; George Saintsbury, Sir Walter Raleigh, and A. C. Bradley in England. Curiously, the leadership was to pass from the hands of the professors until the thirties, when literary criticism once again became closely associated with personalities from the collegiate world, both as writers for and editors of critical journals. By and large the early critics were carrying on the tradition of Matthew Arnold although their lesser colleagues diluted Arnold's "high seriousness" into genteel respectability. In general, they were thoughtful, fair-minded upholders of an intelligent ideal; but they seemed unable to germinate seeds of the criticism of the immediate future. From the present point of view, they were spokesmen of forces that were in process of being rejected.

The job of destroying the images of the past was taken on chiefly by three men: G. B. Shaw, whose quarrel with the gods was articulated as early as 1885, when he entered journalism, and was continued in the prefaces to his many plays; James Gibbons Huneker, whose essays on the various arts appeared in the *New York Sun* from 1900 on; and H. L. Mencken, who became literary critic of *The Smart Set* in 1908. These three marshaled their wit, intelligence, wide reading, and love of shock to unseat the Kronos of Victorianism, although either they had no Zeus to nominate, or their candidates for the office were not entirely acceptable to the future. Their chief contribution to twentieth century criticism now seems to be their successful onslaught against Provincialism, Puritan prudery, and Philistinism—in general, the use of moral respectability as a literary criterion.

In 1911 Randolph Bourne in his *Youth and Life* called for a vigorous reexamination of the past. Van Wyck Brooks responded with his *America's Coming of Age* in 1915, and was soon joined by others (Waldo Frank and Paul Rosenfeld, for example), in looking hard at the American culture, both past and present, and finding it wanting. Something of the same sort of reappraisal could be seen in England, in the war poetry of W. W. Gibson and Siegfried Sassoon. These and others were the spokemen of the young men of that decade whose natural inclination was to reject the past as provincial and outmoded, and the present as materialistic and tradition-bound. Their disillusionment with the manners, methods, and values of the preceding generations extended to the anaemic and respectable art then current.

This is perhaps enough to indicate the role of the Beo-wulfs who struggled against the Grendel-like grip of Victorianism. Meanwhile, others were more positively trying to shape new literary attitudes. In 1910, in his famous address, "The New Criticism," at Columbia University, Joel Spingarn rejected, as literary method, the academic classification of literature into periods and groups. Relying on the aesthetics of Croce, he demanded that each individual work of art be regarded in itself. There is dispute over his view that art is expression and criticism the study of that expression.[1] Paul Elmer More declared that this was to make criticism into impression—that is, the irresponsible adventure of the soul as it experienced a work of art. But it is also possible to understand Spingarn's position as one eschewing impressionism, and calling on the critic to attend scrupulously and rigorously to the particular work of art; in this reading, he looks toward the later formalistic criticism of the thirties. At least in dismissing the professorial tendency to categorize and to seek the moral significance of literature, Spingarn helped create an atmosphere congenial to artistic and critical experiment.

The "literary renaissance" of our time is usually dated from 1912, the year the magazine *Poetry* was founded. Certainly then there was in the air a sense of a second literary coming. The editors of *Poetry* announced, "We believe that

[1] So More summarized it in "The Demon of The Absolute."

there is a public for poetry, that it will grow";[2] and Edwin Marsh, introducing the first volume of *Georgian Poetry*, wrote, "This volume is issued in the belief that English poetry is now once again putting on a new strength and beauty." [3] "Little" magazines began to serve as organs for a more vigor-out art, now unchained from Victorian modes and attitudes; experimentalism flourished: imagism, vorticism, expressionism, Georgian poetry, bitter satire.

Two of these movements suggest the crucial quality of the period. The Georgians seemed not so much to be attacking the old, as trying to retrieve from it what was valid. So they returned, in a period of chaos and urbanism, to the simplicities of rural comforts and beauties, expressed by easily apprehended techniques. The movement was short-lived; the inclusion in their 1916-1917 volume of some bitter war poets indicates that the revulsion against a war-torn, God-abandoned world could not be assuaged by a refusal to face it.

The career of Imagism, too, was brief; but unlike that of the Georgians, it left its mark upon poets and poetry that followed. Its main intellectual force was given by T. E. Hulme, who advocated a "dry and hard" kind of poetry which would repudiate the softness of Romanticism. The enunciated ideals of Imagism show how much the thought, at least, if not the practice was in the vanguard: the emphasis was to be on the precise presentation of visual images, the vocabulary was to be ordinary but exact, the verse technique as experimental as the writers chose, and the selection of subject matter, completely free. In their repudiation of the "high seriousness" of Arnold, and in fact of all values, the Imagists showed their concentration on technique.

So: the taboo-breaking of Shaw, Huneker, and Mencken; a new body of writing, chiefly poetic, that was capable of arousing lively critical attention; yet in literary criticism, still no dominating method. The assaulters of the household gods of the past had relied more or less on the vigor of their own

[2] Quoted in Floyd Stovall, ed., *The Development of American Literary Criticism*, p. 169.
[3] Quoted in David Daiches, *Poetry and the Modern World*, p. 38.

minds and taste. Huneker's frank admission that his essays
were "a record of some personal preferences, not an attempt
at critical evaluation" [4] broadly describes the efforts, I think,
of Shaw and Mencken and even, to some degree, of the
younger firebrand, Ezra Pound.

Pound had reached many of the conclusions of Hulme, independently, from his study of Provençal poetry, Latin and
Greek lyrics, and the classical poetry of the Orient. These
ideas he urged upon almost anyone interested and slightly
sympathetic, but especially, of course, upon T. S. Eliot. These
two extraordinary forces in both creative and critical literature sanctioned the close study of techniques of writing, and
stimulated readers and poets to distinguish between aesthetic
experience, and politics, religion, morality, ethics, and so on.
More than this, they offered examples of the close study of
form. Their early theory and practice are surely the ancestors
of the formalistic criticism of the thirties; and with Huneker,
they extended the subject matter of criticism by introducing
the literature of Europe.

The main conditions necessary to the development of a
critical movement by this time were in existence: release
from the criteria of the past; a new body of creative writing
worthy of critical attention; and a sense of excitement (not
optimism, however) about the future of literature. Oddly
enough, the first group of critics who gathered together with
common ideals of examination and evaluation were not the
aficionados of experiment, but the conservators of the Ar-
noldian tradition: the Neo-Humanists.

[4] Quoted in Floyd Stovall, ed., *op. cit.*, p. 166.

THE MORAL APPROACH:

LITERATURE
AND MORAL IDEAS

Introduction

OF THE VARIOUS TYPES of criticism practiced today, the moral approach has undoubtedly the longest history. Plato was concerned with the moral effect the poet might have in his ideal Republic; Horace gave great weight to the usefulness as well as the beauty of poetry; Renaissance figures, like Sir Philip Sidney, were similarly concerned. Dr. Johnson, the great cham of eighteenth century "common sense" fortified by intellectual power, did not hesitate to judge the moral content of the writers whom he discussed in *The Lives of the Poets*. Matthew Arnold argued the importance of the "high seriousness" of art.

All of these are thoughtful spokesmen of the conviction that the importance of literature is not merely in its way of saying, but also in what it says. The dichotomy—often expressed as "form and content"—has been for our time an important one since the Formalists have argued for the heavy emphasis, in the practice of criticism, upon the way of saying, the arrangement of the parts, the "how" of a poem's meaning, while moral critics have attended to the "what" of meaning.

In the twentieth century, the impulse toward moral evaluation has been expressed chiefly by writers who are grouped by the label, Neo-Humanist. Their chief interest lies in literature as a "criticism" of life. To them, the study of the technique of literature is a study of means, whereas they are concerned with the ends of literature as affecting man, with literature as it takes its place in the human forum of ideas and attitudes.

Their analysis of man is traditional, going back to that of the Renaissance Humanists. Accordingly, man is a being who may be distinguished from the animal by his reason and his possession of ethical standards. He stands as a free being, prone to animalistic urges or egocentric yawps; but is respon-

sible to place these tendencies, insofar as he wishes to culti-
vate his peculiarly human nature, under the control of reason.
Freedom is thus not only liberation from circumstances, but
subjection to "inner law." So the watchwords of Humanism are
order, restraint, discipline.

The twentieth century critical movement which associated
itself with this philosophical position was originally American. Paul Elmer More had been writing since 1904, when the
first of his *Shelburne Essays* appeared, and Irving Babbitt
took a parallel position with *Literature and the American
College* in 1908. At first, there was a very small audience,
even less a sympathetic one. The growing assault on the past
naturally included an attack on those who, like Babbitt and
More, defended the past. It was difficult for them to make
headway in a time of skepticism toward traditional values,
and of self-expressive experiments in the arts. In short, they
were for a while overshadowed by the debunkers, iconoclasts,
and experimenters who were having their day. But in the
twenties, more respectful attention was given them, and they
were joined by a number of writers like Norman Foerster,
Harry Hayden Clark, G. R. Elliott, Robert Shafer, Frank
Jewett Mather, Gorham Munson, and, for a time, Stuart
Sherman Pratt. These were enough to make a school, and the
name "Neo-Humanist" became current as a term to describe
their position in literary criticism.

In practice, they tended to oppose two literary tendencies:
Naturalism, with its debased view of man, denying him free
will and responsibility; and Romanticism, with its excessive
cultivation of the ego and sympathy with comparatively unrestrained expression. These tendencies, of course, included
much of the contemporaneous literature, so that to some
opponents the Neo-Humanists seemed reactionary in taste,
while their strong sense of morality led to a charge of ethical
hyperorthodoxy. Yet many of these Neo-Humanists strove
chiefly to unite moral earnestness, based on a thoughtful and
dignified concept of man's nature, with aesthetic sensitivity.

Something like the end of the movement occurred in the
early thirties. The newer ontological and sociological ap-

proaches (the latter often offering its own kind of moral dogmatism) attracted many of the younger critics. Babbitt's death in 1933 and More's in 1937 took the strongest defenders of Humanism from the ranks. But from our present point of view, it is possible to see that Humanism did not die, so much as it underwent a rebirth with modification, into Religious Humanism.

Early in the century, T. E. Hulme had expressed a division between his own position and that of the Neo-Humanists, although he was as strongly opposed as they to the softness and confusion of Romanticism. The difference came down to this: whether the moralist would or would not acknowledge supernatural sanction for the moral standards he held up to the arts. The Neo-Humanists themselves were unsettled about the question: Paul Elmer More became associated with institutional religion and G. R. Elliott declared positively the necessity of an alliance between religion and morality; but by and large, the group followed Babbitt's lead in remaining secular or religiously noncommittal. In 1927 and 1929, T. S. Eliot forcefully criticized both Babbitt and Foerster for this central weakness as he saw it: morality that has no vindication outside of itself cannot compel reasonable belief.

The result of this intramural turmoil was, finally, to incorporate the warrant of religious persuasion into the recommendation of moral standards. So, when the movement died in its early form, the values survived, and still survive, chiefly in alliance with religion. The term "Christian Humanist," for example, may justly be applied to T. S. Eliot, and is frankly accepted by a number of scholars and critics, like Edmund Fuller and Hyatt Waggoner, as indicating the focus of their critical view.

The moral approach to literature is too basic to human interests to exist only within the confines of a group. F. R. Leavis, among English critics, and Yvor Winters, among Americans, express the traditional concern for the moral ends of literature, although the critical activities of both are too various to permit the term "Humanist" to define their approach. Winters, for example, has been described as making "the same inveterate defense of classical virtues, the same condemnation of eccentric individualism, the same stress on moral values that literature should exemplify, the same adherence to a system of absolutism." [5] Furthermore, much of the criticism of the Marxists is at base moral, though the image of man they propose differs greatly from that of the Humanists, and is related to so special a theory of human forces that the Marxists are best understood as exemplars of "The Social Approach." Even among some of the formalistic critics, the moral view is retained. In "Religion and Literature" T. S. Eliot enunciated an interesting split of judgment: "The 'greatness' of literature cannot be determined solely by literary standards; though we must remember that whether it is literature or not can be determined only by literary standards." This distinction makes it possible for some, like Allen Tate and John Crowe Ransom, who have the moralist's interest in the "greatness" of literature, to concentrate in their critical explications on the "solely literary standards."

[5] Charles J. Glicksberg, *American Literary Criticism 1900–1950*, p. 42.

Bibliographical Note

There are two excellent expositions of the secular humanistic position: the final chapter of Norman Foerster's *American Criticism*, 1928, and Douglas Bush's article, "The Humanistic Critic" in *Kenyon Review* XIII (Winter, 1951). In disagreement, from the point of view of those who share the values, but insist on supernatural sanction for them, there are two essays by T. S. Eliot: "The Humanism of Irving Babbitt" and "Second Thoughts on Humanism"; and one by Alan Tate, "Humanism and Naturalism." The first two appear in Eliot's *Selected Essays 1917-1932*, the last in Tate's *Reactionary Essays on Poetry and Ideas*. In *Humanism in America*, 1930, Norman Foerster edited essays by many of the members of the group at that time.

The major documents of the movement are Irving Babbitt's *The New Laokoön*, 1910, and *Rousseau and Romanticism*, 1919, and *The Shelburne Essays*, 1904-1935, of Paul Elmer More.

Alfred Kazin presents in *On Native Grounds* (pp. 291-311) a hostile study of the Neo-Humanism of Babbitt and More. The *Critique of Humanism*, 1930, edited by C. H. Grattan, is devoted to the limitations and weakness of the approach in its most flourishing days.

Much of the writing of Yvor Winters, whose position has an affinity with that of the Humanists, is collected in *The Defense of Reason*, 1947, consisting of his three books, with an additional essay. The position of F. R. Leavis is also moralistic; some of his works are *New Bearings in English Poetry*, 1932, *The Great Tradition*, 1948, and *The Common Pursuit*, 1952.

Genius and Taste

BY IRVING BABBITT

I

IN *Roderick Random* (1748), the poet Melopoyn, confined
in the Marshalsea for debt, stalks forth "wrapped in a dirty
rug tied about his loins with two pieces of list of different
colors," and, making a profound bow to the assembled pris-
oners, pronounces before them "with great significance of
voice and gesture a very elegant and ingenious discourse upon the difference between genius and taste." Mr. Spingarn's
views on genius and taste, in his *Creative Criticism,* like so
many other views that are being put forth as ultramodern,
take us back to this period in the eighteenth century. A new
movement began to gain head about that time, a movement
in the midst of which we are still living, and the opposition
between this movement and traditional conceptions appears
nowhere more clearly, perhaps, than in its reinterpretation of
such words as genius and taste. In one of his most conservative moods Voltaire defined genius as only "judicious imitation"; which meant in practice the imitation of the approved
models according to certain rules and conventions. But to
imitate thus is to be merely orthodox, and Voltaire maintains
that after all mere orthodoxy, though necessary, does not suffice. In any one who hopes to achieve literary salvation good
works must be supplemented by grace, and grace is accorded
to but few. If Voltaire is to the last degree astringent and restrictive in his attitude towards literary genius, he is hardly less
so in his attitude towards taste. The critic, too, he holds, must
have a special tact and intuition that cannot be acquired. Voltaire estimates that in the whole world there are only a few
thousand men of taste—mainly settled about Paris. In short,
genius and taste as Voltaire views them are very vivid and
vital things, but operate within the limits imposed by the neo-

classic doctrine of imitation, a doctrine that suffered from the start from a taint of formalism.

Those who sought to purge literature of this taint began towards the middle of the eighteenth century to oppose the neoclassical harping on judgment and imitation a plea for imagination and originality. The enthusiast and original genius who emerged at this time and arrayed himself against the wit and man of the world had from the outset a strong leaning towards primitivism. For example, Edward Young's *Conjectures on Original Composition* (1759) will be found in its attacks on imitation, and its exaltation of spontaneity and free expression, to anticipate surprisingly the gospel of recent primitivists like Mr. Spingarn and his master, Benedetto Croce. According to the older school, art aims not at the expression of the individual, but at the universal—the "grandeur of generality." On the contrary, says Young, genius resides in one's ultimate idiosyncrasy, that ineffable something that makes every man different from his fellows. If one wishes to be a creator and not a mechanical imitator, one should simply be one's temperamental self, and above all submit to no constraint upon one's imagination. "In the fairyland of fancy genius may wander wild; there it has a creative power and may reign arbitrarily over its own empire of chimeras." (The empire of Chimeras was later to become the tower of ivory.) If one is not to be contaminated by imitation, it is an advantage, Young insinuates, to be ignorant and brainless. "Many a genius probably there has been which could neither write nor read." This advantage, the primitivist soon came to argue, was enjoyed especially in the early stages of society before originality had been crushed beneath a superincumbent weight of artificial culture, and before critics had begun their pernicious activities. This primitivistic view of genius received a great stimulus from the publication of the Ossianic poems. "Genius," says Diderot, summing up a whole movement, "calls for something enormous, primitive and barbaric."

If genius, according to the primitivist, is something purely expressive, a spontaneous temperamental overflow, taste, as he views it, is likewise at the opposite pole from the taste of the neoclassicist. Voltaire failed to do justice to certain writers—Shakespeare, for example—who were outside the strict neoclassical convention. According to the new doctrine, the critic should cease to be thus exclusive and become comprehensive and sympathetic. This is an important half-truth, though perhaps no half-truth since the beginning of the world has ever been so overworked. For it is not enough, as Mr. Spingarn would have us believe, that the critic should ask what the creator aimed to do and whether he has fulfilled his aim; he must also ask whether the aim is intrinsically worth while. He must, in other words, rate creation with reference to some standard set both above his own temperament and that of the creator. According to the primitivist, on the contrary, the genius has simply to let himself go both imaginatively and emotionally, and the whole business of the critic is to receive so keen an impression from the resulting expression that when passed through his temperament it issues forth as a fresh expression. By thus participating in the creative thrill of genius, the critic becomes creative in turn, and in so far genius and taste are one.

Now taste has been defined as a man's literary conscience. The transformation of the literary conscience that took place in the eighteenth century is only one aspect of the transformation that took place during that period in the conscience in general. Instead of being looked upon, as it always had been traditionally, as an inner check upon impulse and emotion, the conscience came to be regarded as itself an expansive emotion. Once discredit the veto power in human nature, once identify the spirit that says no with the devil, and the rest—for example, the tendency of genius and taste to run together in a common expansiveness, a common eagerness for expression—follows quickly. "The identity of genius and taste," says Mr. Spingarn, "is the final achievement of modern thought on the subject of art; and it means that fundamentally the creative and critical instincts are one and the same." In that case the credit of this discovery belong to critics who antedate by at least a century Signor Croce. For example,

A. W. Schlegel protests in his Berlin lectures (1803) against a "fault-finding criticism that looked upon what is truly positive in poetry—genius—as the evil principle, and wished to subordinate it to the negative principle—so-called good taste; an unreal and purely fanciful contrast. These two things (i.e., genius and taste) are indivisibly one."

II

If the creator has merely to get his own genius, i.e., his own uniqueness, expressed, it is hard to see why the critic should be more disinterested, why he should not be less concerned with the faithfulness of the impression he receives from the work of the creator than with the temperamental modifications he gives this impression, with his remolding of it into a fresh creation so that it may become expressive of *his* genius. These ultimate implications of the expressionistic-impressionistic view have been worked out by no one more consistently, perhaps, than by Oscar Wilde in his dialogue *The Critic as Artist.* "Criticism," Wilde concludes, "is the only civilized form of autobiography." Except that he falls somewhat short of this last affirmation, Mr. Springarn runs very closely parallel to Wilde, to whom indeed he makes due acknowledgment. What underlies this whole movement from the original genius of the eighteenth century down to Wilde and Mr. Spingarn is the craving for an indeterminate vagabondage of imagination and emotion; and far more significant than the emotional emancipation is the emancipation of the imagination from any allegiance to standards, from any central control. The neoclassicists had forgotten in their devotion to what they conceived to be truth and nature, by which they meant normal human nature, the supreme rôle of the imagination, or, if one prefers, of illusion in both art and life. They hoped, as we have seen, to achieve their grandeur of generality by a merely judicious imitation. Yet Voltaire himself had declared that "illusion is the queen of the human heart." The original genius opposed to the unimaginative neoclassic notion of normality an imagination that is subject to no norm whatsoever, that is, in Young's phrase, free to wander wild in its own empire of chimeras. Wilde has the supreme effrontery to put this cult of pure illusion under the patronage of Aristotle. But this should at least serve to remind us that Aristotle, unlike the neoclassicists, recognizes the all-important rôle of illusion. The poet, he says, gives us a truth superior to that of the historian— superior because it is more representative. But in order to give us this representative truth, he goes on to say, the poet must be a master of illusion. In Goethe's phrase, the best art gives us "the illusion of a higher reality"; and this has the advantage of being strictly experimental, of being only a statement of what one actually experiences on reading a great poem or seeing a great picture. Imitation, in the theory of an Aristotle and the practice of a Sophocles or a Phidias, is not merely judicious, but creative, and creative because it is imaginative. For the Greek, genius consists not in getting one's uniqueness uttered, but in the imaginative perception of the universal. Homer, says Aristotle, is the greatest of poets because he never entertains us with his own person, but is the most constantly an imitator. Homer still remains the greatest of poets for this very reason. He paints with his eye on the object, and that object is human nature.

The opposite pole is reached when Lamartine tells us that he wrote solely for "the relief of his heart." The fact that the poet who overflows in this way is widely acclaimed is no sure proof that he has attained the universal. Many men may become abnormal at the same time and in the same way. A whole generation saw itself reflected in *René. René* is already more remote from us than Homer; and that is because the quality of the imagination displayed is, from the point of view of normal human experience, highly eccentric. It has been said, on the other hand, that Shakespeare dwells at the very center of human nature. This is only another way of saying that Shakespeare is one of the most imaginative of men. His imagination, however, is not irresponsible like that of the original genius, but is disciplined to reality. At his best he is ethical in the Greek sense. To be ethical in the

Greek sense is not to preach or to agitate problems, but to see life with imaginative wholeness. It is only too plain that the original genius, in his break with the neoclassic formalist, did not rise to ethical standards—to do this he would have needed to work out a sound view of the imagination and of imaginative imitation—but merely fell from legalism into anarchy. One should add—and this again is a fact that everyone can verify for himself—that the highest type of creator gets his general truth without any sacrifice of his peculiar personal note; he is at once unique and universal. But the original genius tends to identify—here is his underlying error—the normal with the commonplace. What he sees at the center is academic routine, and he gets as far away from this center as he can by inbreeding idiosyncrasy. And then somebody finds that the eccentric position thus assumed is still too central and proceeds to fly off from it; whereupon still another comes along and secedes from this seceder from a secessionist, and so on indefinitely. The extremists in painting have got so far beyond Cézanne, who was regarded not long ago as one of the wildest of innovators, that Cézanne is in a fair way, we read, to "achieve the unhappy fate of becoming a classic."

One should indeed not forget that in the house of art are many mansions. The imagination that is more or less free to wander wild in its own empire of chimeras has its place on the recreative side of life. The question of truth and reality is not in this sort of creation primary. But it is right here that the primitivist is guilty of the gravest confusions. Mr. Spingarn holds that the would-be creator should submit to no test of truth and reality, but should simply "let himself go" emotionally and imaginatively; should get rid of "inner or outer inhibitions," and the result, one is to believe, will not be something more or less re-creative; on the contrary, one will presently find Mr. Spingarn crediting the creator of this type with a "vision of reality" and "spiritual exaltation." Mr. Spingarn promises us that if we follow his prescription, we shall not only have genius—which will turn out to be identical with taste—but that we shall also go mad. One may agree

with him that the man who puts no check on his imagination,
and is at the same time convinced of his "spiritual exaltation,"
is in a fair way to go mad, but one may disagree with him
in deeming this madness a divine madness. In its mildest
forms this whole theory of genius and taste encourages conceit; in its more advanced forms megalomania. Once eliminate
the high impersonal standard, the ethical norm that sets
bounds to the eagerness of the creator to express himself,
and the eagerness of the creator to thrill to this expression,
and it is hard to see what measure of a man's merit is left
save his intoxication with himself; and this measure would
scarcely seem to be truthworthy. Virgil, we are told, wished
to burn the Æneid. The undergraduate, on the other hand,
often has a considerable conceit of his own genius in writing
his daily theme. "Every ass that's romantic," says Wolseley in
his preface to *Valentinian* (1685), "believes he's inspired."

After all, the doctrine of imitation merely means that one
needs to look up to some standard set above one's ordinary
self. Anyone who looked up to the standards established by
the two great traditions, the classical and the Christian,
tended to acquire in some measure the supreme Christian
virtue, humility, and the supreme classical virtue, decorum,
or, if one prefers, a sense of proportion. To repudiate the
traditional Christian and classical checks and at the same
time fail to work out some new and more vital control upon
impulse and temperament is to be guilty of high treason to
civilization.

If, on the one hand, the "spiritual exaltation" of the primitivist makes against the two virtues that sum up in a way all
civilization, humility, and decorum, on the other hand it
encourages the two root diseases of human nature, conceit
and laziness. Mr. Spingarn's exhortation to get rid of both
inner and outer inhibitions and let ourselves go amounts in
effect to this: follow the line of least resistance—and be a
genius. It is easy to be an unchained temperament, difficult to
attain to a proportionate and disciplined view of life. By
preaching sheer imaginative and emotional unrestraint in the

name of expression, Mr. Spingarn is tending to discredit that very modern spirit [1] for which he professes to stand. If to be modern means anything, it means to be positive and experimental in one's attitude towards life. If such a phrase as a "vision of reality" is to have any experimental content, if it is to be anything more than a mask for egotism, the reality of which one has a vision will serve to set bounds to the expansion of one's ordinary self; will be known practically, in short, as an inner inhibition. It should be clear to any one who considers the case of those who have viewed life with some degree of centrality and wholeness that they have won their restraining ethical insight with the aid of the imagination. If a sound type of individualism is to be achieved, and this is the specifically modern problem, it is scarcely possible to stress too strongly the rôle of the ethical or generalizing imagination. Such vision of reality as is vouchsafed to finite man must ever come to him through a veil of illusion. This inseparableness of reality and illusion may embarrass the metaphysician, but not the positivist who discriminates between the sham vision and the true, not on metaphysical grounds, but by their fruits.

Now the fruits of the primitivistic theory of genius and originality have had time to become manifest. If this theory was incubated in eighteenth-century England, it received its chief developments in eighteenth-century Germany, where it was applied by Herder, Fichte, and others, not merely to individuals, but to nations. When an individual becomes unduly exalted over his own "genius," there are various ways in which he may be relieved of his excess of conceit. But when a whole nation gets into a similar state of exaltation and is consumed by the ardor for self-expression, when instead of submission to genuine ethical standards there is a collective inbreeding of temperament and idiosyncrasy, then the case is well-nigh hopeless. One may then properly raise the question

---

[1] For my definition of the modern spirit see *Nation,* August 2, 1917 (article on "Matthew Arnold"). For my use of the word laziness see *ibid.,* October 18, 1917 ("Interpreting India to the West").

that Bishop Butler is said to have debated with himself, whether a whole nation may not go mad. National conceit runs into national megalomania, and the intoxication of a whole people with itself finally comes to be felt by it as an ecstatic "idealism." A nation of this kind may count upon having its "creative" critics, who will hope to show their taste by simply sharing this intoxication and their genius by giving it fresh expression.

III

This whole conception of genius and taste has about it the flavor of a decadent estheticism. The term creative critic, in particular, seems destined to remain a noteworthy example of what Arnold calls the grand name without the grand thing; and this is a pity, for there is an important sense in which the critic should be creative, especially in an age like the present, which has cut loose from its traditional moorings. Before determining what this sense is, let us consider for a moment the true relation between creator and critic, between genius and taste. Not to speak of other and minor differences, the creator differs above all from the critic, not merely in having genius in general, but a mysterious and incommunicable gift. Dr. Johnson goes too far when he defines genius as "only a mind of large general powers accidentally determined to some particular direction." The musical genius of a Mozart, for example, cannot be accounted for in any such fashion. Dr. Johnson was nevertheless right in condemning the whole primitivistic notion of genius and the lazy drifting with temperament that it encouraged. As a seventeenth-century Frenchman put it, it is not enough to have great gifts, one must also know how to manage them. Though a man's genius may not be in his power, the control of this genius to some human end largely is. To determine this end, he must look to standards, standards which, if he is not to be a mere traditionalist, he must create with the aid of the ethical imagination. If he does not seek to humanize his gift, if he is content to be a mere unchained force of nature, he may have genius, almost any amount of it, and yet remain, as Tennyson said of Hugo, only a "weird Titan."

The critic, for his part, cannot afford any more than the creator simply to let himself go. If he is merely content to partake of the creative thrill of genius, he may have gusto, zest, relish, what you will, but he will not have taste. He will begin to have taste only when he refers the creative expression and his impression of it to some standard that is set above both. And if this standard is to be purified of every taint of formalism, it must not be merely traditional or rationalistic, but must rest on an immediate perception of what is normal and human, a perception that the critic, like the creator, can win in its fullness only with the aid of the ethical or generalizing imagination. The best type of critic may therefore be said to be creative in the sense that he creates standards. It is in their common allegiance to standards that critic and creator really come together. They ascend, and not, as in the primitivistic theory, descend, to meet. With the elimination of the restrictive and selective principle—and the presence of standards is always felt as such a principle—what is left is the most dangerous of all forms of anarchy—anarchy of the imagination. This is what Goethe meant when he said that "nothing is so horrible as imagination without taste."

To acquire a true literary conscience, to mediate between the restrictive and selective principle and one's vivid personal impression, to have standards and then to apply them flexibly and intuitively, is not easy. It is to be feared that Voltaire is nearer the truth when he discourses on the small number of the elect in matters of taste than Mr. Spingarn when he utters his facile assurance, so agreeable to democratic ears, that "we are all geniuses; we are all possessed of taste." Mr. Spingarn's message would seem to be the very opposite of what we need in America at the present time. For though we no doubt have "ideals"—at least we seem very certain on this point—we lack standards; and the pathway to standards would scarcely seem to lie through the glorification of impulse and unrestraint. Because certain barriers imposed by neoclassic good taste were found to be arbitrary and artificial, the primitivist assumes that all barriers are arbitrary and artificial; and the consequences of this assumption, if worked out consistently, should give us pause. Civilization, at bottom, rests on the recognition of the fact that man shows his true liberty by resisting impulse, and not by yielding to it, that he grows in the perfection proper to his own nature not by throwing off but by taking on limitations. As a matter of fact, not much is left of the values of civilized life when Mr. Spingarn has finished enumerating the things that must be thrown overboard if the creator is to express himself adequately, and the "new" or "esthetic" critic is to partake of the creator's thrill and reexpress it. Mr. Spingarn says that the opening night of the International Exhibition (1913) was one of the most "exciting adventures" that he had ever experienced. Many of the pictures that have been appearing in this and similar exhibitions of late years, far from being so excitingly novel, would suggest rather that our American partisans of pure expression are coming in at a late stage of a movement that from its rise in the eighteenth century was unable to distinguish between the original and the aboriginal. If Mr. Theodore Dreiser, author of *The Genius,* had set forth his views of originality in Germany about 1775 (*die Geniezeit*), they would have been wrong, but they would at least have had the semblance of novelty. As it is, it is hard for a person even moderately versed in literary history to read these views without yawning. Nothing is more tiresome than stale eccentricity. Is this country always to be the dumping ground of Europe? Americans who wish to display real virility and initiative will scarcely be content to fall in at the end of the procession, especially when the procession is moving, as in this case, towards the edge of a precipice. They will see that we must begin by creating standards, if our other attempts at creation are to have any meaning, and they will not underestimate the difficulty of the task. Primitivism leads to affirmations that are repugnant to the most elementary common sense—for example, to Mr. Spingarn's affirmation that the "art of a child is art quite as much as that of Michelangelo." But it is not enough to oppose to such aberrations mere common sense or reason or judgment. The strength of the primitivist is that he recognizes in his own way the truth proclaimed by Napoleon—that imagination governs the world. Those who believe in the need of a humanistic reaction at present should be careful not to renew the neoclassical error. Thus Dryden attributes the immortality of the Æneid to its being "a well-weighed, judicious poem. Whereas poems which are produced by the vigor of imagination only have a gloss upon them at the first which time wears off, the works of judgment are like the diamond: the more they are polished the more luster they receive." But what is preeminent in Virgil, what gives the immortalizing touch to his work, is not the judgment he displays, but the quality of his imagination. It is no doubt inevitable, in speaking and writing, to divide man up into faculties and contrast judgment with imagination. At the same time one should recollect that this division of man into more or less watertight compartments has about it nothing positive and experimental. What is positive and experimental, let me repeat, is that in creation of the first order, creation that has high seriousness in the Aristotelian sense, the imagination does not wander aimlessly, but is at work in the service of a supersensuous truth that it is not given to man to seize directly; and that the result is "the illusion of a higher reality." Creation of this order, one may report from actual observation, is something more than the intense expression of some expansive ego, whether individual or national; it has a restrained and humanized intensity— intensity on a background of calm. Our whole modern experiment, not only in art and literature, but in life, is threatened with breakdown, because of our failure to work out new standards with the aid of this type of imagination. And this breakdown of the modern experiment is due to its not having lived up to its own program. Those who have put aside the discipline of outer authority have professed to do so because of their thirst for immediacy, of their wish to face unflinchingly the facts of nature and of human nature. Yet the veto power in human nature is nothing abstract, nothing that one needs to take on hearsay, but a matter of immediate perception. It is this fact, the weightiest of all, that the corrupters of the literary conscience and of the conscience in general have failed to face in making of the imagination the irresponsible accomplice of the unchained emotions.

Religion and Literature

By T. S. Eliot

WHAT I HAVE TO SAY is largely in support of the following
propositions: Literary criticism should be completed by criticism from a definite ethical and theological standpoint. In so
far as in any age there is common agreement on ethical and
theological matters, so far can literary criticism be sub-
stantive. In ages like our own, in which there is no such
common agreement, it is the more necessary for Christian
readers to scrutinize their reading, especially of works of
imagination, with explicit ethical and theological standards.
The "greatness" of literature cannot be determined solely
by literary standards; though we must remember that whether
it is literature or not can be determined only by literary
standards.[1]

We have tacitly assumed, for some centuries past, that
there is *no* relation between literature and theology. This is
not to deny that literature—I mean, again, primarily works
of imagination—has been, is, and probably always will be
judged by some moral standards. But moral judgments of
literary works are made only according to the moral code
accepted by each generation, whether it lives according to
that code or not. In an age which accepts some precise
Christian theology, the common code may be fairly orthodox:
though even in such periods the common code may exalt such
concepts as "honor," "glory" or "revenge" to a position quite
intolerable to Christianity. The dramatic ethics of the Elizabethan Age offers an interesting study. But when the common
code is detached from its theological background, and is consequently more and more merely a matter of habit, it is
exposed both to prejudice and to change. At such times

[1] As an example of literary criticism given greater significance
by theological interests, I would call attention to Theodor Haecker:
Virgil . . . [London, 1934].

morals are open to being altered *by* literature; so that we find in practice that what is "objectionable" in literature is merely what the present generation is not used to. It is a commonplace that what shocks one generation is accepted quite calmly by the next. This adaptability to change of moral standards is sometimes greeted with satisfaction as an evidence of human perfectibility: whereas it is only evidence of what unsubstantial foundations people's moral judgments have.

I am not concerned here with religious literature but with the application of our religion to the criticism of any literature. It may be as well, however, to distinguish first what I consider to be the three senses in which we can speak of "religious literature." The first is that of which we say that it is "religious literature" in the same way that we speak of "historical literature" or of "scientific literature." I mean that we can treat the Authorized translation of the Bible, or the works of Jeremy Taylor, as literature, in the same way that we treat the historical writing of Clarendon or of Gibbon— our two great English historians—as literature; or Bradley's *Logic*, or Buffon's *Natural History*. All of these writers were men who, incidentally to their religious, or historical, or philosophic purpose, had a gift of language which makes them delightful to read to all those who can enjoy language well written, even if they are unconcerned with the objects which the writers had in view. And I would add that though a scientific, or historical, or theological, or philosophic work which is also "literature," may become superannuated as anything but literature, yet it is not likely to be "literature" unless it had its scientific or other value for its own time. While I acknowledge the legitimacy of this enjoyment, I am more acutely aware of its abuse. The persons who enjoy these writings *solely* because of their literary merit are essentially parasites; and we know that parasites, when they become too numerous, are pests. I could easily fulminate for a whole hour against the men of letters who have gone into ecstasies over "the Bible as literature," the Bible as "the noblest monument of English prose." Those who talk of the Bible as a "monument of English prose" are merely admiring it as a

monument over the grave of Christianity. I must try to avoid
the bypaths of my discourse: it is enough to suggest that just
as the work of Clarendon, or Gibbon, or Buffon, or Bradley
would be of inferior literary value if it were insignificant as
history, science and philosophy respectively, so the Bible has
had a *literary* influence upon English literature *not* because
it has been considered as literature, but because it has been
considered as the report of the Word of God. And the fact
that men of letters now discuss it as "literature" probably
indicates the *end* of its "literary" influence.

The second kind of relation of religion to literature is that
which is found in what is called "religious" or "devotional"
poetry. Now what is the usual attitude of the lover of poetry
—and I mean the person who is a genuine and firsthand
enjoyer and appreciator of poetry, not the person who follows
the admirations of others—toward this department of poetry?
I believe, all that may be implied in his calling it a *department*. He believes, not always explicitly, that when you qualify
poetry as "religious" you are indicating very clear limitations.
For the great majority of people who love poetry, *"religious*
poetry" is a variety of *minor* poetry: the religious poet is not
a poet who is treating the whole subject matter of poetry in
a religious spirit, but a poet who is dealing with a confined
part of this subject matter: who is leaving out what men
consider their major passions, and thereby confessing his
ignorance of them. I think that this is the real attitude of
most poetry lovers towards such poets as Vaughan, or Southwell, or Crashaw, or George Herbert, or Gerard Hopkins.

But what is more, I am ready to admit that up to a point
these critics are right. For there is a kind of poetry, such as
most of the work of the authors I have mentioned, which is
the product of a special religious awareness, which may
exist without the general awareness which we expect of
the major poet. In some poets, or in some of their works,
this general awareness may have existed; but the preliminary
steps which represent it may have been suppressed, and only
the end product presented. Between these, and those in which
the religious or devotional genius represents the *special* and

limited awareness, it may be very difficult to discriminate. I do not pretend to offer Vaughan, or Southwell, or George Herbert, or Hopkins as major poets: I feel sure that the first three, at least, are poets of this limited awareness. They are not great religious poets in the sense in which Dante, or Corneille, or Racine, even in those of their plays which do not touch upon Christian themes, are great Christian religious poets. Or even in the sense in which Villon and Baudelaire, with all their imperfections and delinquencies, are Christian poets. Since the time of Chaucer, Christian poetry (in the sense in which I shall mean it) has been limited in England almost exclusively to minor poetry.

I repeat that when I am considering Religion and Literature, I speak of these things only to make clear that I am not concerned primarily with Religious Literature, I am concerned with what should be the relation between Religion and all Literature. Therefore the third type of "religious literature" may be more quickly passed over. I mean the literary works of men who are sincerely desirous of forwarding the cause of religion: that which may come under the heading of Propaganda. I am thinking, of course, of such delightful fiction as Mr. Chesterton's *Man Who Was Thursday*, or his *Father Brown*. No one admires and enjoys these things more than I do; I would only remark that when the same effect is aimed at by zealous persons of less talent than Mr. Chesterton the effect is negative. But my point is that such writings do not enter into any serious consideration of the relation of Religion and Literature: because they are conscious operations in a world in which it is assumed that Religion and Literature are not related. It is a conscious and limited relating. What I want is a literature which should be *un*consciously, rather than deliberately and defiantly, Christian: because the work of Mr. Chesterton has its point from appearing in a world which is definitely not Christian.

I am convinced that we fail to realize how completely, and yet how irrationally, we separate our literary from our religious judgments. If there could be a complete separation, perhaps it might not matter: but the separation is not, and never can be, complete. If we exemplify literature by the novel—for the novel is the form in which literature affects the greatest number—we may remark this gradual secularization of literature during at least the last three hundred years. Bunyan, and to some extent Defoe, had moral purposes: the former is beyond suspicion, the latter may be suspect. But since Defoe the secularization of the novel has been continuous. There have been three chief phases. In the first, the novel took the Faith, in its contemporary version, for granted, and omitted it from its picture of life. Fielding, Dickens and Thackeray belong to this phase. In the second, it doubted, worried about, or contested the Faith. To this phase belong George Eliot, George Meredith and Thomas Hardy. To the third phase, in which we are living, belong nearly all contemporary novelists except Mr. James Joyce. It is the phase of those who have never heard the Christian Faith spoken of as anything but an anachronism.

Now, do people in general hold a definite opinion, that is to say religious or antireligious; and do they read novels, or poetry for that matter, with a separate compartment of their minds? The common ground between religion and fiction is behavior. Our religion imposes our ethics, our judgment and criticism of ourselves, and our behavior towards our fellow men. The fiction that we read affects our behavior towards our fellow men, affects our patterns of ourselves. When we read of human beings behaving in certain ways, with the approval of the author, who gives his benediction to this behavior by his attitude towards the result of the behavior arranged by himself, we can be influenced towards behaving in the same way.[2] When the contemporary novelist is an individual thinking for himself in isolation, he may have something important to offer to those who are able to receive it. He who is alone may speak to the individual. But the majority of novelists are persons drifting in the stream, only a little faster. They have some sensitiveness, but little intellect.

[2] Here and later I am indebted to Montgomery Belgion. *The Human Parrot* (chapter on The Irresponsible Propagandist) [London, 1931].

We are expected to be broadminded about literature, to put aside prejudice or conviction, and to look at fiction as fiction and at drama as drama. With what is inaccurately called "censorship" in this country—with what is much more difficult to cope with than an official censorship, because it represents the opinions of individuals in an irresponsible democracy, I have very little sympathy; partly because it so often suppresses the wrong books, and partly because it is little more effective than Prohibition of Liquor; partly because it is one manifestation of the desire that state control should take the place of decent domestic influence; and wholly because it acts only from custom and habit, not from decided theological and moral principles. Incidentally, it gives people a false sense of security in leading them to believe that books which are *not* suppressed are harmless. Whether there *is* such a thing as a harmless book I am not sure: but there very likely are books so utterly unreadable as to be incapable of injuring anybody. But it is certain that a book is not harmless merely because no one is consciously offended by it. And if we, as readers, keep our religious and moral convictions in one compartment, and take our reading merely for entertainment, or on a higher plane, for æsthetic pleasure, I would point out that the author, whatever his conscious intentions in writing, in practice recognizes no such distinctions. The author of a work of imagination is trying to affect us wholly, as human beings, whether he knows it or not; and we are affected by it, as human beings, whether we intend to be or not. I suppose that everything we eat has some other effect upon us than merely the pleasure of taste and mastication; it affects us during the process of assimilation and digestion; and I believe that exactly the same is true of anything we read.

The fact that what we read does not concern merely something called our *literary taste,* but that it affects directly, though only amongst many other influences, the whole of what we are, is best elicited, I think, by a conscientious examination of the history of our individual literary education. Consider the adolescent reading of any person with some literary sensibility. Everyone, I believe, who is at all sensible to the seductions of poetry, can remember some moment in youth when he or she was completely carried away by the work of one poet. Very likely he was carried away by several poets, one after the other. The reason for this passing infatuation is not merely that our sensibility to poetry is keener in adolescence than in maturity. What happens is a kind of inundation, of invasion of the undeveloped personality, the empty (swept and garnished) room, by the stronger personality of the poet. The same thing may happen at a later age to persons who have not done much reading. One author takes complete possession of us for a time; then another; and finally they begin to affect each other in our mind. We weigh one against another; we see that each has qualities absent from others, and qualities incompatible with the qualities of others: we begin to be, in fact, critical; and it is our growing critical power which protects us from excessive possession by any one literary personality. The good critic—and we should all try to be critics, and not leave criticism to the fellows who write reviews in the papers—is the man who, to a keen and abiding sensibility, joins wide and increasingly discriminating reading. Wide reading is not valuable as a kind of hoarding, an accumulation of knowledge, or what sometimes is meant by the term "a well stocked mind." It is valuable because in the process of being affected by one powerful personality after another, we cease to be dominated by any one, or by any small number. The very different views of life, cohabiting in our minds, affect each other, and our own personality asserts itself and gives each a place in some arrangement peculiar to ourself.

It is simply not true that works of fiction, prose or verse, that is to say works depicting the actions, thoughts and words and passions of imaginary human beings, *directly* extend our knowledge of life. Direct knowledge of life is knowledge directly in relation to ourselves, it is our knowledge of *how* people behave in general, of *what* they are like in general, in so far as that part of life in which we ourselves have participated gives us material for generalization. Knowledge of life obtained through fiction is only possible by another stage of self-consciousness. That is to say, it can only be a knowledge of other people's knowledge of life, not of life itself. So far as we are taken up with the happenings in any novel in the same way in which we are taken up with what happens under our eyes, we are acquiring at least as much falsehood as truth. But when we are developed enough to say: "This is the view of life of a person who was a good observer within his limits, Dickens, or Thackeray, or George Eliot, or Balzac; but he looked at it in a different way from me, because he was a different man; he even selected rather different things to look at, or the same things in a different order of importance, because he was a different man; so what I am looking at is the world as seen by a particular mind"—then we are in a position to gain something from reading fiction. We are learning *something* about life from these authors direct, just as we learn something from the reading of history direct; but these authors are only really helping us when we can see, and allow for, their differences from ourselves.

Now what we get, as we gradually grow up and read more and more, and read a greater diversity of authors, is a variety of views of life. But what people commonly assume, I suspect, is that we gain this experience of other men's views of life only by "improving reading." This, it is supposed, is a reward we get by applying ourselves to Shakespeare, and Dante, and Goethe, and Emerson, and Carlyle, and dozens of other respectable writers. The rest of our reading for amusement is merely killing time. But I incline to come to the alarming conclusion that it is just the literature that we read for "amusement," or "purely for pleasure" that may have the greatest and least suspected influence upon us. It is the literature which we read with the least effort that can have the easiest and most insidious influence upon us. Hence it is that the influence of popular novelists, and of popular plays of contemporary life, requires to be scrutinized most closely. And it is chiefly *contemporary* literature that the majority of people ever read in this attitude of "purely for pleasure," of pure passivity.

The relation of what I have been saying to the subject announced for my discourse should not be a little more apparent. Though we may read literature merely for pleasure, of "entertainment" or of "æsthetic enjoyment," this reading never affects simply a sort of special sense: it affects us as entire human beings; it affects our moral and religious existence. And I say that while individual modern writers of eminence can be improving, contemporary literature as a whole tends to be degrading. And that even the effect of the better writers, in an age like ours, may be degrading to some readers; for we must remember that what a writer does to people is not necessarily what he intends to do. It may be only what people are capable of having done to them. People exercise an unconscious selection, in being influenced. A writer like D. H. Lawrence may be in his effect either beneficial or pernicious. I am not even sure that I have not had some pernicious influence myself.

At this point I anticipate a rejoinder from the liberal-minded, from all those who are convinced that if everybody says what he thinks, and does what he likes, things will somehow, by some automatic compensation and adjustment, come right in the end. "Let everything be tried," they say, "and if it is a mistake, then we shall learn by experience." This argument might have some value, if we were always the same generation upon earth; or if, as we know to be not the case, people ever learned much from the experience of their elders. These liberals are convinced that only by what is called unrestrained individualism will truth ever emerge. Ideas, views of life, they think, issue distinct from independent heads, and in consequence of their knocking violently against each other, the fittest survive, and truth rises triumphant. Anyone who dissents from this view must be either a mediævalist, wishful only to set back the clock, or else a fascist, and probably both.

If the mass of contemporary authors were really individualists, every one of them inspired Blakes, each with his separate vision, and if the mass of the contemporary public were really a mass of *individuals* there might be something to be said for this attitude. But this is not, and never has been, and

never will be. It is not only that the reading individual today
(or at any day) is not enough an individual to be able to
absorb all the "views of life" of all the authors pressed upon
us by the publishers' advertisements and reviewers, and to be
able to arrive at wisdom by considering one against another.
It is that the contemporary authors are not individuals
enough either. It is not that the world of separate individuals
of the liberal democrat is undesirable; it is simply that this
world does not exist. For the reader of contemporary literature is not, like the reader of the established great literature
of all time, exposing himself to the influence of divers and
contradictory personalities; he is exposing himself to a mass
movement of writers who, each of them, think that they have
something individually to offer, but are really all working
together in the same direction. And there never was a time, I
believe, when the reading public was so large, or so helplessly
exposed to the influences of its own time. There never was
a time, I believe, when those who read at all, read so many
more books by living authors than books by dead authors; there
never was a time so completely parochial, so shut off from
the past. There may be too many publishers; there are certainly too many books published; and the journals ever incite
the reader to "keep up" with what is being published. Indi-
dividualistic democracy has come to high tide: and it is more
difficult today to be an individual than it ever was before.

Within itself, modern literature has perfectly valid distinctions of good and bad, better and worse: and I do not
wish to suggest that I confound Mr. Bernard Shaw with Mr.
Noel Coward, Mrs. Woolf with Miss Mannin. On the other
hand, I should like it to be clear that I am not defending a
"high"-brow against a "low"-brow literature. What I do wish
to affirm is that the whole of modern literature is corrupted by
what I call Secularism, that is is simply unaware of, simply
cannot understand the meaning of, the primacy of the supernatural over the natural life: of something which I assume to
be our primary concern.

I do not want to give the impression that I have delivered
a mere fretful jeremiad against contemporary literature. As-

suming a common attitude between you, or some of you, and myself, the question is not so much, what is to be done about it? as, how should we behave towards it?

I have suggested that the liberal attitude towards literature will not work. Even if the writers who make their attempt to impose their "view of life" upon us were really distinct individuals, even if we as readers were distinct individuals, what would be the result? It would be, surely, that each reader would be impressed, in his reading, merely by what he was previously prepared to be impressed by; he would follow the "line of least resistance," and there would be no assurance that he would be made a better man. For literary judgment we need to be acutely aware of two things at once: of "what we like," and of "what we *ought* to like." Few people are honest enough to know either. The first means knowing what we really feel: very few know that. The second involves understanding our shortcomings; for we do not really know what we ought to like unless we also know why we ought to like it, which involves knowing why we don't yet like it. It is not enough to understand what we ought to be, unless we know what we are; and we do not understand what we are, unless we know what we ought to be. The two forms of self-consciousness, knowing what we are and what we ought to be, must go together.

It is our business, as readers of literature, to know what we like. It is our business, as Christians, *as well as* readers of literature, to know what we ought to like. It is our business as honest men not to assume that whatever we like is what we ought to like; and it is our business as honest Christians not to assume that we do like what we ought to like. And the last thing I would wish for would be the existence of two literatures, one for Christian consumption and the other for the pagan world. What I believe to be incumbent upon all Christians is the duty of maintaining consciously certain standards and criteria of criticism over and above those applied by the rest of the world; and that by these criteria and standards everything that we read must be tested. We must remember that the greater part of our current reading matter is written for us by people who have no real belief in a supernatural order, though some of it may be written by people with individual notions of a supernatural order which are not ours. And the greater part of our reading matter is coming to be written by people who not only have no such belief, but are even ignorant of the fact that there are still people in the world so "backward" or so "eccentric" as to continue to believe. So long as we are conscious of the gulf fixed between ourselves and the greater part of contemporary literature, we are more or less protected from being harmed by it, and are in a position to extract from it what good it has to offer us.

There are a very large number of people in the world today who believe that all ills are fundamentally economic. Some believe that various specific economic changes alone would be enough to set the world right; others demand more or less drastic changes in the social as well, changes chiefly of two opposed types. These changes demanded, and in some places carried out, are alike in one respect, that they hold the assumptions of what I call Secularism: they concern themselves only with changes of a temporal, material, and external nature; they concern themselves with morals only of a collective nature. In an exposition of one such new faith I read the following words:

"In our morality the one single test of any moral question is whether it impedes or destroys in any way the power of the individual to serve the State. [The individual] must answer the questions: 'Does this action injure the nation? Does it injure other members of the nation? Does it injure my ability to serve the nation?' And if the answer is clear on all those questions, the individual has absolute liberty to do as he will."

Now I do not deny that this is a kind of morality, and that it is capable of great good within limits; but I think that we should all repudiate a morality which had no higher ideal to set before us than that. It represents, of course, one of the violent reactions we are witnessing, against the view that the community is solely for the benefit of the individual; but it is equally a gospel of this world, and of this world alone. My complaint against modern literautre is of the same kind. It is not that modern literature is in the ordinary sense "immoral" or even "amoral"; and in any case to prefer that charge would not be enough. It is simply that it repudiates, or is wholly ignorant of, our most fundamental and important beliefs; and that in consequence its tendency is to encourage its readers to get what they can out of life while it lasts, to miss no "experience" that presents itself, and to sacrifice themselves, if they make any sacrifice at all, only for the sake of tangible benefits to others in this world either now or in the future. We shall certainly continue to read the best of its kind, of what our time provides; but we must tirelessly criticize it according to our own principles, and not merely according to the principles admitted by the writers and by the critics who discuss it in the public press.

The New Compassion in the American Novel

By Edmund Fuller

Never a glycerin tear shed to the tune of "Hearts and Flowers" in a Victorian tear-jerker was so sloppy and false as is the weird sentimentality in some of the roughest and supposedly most "realistic" of modern novels. An inverted pathos has sprung up among what Maxwell Geismar has called "the brutes." For some years, authors, publishers and reviewers have kicked around the word *compassion* so loosely that its meaning may become corrupted and lost.

The present decline of compassion (which also is the decline of tragedy) began in an odd and relatively innocuous way. It started with the vogue of the lovable bums, and at first it was no worse than a foolish romanticizing of the scalawag: a beery, brass-rail sentimentality. This pattern was not completely new—we see a bit of it in all the classical picaros—but never had it been so elaborated as it began to be in the thirties. It had charm and appeal, at times, dealing good-naturedly with human foibles. It is possible to look affectionately upon such people, as with Wilkins Micawber, if you keep your head and don't elevate a mood into a philosophy.

Some writers, especially those talented men William Saroyan, in *The Time of Your Life,* and John Steinbeck, in several books from his early *Tortilla Flat* to his recent *Sweet Thursday,* developed the lovable bums into the fallacy of "the beautiful little people"—which almost always meant the shiftless, the drunk, the amoral, and the wards of society. A corollary was implied: if you didn't love these characters, you were a self-righteous bigot, hard of heart by contrast to the author's compassion and love for the common clay of humanity. Conversely, these books imply another world of respectable and economically stable people who vaguely are not nice, not right, compared to the ineffable and intransigent "little people."

Yet some, though not all, of this stuff called itself "realistic." Its absurdities reached a point in Steinbeck's *The Wayward Bus,* which inspired John Mason Brown to one of the most searching remarks since the little boy said the emperor wasn't wearing any clothes: "If realism isn't real, then isn't it trash?"

A sinister twist came in the path some years ago, and abruptly this new soft streak lost its innocence. The lovable bum began to slip away, and in his place emerged the genial rapist, the jolly slasher, the fun-loving dope pusher. Now we see increasingly a technique of simple identification with the degraded which is miscalled compassion. It lacks the requisites for compassion as much as its subjects lack the requisites for tragedy.

What is compassion, anyhow? It means the sharing of a sorrow, a pity and sympathy, a desire to help—feeling another's pain or plight as if it were one's own, seeing "those in chains as bound with them." It applies to a man's moral as well as material or physical breakdown. In the moral realm it recognizes the sharing of all human guilt, the potentiality of evil in the most blameless, the element which the Christian calls Original Sin and the analyst calls the id. In the traditions of both tragic and pathetic literature there is an abundance of authentic compassion.

A large and generous view of life and a distinct standard of values are necessary to establish compassion. These need not, of course, be formulated, but at least you must be able to discriminate between a happy state and an unhappy one; you must be able to discern the difference between a man destroyed through his own fault and one destroyed through no fault of his own, with all the delicate gradations possible between. You must set a moral value on man's actions and circumstances. Compassion is not a suspension of judgment, it is a judgment tempered and chastened according to the facts under some definable theory of the human condition. Compassion is discernment of the gap between the man that is and the potential man that was.

Two old saws contain much of the truth about the compassionate view of life and, incidentally, remove its unavoidable judgments from any taint of smugness: "There but for the grace of God go I" and "To understand all is to forgive all." How these apply to the phony compassion in many current novels we shall see.

In the enthusiastic critical reception of *From Here to Eternity,* culminating in the National Book Award, the word *compassion* was sprayed all over the scene by the critical fraternity. The writing of James Jones may well have many admirable attributes, but I do not see wherein compassion is one of them.

Like all the other pseudo-tough young writers engaged in this peculiar transposition of values, Mr. Jones is shamelessly and laughably sentimental. This is missed by some simply because he isn't sentimental about Mother or Dad or the Pure Girl or Jesus or Darling Babies. Instead, he is sentimental about incorrigible antisocial and criminal types and whores. He is said to be compassionate toward these—which is as you choose to think. Certainly, though, if you are *not* one of these you may expect short shrift from Mr. Jones, for he has precious little compassion for anyone else.

If you can wipe Mr. Jones's tears out of your eyes, you will see that the famous Private Robert E. Lee Prewitt is not a social being, nor are his buddies. Prewitt is not the most extreme of them, but he is the "hero." His type is a social hazard. Since many men have endured as much in the way of background experience as Prewitt did, he is no more the helpless creation of something outside him than anyone else. His character is partly, even largely, self-created, as is true, for practical purposes, of most of us.

But, says Compassionate Jones: Prewitt, Maggio, Stark and the others, drinking and whoring, knifing and slugging, rolling homosexuals, defying authority indiscriminately and eternally, are good, good people. All authority, all sobriety, all the rest of the world, are bad. He is vindictive against the socially adjusted or constructive. If you listen to him long you'll be ashamed to be sober and out of jail. This is not compassion; it is paranoia.

And this is why some of us regard *From Here to Eternity* not as a controlled work of art but as a clinically interesting projection of personalities by a man endowed with genuine gifts for narrative and pictorial characterization. Whether we are right or wrong, the minority holding this opinion must state it, in the face of reviews, sales and awards.

The most interesting case I've seen since Jones is a first novel of some seasons ago by George Mandel, *Flee the Angry Strangers*. It made no special mark in hard covers, though circulated widely in paper reprint. I choose it as a peculiarly apt illustration of a tendency which can be demonstrated in variations in many novels. In it the false compassion takes the ever more common form of complete negation of values and denial of responsibility. The author's interpreter, in the books, looks on the world of dope addiction and shrugs away any helpful intervention on these grounds: "Who the hell am I to stop it? Who am I to decide about people? There's no harm in anything. You can't stop any of that. You have no right. Nobody has."

With this view, he concludes that all the fallen are the result of repressive nay-saying by the unfallen. (Why the unfallen didn't fall is never explained.) And again emerges the teary slobbering over the criminal and degraded, the refusal to assign any share of responsibility to them, and a vindictive lashing out against the rest of the world.

This particular "compassion" is the sentimental pretense that things are not what they are. Mr. Mandel's eighteen-year-old heroine, addicted to drugs, sexually delinquent, mother of an illegitimate child, finally has been put in an institution. Mr. Mandel supports her in the outraged lament, "My own mother put me there."

As this girl escapes, steps up the dope, takes on more men indiscriminately, and tries a little prostitution, she can still say, reproachfully, "You think I'm a tramp."

"Shucks, kid," is the general attitude of the new-compassion boys, "just going around and doing everything a tramp does, doesn't make a good, sweet, clean little kid like you a tramp."

In short, the new compassion is the denial that men and

women are what their consistent, voluntary (and involuntary) patterns of action make them. The elements of true tragedy and compassion—the fall from a standard, responsibility however extenuated, repentance, and the struggle for rehabilitation—are not in this philosophy.

What is wrong with Mandel's approach to his delinquent heroine? He feels sorry for her—don't we all? Can he deny that she has become a tramp? Compassion is to see precisely what she is (which he evades), analyze how she got that way (which he distorts or oversimplifies), and seek for what can be done to rehabilitate her (which he refuses). This is the weakness of many such novels.

It is no casual matter that authors, publishers, and reviewers should blandly accept such attitudes as compassion. It may be the most unwholesome and dangerous single symptom in modern literature, for as there is nothing more appealing than the cloak of compassion, there is nothing more treacherous when it is false. In literary art, this is the absolute end product of ethical relativism. No valid compassion can exist without a moral framework. The Greeks had such a framework. The Judeo-Christian tradition has one. Only in recent years, in the work of some groups of writers, especially in the French existentialist movement, has the moral framework quietly and completely dropped away. This new compassion is a danger to the art of writing, and a deadly one when it is accepted on its claims.

These writers are trapped in a terrible contradiction. Their form of compassion is not to blame, and they find that they cannot portray life at all without assigning blame. Therefore, since their concept of compassion will not permit them to blame anything upon the criminal, the degraded, and the destroyed, they blame everything upon the noncriminal, the nondegraded and the undestroyed. It is a kind of counter-puritanism.

The irony is that these writers have no intermediate ground. Many so-called good people are responsible for the destruction of others. All of us are involved in the guilt of mankind. Throughout literature and life we see it. But you have to have a standard of values in order to see how corrupt, warped, misdirected values destroy themselves and others. That's the realm of tragedy, of individuality and subtlety. If you have no values, and see no values, you cannot distinguish the hypocrite from the virtuous man, the self-righteous man from the genuinely good, the Uriah Heep from the man of honest humility. The world contains them all, and more. Beginning by seeing only bad, the new compassion ends by inverting it to be a curious "good" to which normal life stands as a kind of "bad." "Evil, be thou my good": this is the key to our paranoid novelists.

The existentialists and those influenced by them, and many who unconsciously have been practicing existentialists without the fancy jargon, portray human depravity and degradation without comment, presumably as they see it. This is a kind of moral neutralism. It makes no judgment, on the grounds that there is no judgment. But these writers show phenomena without meaning. If we give depravity no significance we imply that it has no significance. Far from being neutral or unmoralistic or undogmatic, this is a highly partisan, positive philosophical position indeed.

The conflict between good and evil is a common thread running through all the great literature and drama of the world, from the Greeks to ourselves. The principle that conflict is at the heart of all dramatic action, when illustrated by concrete example, almost always turns up some aspect of the struggle between good and evil.

The idea that there is neither good nor evil—in any absolute moral or religious sense—is widespread in our times. There are various relativistic, behavioristic standards of ethics. If they even admit the distinction between good and evil they see it as a relative matter and not as the whirlwind of choices at the center of living. In any such state of mind, conflict can be only a petty matter at best, lacking true universality. The acts of the evildoer and of the virtuous man alike become dramatically neutralized. Imagine *Crime and Punishment* or *The Brothers Karamazov* if Dostoevsky had thought that the good and the evil in those books were wholly a relative matter and had had no conviction about them.

You can't have a vital literature if you ignore or shun evil. What you get then is the goody-goody in place of the good, the world of Pollyanna. *Cry, the Beloved Country* is a great and dramatic novel because Alan Paton, in addition to his skill of workmanship, sees with clear eyes both good and evil, differentiates them, pitches them into conflict with each other, *and takes sides*. He sees that the native boy, Absalom Kumalo, who has murdered, cannot be judged justly without taking into account the environment that has partly shaped him. But he sees, too, that Absalom the individual, not society the abstraction, did the act and has responsibility. Mr. Paton understands mercy. He knows that this precious thing is not shown on sentimental impulse, but after searching examination of the realities of human action. Mercy follows a judgment; it does not precede it.

One of the novels of the talented Paul Bowles, *Let It Come Down,* is full of motion, full of sensational depravities, and is a crashing bore. For the book recognizes no good, admits no evil, and is coldly indifferent to the moral behavior of its characters. It is a long shrug. Such a view of life is nondramatic, negating the vital essence of drama.

Charles Jackson is a novelist unmistakably sensitive and gifted. His novels are terrifyingly preoccupied with modes of demoralization and collapse. They depict these faithfully, but take in no other aspects of life at all. He admires and partly emulates Dostoevsky, but he does not appear to realize that the difference between the dark tones of his own work and those in Dostoevsky's novels is precisely that Dostoevsky took sides. He was not neutral in the conflict between good and evil. The gulf fixed between Jackson and Dostoevsky is not one of literary craftsmanship but of moral sense.

Dostoevsky views Raskolnikov with compassion, for he sees and interprets for us the moral fallacy that entrapped Raskolnikov. If there were no such fallacy, if Dostoevsky had perceived no moral standard to be warped, Raskolnikov (whose name means "the dissenter") would have been a mere Russian Robert E. Lee Prewitt, and there would have been no tragedy. The great depth of *Crime and Punishment* (the very title states it) is that both Dostoevsky the author and

Raskolnikov the created character are conscious of the moral dilemma.

Dreiser, in *An American Tragedy,* sees Clyde Griffiths with compassion because he shows us how the boy has been undermined by a shoddy set of material values and is poorly equipped to appraise them. Dreiser sees the good and evil in the American era he portrays; the social tragedy is that there are those like Clyde who can see them only dimly, if at all.

The original muckrakers portrayed horrors with a fierce indignation against the social injustice they saw as causative, if sometimes too simply. So it is in Upton Sinclair's *The Jungle.* But these men were reformers. Their eyes were fixed upon a good of which they saw men deprived, and which they were determined passionately to restore. In the writers we are discussing, the vision of the good is lost. They stare hypnotized upon the mess as if they conceived it to be the sole, or total, reality of life.

Many novelists of talent other than those named are more or less involved in the confusion of identification with compassion, in the process of representing a facet of life as if it were the whole and of presenting phenomena without the evaluation which the greatest of writers, and even the mere reformers, never have shrunk from offering. They feel that by detailing innumerable horrors without visible revulsion they are somehow demonstrating sympathy. They conceive their virtue as not casting stones at the sinner, but many cast stones in other directions, and some reverse the words of Jesus to say, in effect, "Neither do I condemn you—go and sin some more."

National Book Award juries have shown an affinity for new-compassion novels. In addition to *From Here to Eternity,* they have given the palm to Nelson Algren's *The Man with the Golden Arm* and Saul Bellow's *The Adventures of Augie March.* In Algren's skillful work, including the recent *A Walk on the Wild Side,* there may be sympathy, but it remains the one-sided sympathy of the new compassion. The promising talent of Norman Mailer has collapsed utterly into this genre in *Barbary Shore* and *The Deer Park.* Leonard Bishop's novels belong there, and Irving Shulman's at least lean that way. The total catalogue of writers and books within this category would be burdensome to compile.

Some borderline books of the kind we are discussing are no more than crying novels or—to be more blunt about a few—sniveling novels. A vast and blurred self-pity is appliquéd upon the fictional characters—as if to do this represented compassion in the author. In some cases it is simple transference of the author's own self-pity, as shown by the inability to see or move beyond it in portraying life. In some, the assiduous stock-piling of depravities has an unmistakable element of reveling, of wallowing, of bad-boy's glee. Many of these writers cry, "Look, Ma, I'm blaspheming."

There are merely fitful glimmerings of life and agitated motions in the books of such novelists. The vital questions which would bring them to profound life have been nullified. You cannot say of their attitude toward their characters, "To understand all is to forgive all." They see much but understand nothing. They do not understand all—they *devalue* all. They do not forgive all. They do not forgive anything. They say there is nothing to forgive. They take murder, rape, perversion and say, belligerently, "What's wrong with it?"

You cannot say of their characters, "There but for the grace of God go I," because you cannot find in their work any chain of moral cause and effect by which *you* could get from where *you* are to where their characters are (as you can in Dostoevsky and Paton). The placement of these characters in their situations is arbitrary and mechanical, as is the inversion of good and bad.

The irony of ironies is that these are not the most compassionate, but the most vindictive writers working today; not the most humble, but the most arrogant; not the binders of the wounds of their fallen brothers, but the destroyers of the social order. "Down! Down everybody!" they scream. "Down with us all!"

Dostoevsky anticipated this moral phenomenon as he did so many others. These paranoid novels are books that some of his brilliantly studied characters might have written. Ivan

Karamazov said, "Everything is permitted," and Smerdyakov, acting accordingly, murdered. Raskolnikov saw moral law as inapplicable to some men, and acting accordingly, murdered. Ideas are more than abstractions, Dostoevsky shows us again and again. Ideas have consequences. God preserve us from the consequences of the ideas implicit in the novels of the new compassion.

THE PSYCHOLOGICAL APPROACH:

LITERATURE AND PSYCHOLOGICAL THEORY

Introduction

BY THE EARLY YEARS of our second decade, most writers were acquainted with the ideas of Freud. A. A. Brill had translated into English *Three Contributions to the Theory of Sex* in 1910, and in 1912, *The Interpretation of Dreams.* Also as early as 1910, Dr. Ernest Jones had published his first attempt to interpret *Hamlet* from a Freudian point of view.[1] These works were of special interest to writers, seeming to offer a key—perhaps *the* key—to the processes of art, the unconscious intentions of artists, and the motives of fictitious characters.

The attraction of Freudian theory to creative writers is easily explained. Literary Naturalism (especially French) had presented an image of man as a victim of environment and/or biology. Freudian ideas substantiated these insights, offering a "scientific" terminology by which to interpret man's bondage to his libidinous compulsions, or to the repressions society forced upon him. The Freudian judgment—that man is sick rather than villainous—fit neatly with the Naturalist's refusal to condemn a being who was not responsible, but was the dupe of natural and preterhuman forces. Psychology likewise seemed to give sanction to the Romantic impulse toward self-expression and the exploitation of the perverse. Much of the "madness" of the French Symbolists and the experimentalists who followed them could now be regarded as the method of the unconscious.

So with the spreading of Freud's theories and a new terminology, writers of both Romantic and Realistic persuasions were enabled and encouraged to probe deeper in their dramatizations of the human situation. In time the impact of psy-

[1] "The Oedipus Complex as an Explanation of Hamlet's Mystery," in *The American Journal of Psychology,* XXI (1910). This later was expanded and revised, until it reached its final form as *Hamlet and Oedipus,* 1949, the classic example of the psychological interpretation of a fictitious character.

chology upon creative literature was strengthened by the additional influence of Adler's concept of the inferiority complex, and of Jung's theory of the collective unconscious. But the earliest force was Freudian. Its presence in the work of Lawrence, Mann, Sherwood Anderson and others has been studied by F. J. Hoffman in *Freudianism and the Literary Mind,* 1945, and one can also note without difficulty the part psychology has played in the writings of May Sinclair, Joyce, Katherine Mansfield, Graham Greene, and Dylan Thomas.

It was inevitable that critics as well as creative writers should turn to the new field of knowledge for illumination. The first result seems to have been the enlistment of the new "science" in the war against the Past, particularly the Puritan culture in America, and the Victorian in England. The values of both these traditions, devoted to kinds of "high seriousness," were especially vulnerable to the new weapon. If the virtues of reticence, chastity, gentility, respectability, and so on, could be exposed as unhealthy repressions of the id rather than as revelations of divinity, then those who argued for the retention of such traditional values could be effectively accused of ignorance or deliberate and regressive blindness. Randolph Bourne's "The Puritan's Will to Power" [2] is one of many examples of the attempt to destroy, with the aid of psychology, those traditional values which the Neo-Humanists were concerned to salvage.

The flourishing use of psychology in literary criticism began with Conrad Aiken's *Skepticisms: Notes on Contemporary Poetry,* 1919. Max Eastman and Floyd Dell, as editors of *The Masses,* despite their inclination to stress sociological values, certainly helped to popularize the psychological approach. In England Robert Graves wrote from the new point of view, although in his case the point of view was rather particular, being the application of W. H. Rivers' theory of the conflict of unconscious personalities. And Herbert Read pleaded for the use of the new field of knowledge in criticism in his *Reason and Romanticism,* 1926.

[2] In *The Seven Arts,* April 1917.

Of course in the first unqualified enthusiasm, many critics used the tools injudiciously. Some had only a superficial comprehension of psychology and applied it indiscriminately to ferret out erotic motive and meaning behind the work of art. But this is the sort of error that is an inevitable result of such a delicious and heady draft. As critics came to hold themselves more soberly responsible for psychological theory, and as growing restraint checked the excesses, the light cast by psychology upon literature began to appear more substantial.

In general the application of psychological knowledge to art can generate three kinds of illumination. First, as I. A. Richards has illustrated, the new field provides a more precise language with which to discuss the creative process. In *Principles of Literary Criticism,* 1924, Richards analyzed the constituents of the æsthetic experience, following the definition he and his collaborators, Ogden and Wood, had established earlier:[3] Beauty is "that which is conducive to synæsthetic equalibrium"—that is, a particular and harmonious kind of response in the audience, brought about by the stimulus of a work of art. Although many had quarreled with one part or another of his work, almost no critic since Richards published his studies has been able to work without recognizing some of his insights. The use to which his kind of analysis has been put can be seen in Kenneth Burke's essay, "Antony in Behalf of the Play"[4] in which this critic brilliantly examines the unconscious relations between writer and reader.

A second application goes back, as Edmund Wilson has pointed out, to literary biography, to the study of the lives of authors as a means of understanding their art. Psychology, of course, enables biographers to speculate upon the "interior" parts of a life. The criticism that employs this approach assumes that an important part of the relationship between artist and art is similar to that between patient and dream; assumes that, as D. H. Lawrence put it, the writer

[3] In *The Foundations of Aesthetics,* 1922.
[4] In *The Philosophy of Literary Form,* 1941.

has "shed his sickness" in his books. The critic then becomes the analyst, taking the art as the symptom, by interpretation of which he can discover the unconscious repressions and drives of the artist. These discoveries may lead in turn to an understanding, even an interpretation, of the work of art itself. Essays in Wilson's *The Wound and the Bow* exemplify how effectively this approach can be used to lead us to understand not only the personal problems of writers, but also the underlying patterns of their writings.

Third, psychology can be used to explain fictitious characters. F. L. Lucas in *Literature and Psychology,* 1951, provides numerous instances from life which clarify the actions and reactions of created characters who might otherwise be puzzling or implausible. The critic who brings this interest to fiction becomes, again, a psychoanalyst, searching for the subconscious patterns which motivate a character. The classic example is, of course, Ernest Jones's study of Hamlet in which he expands the theory he had sketched in 1910. Dr. Jones provides an answer to the puzzle of Hamlet's delay in avenging his father—an answer that could perhaps not have been conceived, certainly not easily expressed, before the development of Freudian psychology. The effect that such an approach to literature can make upon the interpretation of art can be seen almost as remarkably in the numerous psychological studies of Henry James's *The Turn of the Screw,* beginning with Edna Kenton's essay in 1924.[5]

Attacks upon the psychological approach have been of two sorts. One charge is oversimplification, such as occurred early when the tools were new and the spirit of the users was uncritical. Van Wyck Brooks's *The Ordeal of Mark Twain,* 1920, and Lewisohn's *Expression in America,* 1932, have both been attacked on these grounds, although both books nonetheless offer interesting and valuable insights. Another criticism has been more central: that art is significantly different from dream in that the artist is largely, or at least to some extent, in control of his product, as the dreamer is not. The

[5] The main documents have been collected by Gerald Willen in *A Casebook on Henry James's "The Turn of the Screw,"* 1960.

dream may be compulsive confession; art is composed expression. Lionel Trilling and Kenneth Burke have intelligently explored this sort of distinction and related matters in essays which aim to define the uses and limits of psychology for both writer and critic.

A final note. One branch of psychological criticism deals with the unconscious—not of the individual writer or character, but of the race or culture. This approach seems to merit separate attention, especially since it has relations with another field of knowledge, social anthropology, and therefore is best considered under the heading, "The Archetypal Approach."

Bibliographical Note

There are many essays and books which merit attention, in addition to the numerous works already cited. Broad matters of literary concern are treated in F. C. Prescott, *The Poetic Mind*, 1922; Thomas Beers, *The Mauve Decade*, 1926; Herbert Muller, *Modern Fiction*, 1937—one of the few Gestalt approaches; Hanns Sachs, *The Creative Unconscious*, 1942; Roy Basler, *Sex, Symbolism and Psychology in Art*, 1948; and Simon O. Lesser, *Fiction and the Unconscious*, 1957.

Some critical biographies using the materials of psychology: Sir Harold Nicolson, *Tennyson: Aspects of his Life, Character and Poetry*, 1923 and 1932; the same author's *Swinburne*, 1926; Joseph Wood Krutch, *Edgar Allan Poe: A Study in Genius*, 1926; Lewis Mumford, *Herman Melville*, 1929; John Middleton Murry, *The Son of Woman: The Story of D. H. Lawrence*, 1931; Enid Starkie, *Baudelaire*, 1933 (revised 1957); and Marie Bonaparte, *Life and Works of Edgar Allan Poe*, 1953. An excellently illustrative chapter from her book appears, in English translation, in *Partisan Review*, XVII (November, 1950).

Several single essays are worth special mention: William Troy, "Stendhal," in *Partisan Review*, IX (January-February, 1942); Saul Rosenzweig, "The Ghost of Henry James," in *Partisan Review*, XI (Fall, 1944); M. I. Seiden, "A Psychoanalytical Study" (of Yeats's early poems) in *Accent*, VI (Spring, 1946); and Ernst Kris, "Prince Hal's Conflict" in *Psychoanalytical Quarterly*, XVIII (October, 1948).

William Phillips, of *Partisan Review*, has introduced and edited a fine collection of essays which relate psychology to literature, under the title *Art and Psychoanalysis*, 1957.

The Poetic Process

By Kenneth Burke

IF WE WISH to indicate a gradual rise to a crisis, and speak of this as a climax, or a crescendo, we are talking in intellectualistic terms of a mechanism which can often be highly emotive. There is in reality no such general thing as a crescendo. What does exist is a multiplicity of individual artworks each of which may be arranged as a whole, or in some parts, in a manner which we distinguish as climactic. And there is also in the human brain the potentiality for reacting favorably to such a climactic arrangement. Over and over again in the history of art, different material has been arranged to embody the principle of the crescendo; and this must be so because we "think" in a crescendo, because it parallels certain psychic and physical processes which are at the roots of our experience. The accelerated motion of a falling body, the cycle of a storm, the procedure of the sexual act, the ripening of crops—growth here is not merely a linear progression, but a fruition. Indeed, natural processes are, inevitably, "formally" correct, and by merely recording the symptoms of some physical development we can obtain an artistic development. Thomas Mann's work has many such natural forms converted into art forms, as, in *Death in Venice,* his charting of a sunrise and of the progressive stages in a cholera epidemic. And surely, we may say without much fear of startling anyone, that the work of art utilizes climactic arrangement because the human brain has a pronounced potentiality for being arrested, or entertained, by such an arrangement.

But the concept "crescendo" does not have the emotive value of a crescendo. To arouse the human potentiality for being moved by the crescendo, I must produce some particular experience embodying a crescendo, a story, say, about A and B, where A becomes more and more involved in difficulties with B and finally shoots him. Here I have replaced the concept by a work of art illustrating it, and now for the first time I have an opportunity of making the crescendo play upon the human emotions.

In this way the work of art is seen to involve a principle of individuation. A shoots B in a crescendo, X weathers a flood and rescues Y in a crescendo—the artist may particularize, or individuate, the crescendo in any of the myriad aspects possible to human experience, localizing or channelizing it according to the chance details of his own life and vision. And similarly, throughout the permutations of history, art has always appealed, by the changing individuations of changing subject matter, to certain potentialities of appreciation which would seem to be inherent in the very germ-plasm of man, and which, since they are constant, we might call innate forms of the mind. These forms are the "potentiality for being interested by certain processes or arrangements," or the "feeling for such arrangements of subject matter as produce crescendo, contrast, comparison, balance, repetition, disclosure, reversal, contraction, expansion, magnification, series, and so on." Such "forms of the mind" might be listed at greater length. But I shall stop at the ones given, as I believe they illustrate to the extent of being a definition of my meaning. At bottom these "forms" may be looked upon as minor divisions of the two major "forms," unity and diversity. In any case, both unity and diversity will be found intermingling in any example of such forms. Contrast, for instance, is the use of elements which conflict in themselves but are both allied to a broader unity (as laughter on one page, tears on the next, but each involving an incident which furthers the growth of the plot). But the emotions cannot enjoy these forms, or laws (naturally, since they are merely the *conditions of emotional response*) except in their concreteness, in their quasi-vitiating material incorporation, in their specification or individuation.

This statement can be made clearer by comparing and contrasting it with the doctrines of Plato. Plato taught that the world of our senses is the manifestation of divine law through material. Thus, he supposed certain archetypes, or pure ideas, existing in heaven, while the objects of sensuous experience were good, true, and beautiful in proportion as they exemplified the pure form or idea behind them. Physical, or sensuous beauty, is valuable in so far as it gives us glimpses of the divine beauty, the original form, of which it is an imperfect replica.

Scholastic philosophy concerned itself principally with the problems raised by this teaching. The divine forms were called universals, and the concept of a principle of individuation was employed to describe the conditions under which we could experience these divine forms. *"Universale intelligitur, singulare sentitur,"* their position was finally stated: "We think in terms of universals, but we feel particulars." Or, to illustrate, "We may make an intellectual concept of goodness, but we can experience only some particular good thing."

Thus, the Platonic teaching was gradually reversed, and finally became branded as representative of a typically erroneous attitude. To say that an object is good in that it reflects the divine idea, or archetype, of goodness is, according to the nominalists, the mistake of hypostatization, of mistaking a linguistic convenience for a metaphysical reality. What really happens, they say, is that we find certain objects appealing in one way or another (tasty, beneficial, mild, obedient) and in the economy of speech use the word "good" for all these aspects of appeal. And since another economy of speech is the conversion of adjectives into nouns, we next turn "good" into "goodness" and suppose that there is some actual thing, sitting somewhere, which corresponds to this word. This is to misunderstand the nature of language, they assert: and this misunderstanding results from the naïve supposition that, since each object has a word to designate it, so each word designates an object. Thus, they see no need for going from the particular to the universal; and they might, rather, define goodness as a complex of conditions in the human mind, body, and environment which make some objects, through a variety of ways, more appealing than others.

So eager were the nominalists to disavow Plato in detail, that they failed to discover the justice of his doctrines in essence. For we need but take his universals out of heaven and situate them in the human mind (a process begun by Kant), making them not metaphysical, but psychological. Instead of divine forms, we now have "conditions of appeal." There need not be a "divine contrast" in heaven for me to appreciate a contrast; but there *must be* in my mind the sense of contrast. The researches of anthropologists indicate that man has "progressed" in cultural cycles which repeat themselves in essence (in form) despite the limitless variety of specific details to embody such essences, or forms. Speech, material traits (for instance, tools), art, mythology, religion, social systems, property, government, and war—these are the nine "potentials" which man continually reindividuates into specific cultural channels, and which anthropologists call the "universal pattern." And when we speak of psychological universals, we mean simply that just as there is inborn in the germ-plasm of a dog the potentiality of barking, so there is inborn in the germ-plasm of man the potentiality of speech, art, mythology, and so on. And while these potentialities are continually changing their external aspects, their "individuations," they do not change in essence. Given the potentiality for speech, the child of any culture will speak the language which it hears. There is no mental equipment for speaking Chinese which is different from the mental equipment for speaking English. But the potentiality externalizes itself in accordance with the traditions into which the individual happens to be born. And by education we do not mean the "awaking" of a moral, or religious, or social, or artistic sense, but the leading of such potentialities into one specific channel. We cannot teach the moral sense any more than we can teach abstract thought to a dog. But we can individuate the moral sense by directing it into a specific code or tradition. The socialists today imply this fact when they object to the standard *bourgeois* education, meaning that it channelizes the potentialities of the child into a code which protects the *bourgeois* interests, whereas they would have these same potentialities differently individuated to favor the proletarian revolution.

This, I hope, should be sufficient to indicate that there is no hypostatization in speaking of innate forms of the mind, and mentioning "laws" which the work of art makes accessible to our emotions by individuation. And for our purposes we might translate the formula *"universale intelligitur, singulare sentitur"* into some such expansion as this: "We can discuss the basic forms of the human mind under such concepts as crescendo, contrast, comparison, and so on. But to experience them emotionally, we must have them singularized into an example, an example which will be chosen by the artist from among his emotional and environmental experiences."

Whereupon, returning to the Poetic Process, let us suppose that while a person is sleeping some disorder of the digestion takes place, and he is physically depressed. Such depression in the sleeper immediately calls forth a corresponding psychic depression, while this psychic depression in turn translates itself into the invention of details which will more or less adequately symbolize this depression. If the sleeper has had some set of experiences strongly marked by the feeling of depression, his mind may summon details from this experience to symbolize his depression. If he fears financial ruin, his depression may very reasonably seize upon the cluster of facts associated with this fear in which to individuate itself. On the other hand, if there is no strong set of associations in his mind clustered about the mood of depression, he may invent details which, on waking, seem inadequate to the mood. This fact accounts for the incommunicable wonder of a dream, as when at times we look back on the dream and are mystified at the seemingly unwarranted emotional responses which the details "aroused" in us. Trying to convey to others the emotional overtones of this dream, we laboriously recite the details, and are compelled at every turn to put in such confessions of defeat as "There was something strange about the room," or "For some reason or other I was afraid of this boat, although there doesn't seem to be any good reason now." But the details were not the cause of the emotion; the emotion, rather, dictated the selection of the details. Especially when the emotion was one of marvel or mystery, the invented details seem inadequate—the dream becoming, from the standpoint of communication, a flat failure, since the emotion failed to individuate itself into adequate symbols. And the sleeper himself, approaching his dream from the side of consciousness after the mood is gone, feels how inadequate are the details for conveying the emotion that caused them, and is aware that even for him the wonder of the dream exists only in so far as he still remembers the quality pervading it. Similarly, a dreamer may awaken himself with his own hilarious laughter, and be forthwith humbled as he recalls the witty saying of his dream. For the delight in the witty saying came first (was causally prior) and the witty saying itself was merely the externalization, or individuation, of this delight. Of a similar nature are the reminiscences of old men, who recite the facts of their childhood, not to force upon us the trivialities and minutiæ of these experiences, but in the forlorn hope of conveying to us the "overtones" of their childhood, overtones which, unfortunately, are beyond reach of the details which they see in such an incommunicable light, looking back as they do upon a past which is at once themselves and another.

The analogy between these instances and the procedure of the poet is apparent. In this way the poet's moods dictate the selection of details and thus individuate themselves into one specific work of art.

However, it may have been noticed that in discussing the crescendo and the dream I have been dealing with two different aspects of the art process. When art externalizes the human sense of crescendo by inventing one specific crescendo, this is much different from the dream externalizing depression by inventing a combination of details associated with depression. If the artist were to externalize his mood of horror by imagining the facts of a murder, he would still have to externalize his sense of crescendo by the arrangement of these facts. In the former case he is individuating an "emotional form," in the latter a "technical form." And if the emotion makes for the consistency of his details, by determining their selection, technique makes for the vigor, or saliency, or power of the art-work by determining its arrangement.[1]

We now have the poet with his moods to be individuated into subject matter, and his feeling for technical forms to be individuated by the arrangement of this subject matter. And as our poet is about to express himself, we must now examine the nature of self-expression.

First, we must recognize the element of self-expression which is in all activity. In both metaphysics and the sphere of human passions, the attraction of two objects has been called will, love, gravitation. Does water express itself when it seeks its level? Does the formation of a snow crystal satisfy some

---

[1] This saliency is, of course, best maintained by the shifting of technical forms. Any device for winning the attention, if too often repeated, soon becomes wearisome. Chesterton's constant conversion of his thoughts into paradox, for instance, finally inoculates us against the effect intended. Yet any one thought, given this form, is highly salient. The exploitation of a few technical forms produces *mannerism*, while the use of many produces *style*. A page of Shakespeare can be divided endlessly into technical devices (no doubt, for the most part, spontaneously generated): shifting rhythms within the blank verse, coincidences and contrasts of vowel quantity, metaphors, epigrams, miniature plot processes where in a few lines some subject rises, blossoms, and drops— while above the whole is the march and curve of the central plot itself. Yet even Shakespeare tends to bludgeon us at times with the too frequent use of metaphor, until what was an allurement threatens to become an obstacle. We might say that the hypertrophy of metaphor is Shakespeare at his worst, and fills in those lapses of inspiration when he is keeping things going as best he can until the next flare-up. And thus, as with the music of Bach, if he at times attains the farthest reaches of luminosity and intensity, he never falls beneath the ingenious. . . . A writer like Proust, any single page of whom is astounding, becomes wearisome after extended reading. Proust's technical forms, one might say, are limited to the exploitation of parenthesis within parenthesis, a process which is carried down from whole chapters, through parts of chapters, into the paragraph, and thence into the halting of the single sentence.

spiritual hunger awakened by the encroachment of chill upon dormant clouds? Foregoing these remoter implications, avoiding what need not here be solved, we may be content with recognizing the element of self-expression in all human activities. There is the expression of racial properties, types of self-expression common to all mankind, as the development from puberty to adolescence, the defense of oneself when in danger, the seeking of relaxation after labor. And there is the self-expression of personal characteristics: the development from puberty to adolescence manifesting itself in heightened religiosity, cruelty, sentimentality, or cynicism; the defense of oneself being procured by weapons, speech, law, or business; the relaxation after labor being sought in books rather than alcohol, alcohol rather than books, woman rather than either —or perhaps by a long walk in the country. One man attains self-expression by becoming a sailor, another by becoming a poet.

Self-expression today is too often confused with pure utterance, the spontaneous cry of distress, the almost reflex vociferation of triumph, the clucking of the pheasant as he is startled into flight. Yet such utterance is obviously but one small aspect of self-expression. And, if it is a form of self-expression to utter our emotions, it is just as truly a form of self-expression to provoke emotions in others, if we happen to prefer such a practice, even though the emotions aimed at were not the predominant emotions of our own lives. The maniac attains self-expression when he tells us that he is Napoleon; but Napoleon attained self-expression by commanding an army. And, transferring the analogy, the self-expression of the artist, *qua* artist, is not distinguished by the uttering of emotion, but by the evocation of emotion. If, as humans, we cry out that we are Napoleon, as artists we seek to command an army.

Mark Twain, before setting pen to paper, again and again transformed the bitterness that he *wanted* to utter into the humor that he *could* evoke. This would indicate that his desire to evoke was a powerful one; and an event which is taken by Mr. Van Wyck Brooks as an evidence of frustration can just as easily be looked upon as the struggle between two kinds of self-expression. We might say that Mark Twain, as artist, placed so much greater emphasis upon evocation than utterance that he would even change the burden of his message, evoking what he best could, rather than utter more and evoke less. Certain channels of expression will block others. To become an athlete, for instance, I must curb my appetite for food and drink; or I may glut and carouse, and regret to the end of my days the flabbiness of my muscles. Perhaps those critics, then, who would see us emancipated, who would show us a possible world of expression without frustration, mean simply that we are now free to go and storm a kingdom, to go and become Napoleons? In this they provide us with a philosophy of action rather than a method, and in the last analysis I fear that their theories are the self-expression of utterance, not a rigid system for compelling conviction, but a kind of standard for those of their own mind to rally about.

Thus, we will suppose that the artist, whom we have left for some time at the agonizing point of expressing himself, discovers himself not only with a message, but also with a desire to produce effects upon his audience. He will, if fortunate, attempt to evoke the feelings with which he himself is big; or else these feelings will undergo transformations (as in the case of Twain) before reaching their fruition in the art-work. Indeed, it is inevitable that all initial feelings undergo some transformation when being converted into the mechanism of art, and Mark Twain differs from less unhappy artists not in kind, but in degree. Art is a translation, and every translation is a compromise (although, be it noted, a compromise which may have new virtues of its own, virtues not part of the original). The mechanism invented to reproduce the original mood of the artist in turn develops independent requirements. A certain theme of itself calls up a countertheme; a certain significant moment must be prepared for. The artist will add some new detail of execution because other details of his mechanism have created the need for it; hence while the originating emotion is still in ferment, the artist is concerned with impersonal mechanical processes.

This leads to another set of considerations: *the artist's*

means are always tending to become ends in themselves. The
artist begins with his emotion, he translates this emotion into
a mechanism for arousing emotion in others, and thus his
interest in his own emotion transcends into his interest in the
treatment. If we called beauty the artist's means of evoking
emotion, we could say that the relationship between beauty
and art is like that between logic and philosophy. For if logic
is the implement of philosophy, it is just as truly the end of
philosophy. The philosopher, as far as possible, erects his
convictions into a logically progressive and well ordered
system of thought, because he would rather have such a system than one less well ordered. So true is this, that at certain
stages in the world's history when the content of philosophy
has been thin, philosophers were even more meticulous than
usual in their devotion to logical pastimes and their manipula-
tion of logical processes. Which is to say that the philosopher
does not merely use logic to convince others; he uses logic
because he loves logic, so that logic is to him as much an end
as a means. Others will aim at conviction by oratory, because
they prefer rhetoric as a channel of expression. While in the
Inquisition conviction was aimed at through the channel of
physical torture, and presumably because the Inquisitors cate-
gorically enjoyed torture.[2] This consideration shows the poet
as tending towards two extremes, or unilaterals: the extreme
of utterance, which makes for the ideal of spontaneity and
"pure" emotion, and leads to barbarism in art; and the extreme of pure beauty, or means conceived exclusively as end,
which leads to virtuosity, or decoration. And, in that fluctua-
ting region between pure emotion and pure decoration, humanity and craftsmanship, utterance and performance, lies
the field of art, the evocation of emotion by mechanism, a
norm which, like all norms, is a conflict become fusion.

The poet steps forth, and his first step is the translation of

[2] Such a position, it has been contended, does not explain Demosthenes employing eloquence in his defense. We answer that it
explains Demosthenes at a much earlier period when, with pebbles
in his mouth, he struggled to perfect that medium which was
subsequently to make his defense necessary. The medium which
got him into trouble, he had to call upon to get him out of
trouble.

his original mood into a symbol. So quickly has the mood become something else, no longer occupying the whole of the artist's attention, but serving rather as a mere indicator of direction, a principle of ferment. We may imagine the poet to suffer under a feeling of inferiority, to suffer sullenly and mutely until, being an artist, he spontaneously generates a symbol to externalize this suffering. He will write, say, of the King and the Peasant. This means simply that he has attained articulacy by linking his emotion to a technical form, and it is precisely this junction of emotion and technical form which we designate as the "germ of a plot," or "an idea for a poem." For such themes are merely the conversion of one's mood into a relationship, and the consistent observance of a relationship is the conscious or unconscious observance of a technical form. To illustrate:

In "The King and the Peasant" the technical form is one of contrast: the Humble and the Exalted. We might be shown the King and the Peasant, each in his sphere, each as a human being; but the "big scene" comes when the King is convoyed through the streets, and the Peasant bows speechless to the passing of the royal cortège. The Peasant, that is, despite all the intensity and subtlety of his personal experiences, becomes at this moment Peasant in the abstract—and the vestiture of sheer kingliness moves by. . . . This basic relationship may be carried by variation into a new episode. The poet may arrange some incidents, the outcome of which is that the King and the Peasant find themselves in a common calamity, fleeing from some vast impersonal danger, a plague or an earthquake, which, like lightning, strikes regardless of prestige. Here King and Peasant are leveled as in death: both are Humble before the Exalted of unseen forces. . . . The basic relationship may now be inverted. The King and the Peasant, say, are beset by brigands. There is a test of personal ingenuity or courage, it is the Peasant who saves the day, and lo! the Peasant is proved to be a true King and the King a Peasant.[3]

[3] This is, of course, an overly simplified example of technical form as a generative principle, yet one can cite the identical procedure in a noble poem, *Lycidas*. After repeating for so long in

Our suppositional poet is now producing furiously, which prompts us to realize that his discovery of the symbol is no guarantee of good writing. If we may believe Jules Gaultier, Flaubert possessed genius in that he so ardently desired to be a genius; and we might say that this ratio was reindividuated into the symbol of Madame Bovary, a person trying to live beyond her station. This symbol in turn had to be carried down into a myriad details. But the symbol itself made for neither good writing nor bad. George Sand's symbols, which seemed equally adequate to encompass certain emotional and ideological complexities of her day, did not produce writing of such beauty. While as for Byron, we approach him less through the beauty of his workmanship than through our interest in, sympathy with, or aversion to, Byronism—Byronism being the quality behind such symbols as Manfred, Cain, and Childe Harold: the "man against the sky."

This brings up the matter of relationship between the symbol and the beautiful.

This symbol, I should say, attracts us by its power of formula, exactly as a theory of history or science. If we are enmeshed in some nodus of events and the nodus of emotions surrounding those events, and someone meets us with a diagnosis (simplification) of our partially conscious, partially unconscious situation, we are charmed by the sudden illumination which this formula throws upon our own lives. Mute Byrons (potential Byrons) were waiting in more or less avowed discomfiture for the formulation of Byronism, and when it came they were enchanted. Again and again through Byron's pages they came upon the minutiæ of their Byronism (the ramifications of the symbol) and continued enchanted. And thus, the symbol being so effective, they

---

varying details the idea that Lycidas is dead while others are left behind to mourn him ("But, oh! the heavy change, now thou art gone . . .") Milton suddenly reverses the ratio:

"Weep no more, woeful shepherds, weep no more,
     For Lycidas, your sorrow, is not dead."

Lycidas lives on in Heaven. Which is to say, it is Lycidas, and not his mourners, who is truly alive!

called the work of Byron beautiful. By which they meant that it was successful in winning their emotions.

But suppose that I am not Byronic, or rather that the Byronic element in me is subordinated to other much stronger leanings. In proportion as this is so, I shall approach Byron, not through his Byronism, but through his workmanship (not by the ramifications of the symbol, but by the manner in which these ramifications are presented). Byronism will not lead me to accept the workmanship; I may be led, rather, by the workmanship to accept Byronism. Calling only those parts of Byron beautiful which lead me to accept Byronism, I shall find less of such beauty than will all readers who are potential Byrons. Here technical elements mark the angle of my approach, and it will be the technical, rather than the symbolic, elements of the poet's mechanism that I shall find effective in evoking my emotions, and thus it will be in these that I shall find beauty. For beauty is the term we apply to the poet's success in evoking our emotions.

Falstaff may, I think, be cited as an almost perfect symbol from the standpoint of approach through workmanship, for nearly all readers are led to Falstaff solely through the brilliancy of his presentation. The prince's first speech, immediately before Falstaff himself has entered, strikes a theme and a pace which startles us into attention. Thereafter, again and again the enormous obligations which the poet has set himself are met with, until the character of this boisterous "bedpresser" becomes for us one of the keenest experiences in all literature. If one needs in himself the itch of Byronism to met Byron halfway, for the enjoyment of Falstaff he needs purely the sense of literary values.

Given the hour, Flaubert must share the honors with George Sand. But when the emphasis of society has changed, new symbols are demanded to formulate new complexities, and the symbols of the past become less appealing of themselves. At such a time Flaubert, through his greater reliance upon style, becomes more "beautiful" than Sand. Although I say this realizing that historical judgments are not settled once and for all, and some future turn of events may result in

Sand's symbols again being very close to our immediate concerns, while Flaubert might by the same accident become remote: and at such a time Flaubert's reputation would suffer. In the case of his more romantic works, this has already happened. In these works we feel the failures of workmanship, especially his neglect of an organic advancement or progression, a neglect which permits only our eye to move on from page to page while our emotions remain static, the lack of inner coordination making it impossible for us to accumulate momentum in a kind of work which strongly demands such momentum, such "anticipation and remembering." This becomes for us an insurmountable obstacle, since the symbols have ceased to be the "scandals" they were for his contemporaries, so that we demand technique where they inclined more to content themselves with "message." And thus only too often we find the *Temptations of Saint Anthony* not beautiful, but decorative, less an experience than a performance.

Yet we must not consider the symbol, in opposition to style, as outside of technical form. The technical appeal of the symbol lies in the fact that it is a principle of logical guidance, and makes for the repetition of itself in changing details which preserve as a constant the original ratio. A study of evolution, for instance, may be said to repeat again and again, under new aspects, the original proposition of evolution. And in the same way the symbol of art demands a continual restatement of itself in all the ramifications possible to the artist's imagination.[4]

---

[4] It is usually in works of fantasy that this repetition of the symbol under varying aspects can be followed most easily. In *Gulliver's Travels*, for instance, the ratio of discrepancy between Gulliver and his environment is repeated again and again in new subject matter. The ratio of the *Odyssey* is ramified in a manner which is equally obvious, being, we might say, the discovery of the propositions which were, for Homer, inherent in the idea of "man in the wide, wide world." In its purity, this repetition of the symbol's ratio usually makes for episodic plot, since precisely this repetition is the *primum mobile* of the story. Baudelaire's sonnet, *La Géante*, is a perfect instance of the episodic in miniature. Thus, in the

In closing: We have the original emotion, which is channelized into a symbol. This symbol becomes a generative force, a relationship to be repeated in varying details, and thus makes for one aspect of technical form. From a few speeches of Falstaff, for instance, we advance unconsciously to a synthesis of Falstaff; and thereafter, each time he appears on the stage, we know what to expect of him in essence, or quality, and we enjoy the poet's translation of this essence, or quality, into particulars, or quantity. The originating emotion makes for *emotional* consistency within the parts; the symbol demands a *logical* consistency within this emotional consistency. In a horror story about a murder, for instance, the emotion of horror will suggest details associated with horror, but the specific symbol of murder will limit the details of horror to those adapted to murder.[5]

The symbol faces two ways, for in addition to the technical form just mentioned (an "artistic" value) it also applies

more exuberant days, when nature created monsters, the poet would have liked to live with a giantess, like a cat with a queen; he would have peered into the fogs of her eyes; he would have crawled over the slope of her enormous knees; and when, tired, she stretched out across the countryside, he would have "slept nonchalantly beneath the shadows of her breasts, like a peaceful hamlet at the foot of a mountain." . . . This same deduction is, of course, at the bottom of every successful art-work, although where accumulation is more in evidence than linear progression (incidents of plot being "brought to a head") these simple ratios are more deeply embedded, and thus less obvious. In his monologues, his conversations with the ghost, with Polonius, with Ophelia, with his mother—in each of these instances Hamlet repeats, under a new aspect, the same "generative ratio," that symbol and enigma which is Hamlet. "A certain kind of person" is a static symbol; a murder is a dynamic one; but beneath the dynamic we will find the static.

[5] Some modern writers have attempted, without great success, to eliminate the symbol, and thus to summon the *emotional* cluster without the further limitation of a *logical* unity. This is also true of modern music. Compare, for instance, the constant circulation about a theme in classical music with the modern disregard of this "arbitrary" unity. As story today gravitates towards lyric, so sonata gravitates towards suite.

to life, serving here as a formula for our experiences, charming us by finding some more or less simple principle underlying our emotional complexities. For the symbol here affects us like a work of science, like the magic formula of the savage, like the medicine for an ill. But the symbol is also like a "message," in that once we know it we feel no call to return to it, except in our memories, unless some new element of appeal is to be found there. If we read again and again some textbook on evolution, and enjoy quoting aloud pages of it, this is because, beyond the message, there is style. For in addition to the symbol, and the ramifications of the symbol, poetry also involves the *method of presenting* these ramifications. We have already shown how a person who does not avidly need the symbol can be led to it through the excellence of its presentation. And we should further realize that the person who does avidly need the symbol loses this need the more thoroughly the symbol is put before him. I may be startled at finding myself Faust or Hamlet, and even be profoundly influenced by this formulation, since something has been told me that I did not know before. But I cannot repeat this new and sudden "illumination." Just as every religious experience becomes ritualized (artistic values taking the place of revelation) so when I return to the symbol, no matter how all-sufficient it was at the first, the test of repetition brings up a new factor, which is style.

"What we find words for," says Nietzsche, "is that for which we no longer have use in our own hearts. There is always a kind of contempt in the act of speaking." Contempt, indeed, so far as the original emotion was concerned, but not contempt for the act of speaking.

The Myth in Jane Austen

By Geoffrey Gorer

EVERYBODY, OR AT any rate nearly everybody, who is fond of English literature is devoted to the works of Jane Austen; that is pretty generally agreed. It is so generally agreed that it never seems to have occurred to anybody to inquire why these "pictures of domestic life in country villages," to use her own phrase, are able to excite such passionate adoration, or, if the inquiry is made, it is answered in terms of technique and observation. But I do not consider this answer adequate —after all, the almost unread Miss Emily Eden was not lacking in either of these qualities—and I wish to suggest that there are profounder reasons for the excessive love which she excites in so many of her admirers from Scott and Macaulay to Rudyard Kipling and Sir John Squire. The adoration of Miss Austen has at times nearly approached a cult—the sect of "Janeites"—and I propose to try to uncover the mystery behind the worship. The mystery is no unfamiliar one.

It is necessary to mention a few dates. Jane Austen was born in 1775, the youngest daughter of a country clergyman; her father died in 1805, and she then lived with her mother till her own death in 1817. She never married. In her correspondence she appears to have been devoted to her brothers and sisters, particularly her next eldest sister Cassandra: two of her brothers were in the navy. She started writing very young, and the first motive which turned her to writing was, as is clearly shown by the juvenile *Love and Friendship,* satire, or, to use the contemporary phrase, debunking. During Jane Austen's youth the Gothic novel, with its exaggerated emotions and incredible occurrences, was at the height of its fantastic popularity. At that period as at all others in later European history, the emotions depicted in the most popular poetry and fiction of the time were reflected by the majority of their ardent readers. (Until Hemingway and

91

Scott Fitzgerald wrote, the behavior of "the lost generation" was not stereotyped.) The Gothic novel and the contemporary poetry—Byron and Scott—evoked greatly enhanced and self-indulged sensibility and poignant feeling. Jane Austen was temperamentally unable to feel these violent emotions and, as a realist, did not believe they were genuine. An example of her early attitude occurs in *Love and Friendship,* in which the heroine advises the narrator that, when she is overcome by powerful emotions, she should choose to run mad, rather than to go into fainting fits; the reason being that with running mad one gets some healthful exercise, whereas with continuous fainting one is likely to fall on damp places and catch pneumonia.

It was in this spirit of mockery that she wrote *Love and Friendship,* and to a great extent *Northanger Abbey* which was written in 1798; it was also one of the primary motivations in writing *Sense and Sensibility,* which was begun in 1797, but from internal evidence, was almost completely revised before it was published in 1813. *Pride and Prejudice,* which we know to have been completely recast from the first draft made in 1796, was published the same year. *Mansfield Park* was written in 1812-1813, *Emma,* in 1814-1815, and *Persuasion* in 1815-1816. The order in which the books were written is important to my thesis.

Northanger Abbey is to a very great extent satirical, and much of the plot springs from the originals it is debunking; it shows certain features in common with the other novels, but I do not propose to study it in detail. *Persuasion,* the last novel of all, is so important as to need separate treatment. At the moment I wish to discuss the four central novels, *Sense and Sensibility, Pride and Prejudice, Mansfield Park, Emma,* to give the order in which they were written and in which I shall refer to them.

These four novels, though differing in details and characters, have all the same central theme; and it is this theme which I call Jane Austen's myth. All four novels are about young women (Marianne, Elizabeth, Fanny, Emma) who are made love to by, but finally reject, the Charming but Worthless lover (Willoughby, Wickham, Crawford, Frank Churchill) and finally marry a man whom they esteem and admire rather than love passionately (Colonel Brandon, Darcy, Edmund Bertram, Mr. Knightley). But the similarities in the novels do not end here; in all except the last to be written, *Emma,* when Mrs. Woodhouse is dead before the novel opens, the heroine's misfortunes and discomforts are to a very great extent due to the folly, stupidity or malice of her mother (Mrs. Dashwood encourages Marianne in her romanticism; Mrs. Bennet's behavior is directly responsible for Elizabeth's and Jane's unhappiness (ch. 35) and, it is suggested, for Lydia's elopement; poor Fanny Price has no less than three stupid, incompetent and spiteful mothers—Mrs. Price, Aunt Bertram and Aunt Norris—and, though Emma is motherless, her dangerous flirtation with Frank Churchill is forwarded by her mother-surrogate, Mrs. Weston). As in three out of four of the novels the heroine actively dislikes her mother, so, in three out of four of the novels she marries a man who stands in an almost paternal relationship to her. Marianne Dashwood finally marries Colonel Brandon of whom she says (ch. 7) "He is old enough to be *my* father. . . . When is a man to be safe from such wit, if age and infirmity will not protect him?" Fanny Price marries Edmund Bertram who had been "loving, guiding, protecting her as he had been doing ever since she was ten years old, her mind in so great a degree formed by his care . . . etc." (ch. 48). It is true that Miss Austen insists that their relationship is that of brother and sister (chs. 37, 46), but it is an unusual fraternal relationship, with protection entirely on one side and respect on the other. Mr. Knightley stands in a quite overtly paternal relationship to Emma; indeed, with his feebleness and hypochondria Mr. Woodhouse seems more like the grandfather than the father of a young woman. Mr. Knightley on the other hand fills every office of a father; "from family attachment and habit, and through excellence of mind, he had loved her and watched over her from a girl, with an endeavor to improve her, and an anxiety for her doing right, which no other creature had at all shared" (ch. 48). He scolds her and gives her advice (e.g. chs. 1, 43) and watches the progress of her studies (ch. 5), and, when she dances, stays with the other parents who watch the young people amusing themselves (ch. 38). It is the most obvious of the identifications.

Elizabeth, in *Pride and Prejudice,* does, it is true, marry young Mr. Darcy, but has anybody, even the author, been convinced that she loved him, or that she entertained any feelings warmer than respect or gratitude? Surely her own remark, that she must date her affection "from my first seeing his beautiful grounds at Pemberley" (ch. 59), represents the psychological truth. Moreover, there are other passages in which Miss Austen reveals the type of emotion which connected Elizabeth and Darcy. A couple of days before she does finally accept him Elizabeth muses to herself, "if he is satisfied with only regretting me, when he might have obtained my affections and hand I shall soon cease to regret him at all" (ch. 57). The really warm relationship in the novel is that between Elizabeth and her father, Mr. Bennet; Elizabeth is his favorite daughter (ch. 1) and they are able to share in private intimate jokes from which even the rest of the family are excluded; they are so attached that, when Elizabeth plans to go away for a short visit "the only pain was in leaving her father, who would certainly miss her, and who, when it came to the point, so little liked her going, that he told her to write to him, and almost promised to answer her letter" (ch. 27). And one of the chief consolations of her marriage with Darcy was that Mr. Bennet "delighted in going to Pemberley, especially when he was least expected" (ch. 61).

If these various features had occurred in only one novel they could be set down to inventiveness; their fourfold repetition shows that they were overwhelmingly important, at any rate for the author. This central myth—the girl who hates and despises her mother and marries a father-surrogate—is not the exclusive invention of Miss Austen; though, until she wrote, the sexes had been reversed and the subject considered fitter for tragedy than comedy. The most famous example is Sophocles' *Oedipus Rex.* For psychoanalysts, there will be little cause for surprise at the ease with which most of her readers so passionately identify with her heroines.

I have seen it suggested somewhere that Bernard Shaw owes much of his success to the fact that he refuses to take love seriously, and Mr. Maugham has written that "the English are not a sexual nation, and you cannot easily persuade them that a man will sacrifice anything important for love." If these diagnoses are true, there is an added reason for Miss Austen's popularity. There has probably never been a more ferocious debunker of passionate or sexual love than Jane Austen in the four central novels. The Charming but Worthless lovers in the four central novels have already been listed; the same stereotype occurs in *Northanger Abbey* (Captain Tilney: Mrs. Allen is a Silly Mother in the same book) and in *Persuasion* (W. W. Elliot). In four of the books the heroine is attracted momentarily by this stereotype, while in two (*Mansfield Park, Persuasion*) she resists their insidious (sexual) charm; but in all sexual love is portrayed as a snare and a sham, leading only to guilt, misery, and cooled affections.

Persuasion, the last of the novels to be written, is in remarkable contrast to the other four. The central figures of the myth are still present, but their roles are considerably modified. There are two "mothers," one dead before the story opens but stated to have every good quality (Emma's mother was completely characterless); and although the other "mother," Lady Russell, is, as usual, the chief cause of the heroine's unhappiness, the author treats her far more leniently than she had done before, even suggesting that there may be some excuses for her behavior. There are two Charming lovers, one, W. W. Elliot, the Worthless stereotype of the earlier novels; but though the heroine, Anne, had, ten years before the story opened, dismissed the other lover, Captain Wentworth, in exactly the same way as all Jane Austen's heroines dismiss all their Charming lovers, the sentiments he had excited had not disappeared with his dismissal; she still loves him and at the end of the book marries him. But it is the treatment of the father which is the most revolutionary;

Sir Walter Elliot, alone of the fathers in the six novels, is portrayed unmercifully as a vain, proud, stupid and endlessly selfish man; it is the most bitterly drawn character in all the novels, untempered by affection or sympathetic amusement. Not even the numerous "mothers" are treated with such active dislike.

Coming after the obsessive portrayal of the "father-daughter" relationships in the other novels, this sudden reversal is the more surprising. Indeed, it seems to suggest the possibility of a deeply personal motivation. Although it is impossible to know the childhood history of Jane Austen or to do more than guess at what her character was, I suggest that in her youth, probably 1797 or 1798, just before writing *Sense and Sensibility*, Jane Austen did in fact refuse a Charming lover; this may have been at the persuasion of her father or because she could not support the idea of leaving him alone, and could not break the bond which bound them so closely to one another. Through the intervening years she wrote and rewrote her personal dilemma proving to herself that all had been for the best, even though meanwhile father had died, leaving her alone with her mother (and the novels show her belief was that the only good mothers were dead mothers).

We know very little about the personal motives which impel writers of imaginative works to develop their fictions; but I should like to suggest that, at least in Jane Austen's case, the central fantasy corresponds very closely to the manifest content of a dream; and I should further like to suggest that the elaboration of the fantasy into a novel corresponds in some way to the analytic interpretation of a dream and the working through of the dilemma that the dream represents. In this connection it is necessary to stress the fact that the five major novels, in the form in which we have them, were written in as many years, and apparently one immediately after the other; considering the short time taken in writing, the output is enormous. *Northanger Abbey* seems never to have been revised. If we take the central plots of these five novels as dreams, we can clearly trace the gradual working out and alteration of Jane Austen's attitudes toward the members of her family constellation. It is necessary to remember that her father was a clergyman, her favorite brother a sailor, and her sister Cassandra her greatest confidante and friend.

In *Sense and Sensibility* the identification between the sisters is so complete that they seem like the split facets of a single personality. They are completely devoted to one another. One of these sisters, Marianne, marries an elderly man, after having first been attracted by a Worthless lover; the other, Elinor, has always loved, and finally marries a clergyman. The sisters' mother is silly and well meaning, and increases her daughters' unhappiness; the clergyman's mother does everything to thwart her son. The girls' father is dead.

In *Pride and Prejudice* the love between the heroine and one sister, Jane, is extremely strong; but there are three other sisters who are despised. The heroine finally makes up her mind to marry a rich and desirable young man, by which means she gets away from her hated mother and silly sisters and has her father from time to time to herself. She rejects a silly clergyman, and also a Worthless lover. Her mother and sisters are the cause of her misery. Her father is the most beloved person in the book.

In *Mansfield Park* the heroine has no sisters whom she loves. She has two sister substitutes, whom she hates, and a real sister whom she meets late in life and likes temperately. She immediately loves and eventually marries a clergyman, considerably older than herself, who stands midway between the role of father and brother. She has a brother, a sailor, to whom she is very attached. She has three silly and spiteful mothers. She rejects a Worthless lover. Apart from the father-brother, there are two other fathers, one of whom is unsympathetic and the other coarse.

In *Emma* the heroine has one sister, whom she looks down on as foolish and overdomesticated. She marries an elderly man who had always stood in the role of a father. She rejects a silly clergyman and a Worthless lover. Her characterless mother is dead, and the mother-substitute is kind and foolish.

Besides the man she marries, there is another father, senile, hypochondriacal, and gently selfish.

In *Persuasion* the heroine has two sisters whom she hates, and who exploit and neglect her. She has always loved and finally marries a sailor, a man of her own age, though, under the persuasion of a mother-substitute, she had once rejected him. She rejects a Worthless lover. The clergyman is married to a tepidly liked sister-substitute. Her ideal mother is dead, the mother-substitute is well meaning but foolish and inadvertently causes the heroine great distress. The father is hated, proud, silly and endlessly selfish.

It seems as though, by thus reworking her fantasies, Jane Austen had finally uncovered for herself the hidden motives behind the too warm, too loving, family relationships which circumscribed her life. Using symbols, she analyzed her own problems; *Persuasion* was her final solution. In this book she cried out against her starved life, and the selfishness of the father and sisters on whose account it had been starved. When she wrote this book she was nearly at the end of her life, lonely, middle-aged, and nearing the menopause. She could now only voice her regret, her despair. It is this note which makes *Persuasion,* with its poignant and sustained emotion, so completely different to her earlier and more exuberant novels. In the midst of her satirical observation Jane Austen had hidden a myth which corresponded to a facet of universal apprehension, a hidden myth which probably holds good for her myriad admirers; but in her last novel she rejected her myth, her fantasy, because she had learned that, like all myths, it was eventually an enemy of life.

The Image of the Father

*A Reading of "My Kinsman, Major Molineux"
and "I Want to Know Why"*

By Simon O. Lesser

THE SCENE of Hawthorne's story "My Kinsman, Major Molineux" is a New England colony; the time, like the place not too precisely fixed, a "moonlight" night during that period before the Revolution when Great Britain "had assumed the right of appointing the colonial governors."

A young boy of eighteen, named Robin, has come to town to seek his relative, Major Molineux. The Major is either governor of the colony or a subordinate of high rank—just which is not made clear. The boy has good reasons for wanting to find him. He is the second son of a poor clergyman. His elder brother is destined to inherit the farm "which his father cultivated in the interval of sacred duties." The Major is not only rich and influential but childless, and, during a visit paid his cousin the clergyman a year or two before the story opens, has shown an interest in Robin and his brother and hinted he would be happy to establish one of them in life. Robin has been selected for the honor, handsomely fitted out in homespun, and, to cover the expenses of his journey, given half the remnant of his father's salary of the year before.

Just before reaching the town Robin has had to cross a river, and it occurs to him that he should have perhaps asked the ferryman to direct him to the home of his kinsman or perhaps even accompany him as a guide. But he reflects that the first person he meets will serve as well. To his surprise, however, he experiences rebuff after rebuff, difficulty upon difficulty. He asks an elderly gentleman to direct him, but the man not only disclaims any knowledge of the Major; he rebukes Robin so angrily—the youth has impulsively gripped

the old man's coat—that some people nearby roar with
laughter. Robin now wanders through a maze of deserted
streets near the waterfront. Coming to a still-open tavern, he
decides to make inquiry there. He is at first cordially received,
but as soon as he asks to be directed to his relative, the inn-
keeper begins to read the description of an escaped "bounden
servant," looking at Robin in such a way as to suggest that
the description fits him exactly. Robin leaves, derisive laughter
ringing in his ears for the second time that night.

Now the youth loiters up and down a spacious street, looking at each man who passes by in the hope of finding the
Major. He is now so tired and hungry that he begins to consider the wisdom of lifting his cudgel and compelling the
first passerby he meets to direct him to his kinsman. While
toying with this idea, he turns down an empty and rather
disreputable street. Through the half-open door of the third
house he passes he catches a glimpse of a lady wearing a
scarlet petticoat and decides to address his inquiry to her. His
appearance and voice are winning, and the lady steps outside
to talk to him. She proves both attractive and hospitable.
Intimating that she is the housekeeper of the Major, who she
says is asleep, she offers to welcome the youth in his stead.
Though Robin only half believes her, he is about to follow
her when she is startled by the opening of a door in a nearby
house and leaves him to run into her own.

A watchman now approaches, muttering sleepy threats.
They are perfunctory, but sufficient to discourage Robin
temporarily from inquiring for his kinsman. He shouts an
inquiry just as the watchman is about to vanish around a
corner, but receives no reply. Robin thinks he hears a sound
of muffled laughter. He quite clearly hears a pleasant titter
from an open window above his head, whence a round arm
beckons him. Being a clergyman's son and a good youth,
Robin flees.

He now roams through the town "desperately, and at
random, . . . almost ready to believe that a spell was on
him."

Encountering a solitary passerby in the shadow of a church

steeple, Robin insists on being directed to the home of his kinsman. The passerby unmuffles his face. He proves to be a man Robin had noticed earlier at the tavern, but now half of his face has been painted a livid red, the other half black. Grinning at the surprised youth, the man tells him that his kinsman will pass that very spot within the hour. Robin settles down on the church steps to wait. As he struggles against drowsiness, strange and extraordinarily vivid fantasies flit through his mind. He dozes but, hearing a man pass by, wakes and inquires, with unwarranted peevishness, if he must wait there all night for his kinsman, Major Molineux. The stranger approaches and, seeing a country youth who is apparently homeless and without friends, offers to be of help. After hearing Robin's story he joins him to wait the arrival of the Major.

Shortly a mighty stream of people come into view. Robin gradually makes out that some of them are applauding spectators, some participants in a curious procession. It is headed by a single horseman, who bears a drawn sword and whose face is painted red and black: he is the man who has told Robin that his kinsman would pass that way within the hour. Behind the horseman come a band of wind instruments, men carrying torches, and then men in Indian and many other kinds of costume.

Robin has a feeling that he is involved in this procession, a feeling which is quickly confirmed. As the torches approach him, the leader thunders a command, the parade stops, the tumult dies down.

> Right before Robin's eye was an uncovered cart. There the torches blazed the brightest, there the moon shone out like day, and there, in tar-and-feathery dignity, sat his kinsman, Major Molineux!

The Major is a large and majestic man, but now his body is "agitated by a quick and continual tremor" he cannot quell. The encounter with Robin causes him to suffer still more deeply. He recognizes the youth on the instant.

Staring at his kinsman, Robin's knees shake and his hair bristles. Soon, however, a curious change sets in. The adventures of the night, his fatigue, the confusion of the spectacle, above all "the spectre of his kinsman reviled by that great multitude . . . [affect] him with a sort of mental inebriety." In the crowd he sees the watchman he has encountered earlier, enjoying his amazement. A woman twitches his arm: it is the minx of the scarlet petticoat. Finally, from the balcony of the large house across from the church comes a great, broad laugh which momentarily dominates everything: it is the formidable old man of whom Robin made his first inquiries and whom he later went out of his way to avoid.

> Then Robin seemed to hear the voices of . . . all who had made sport of him that night. The contagion was spreading among the multitude, when all at once, it seized upon Robin, and he sent forth a shout of laughter that echoed through the street,—every man shook his sides, every man emptied his lungs, but Robin's shout was the loudest there.

When the laughter has momentarily spent its force, the procession is resumed. Robin asks the gentleman who has been sitting beside him to direct him to the ferry. The Major, the boy realizes, will scarcely desire to see his face again. In the friendliest possible way the gentleman refuses Robin's request. He tells the youth that he will speed him on his journey in a few days if he still wants to leave. But he suggests another possibility. " '. . . if you prefer to remain with us, perhaps, as you are a shrewd youth, you may rise in the world without the help of your kinsman, Major Molineux.' "

"My Kinsman, Major Molineux" belongs, I believe, among Hawthorne's half-dozen greatest short stories. But unexpected difficulties arise when one attempts to account for the spell the story casts. Although it seems clear enough as it is read, it resists analysis. Above all, its climax is puzzling. "Mental inebriety" is hardly an adequate explanation for a youth's bare-faced mockery of an elderly relative for whom he had been searching, whose ill-treatment might have been expected to inspire feelings of compassion and anger.

Of the half-dozen critics who have discussed the story, surprisingly, no more than two seem aware that it presents any difficulties. The rest accept Hawthorne's explanation at face value. They regard "My Kinsman, Major Molineux" as the story of an ignorant country youth who, happening to wander upon the scene at an inopportune time, is first frustrated in his search as a result of the preparation the colonists are making and then becomes a reluctant and confused spectator at their humiliation of his kinsman. Such an interpretation not only fails to explain many aspects of the story; it hardly suggests why the story should interest us. It is perhaps significant that the critics who recognize that the story is by no means so one-dimensional as this, Malcolm Cowley and Q. D. Leavis, also show the keenest awareness of its greatness. Unfortunately even these critics have not succeeded, in my opinion, in penetrating to the story's richest veins of meaning.

Malcolm Cowley describes the story as "the legend of a youth who achieves manhood through searching for a spiritual father and finding that the object of his search is an imposter" (Introduction to *The Portable Hawthorne*). Leaving to one side the question of whether Robin is searching for a spiritual father, it may be said at once that there is no evidence that Major Molineux is an imposter. The first paragraph of the story tells us that the colonial servants appointed by Great Britain were likely to be resented even when they carried out instructions with some lenience; and we are later told that the Major's head had "grown gray in honor."

Mrs. Leavis regards "My Kinsman, Major Molineux" as a "prophetic forecast of . . . the rejection of England that was to occur in fact much later" ("Hawthorne as Poet," *Sewanee Review*, Spring, 1951). This is by no means as farfetched a reading of the story as it may at first appear. It has the merit of calling attention to a rebelliousness in Robin for which, as we shall see, there is a great deal of evidence. But as I think will become clear, Mrs. Leavis has perceived a secondary implication of that rebelliousness; it has a much more intimate source and reference.

The remaining critics who have commented on "Major Molineux" have evidently based their remarks almost entirely on their conscious reactions to the story's manifest level of meaning. At best, I believe, such criticism is of limited value; in connection with such a work as this it is sometimes actually misleading. Like some other stories by Hawthorne and by such writers as Melville, Kafka, Dostoevsky and Shakespeare, "My Kinsman, Major Molineux" is Janus-faced. It says one thing to the conscious mind and whispers something quite different to the unconscious. The second level of meaning is *understood* readily enough, immediately and intuitively. Our acceptance of Robin's behavior—which, as we shall see, is bizarre not only during his ultimate encounter with his kinsman but throughout the story—is only explicable, I believe, on the assumption that we understand it without difficulty. To respond to the story, to find Robin's behavior not only "right" but satisfying, we must perceive a great many things nowhere explicitly developed. These hidden implications are not meant to come to our attention as we read; they would arouse anxiety if they did. Even to get at them after one has read the story requires a deliberate exertion of will. There is still another difficulty. To deal with these implications at all systematically, one is almost compelled to make some use of depth psychology. This is a kind of knowledge most critics are curiously loathe to employ.

As soon as we look at "My Kinsman, Major Molineux" more closely, we discover that it is only in part a story of baffled search: Robin is never so intent on finding his illustrious relative as he believes he is and as it appears. The story even tells us why this is so. To some extent we understand from the very beginning; the explanations offered serve basically to remind us of things we have experienced ourselves.

As Robin walks into the town, it will be remembered, he realizes that he should probably have asked the ferryman how to get to the home of Major Molineux. Today we have scientific evidence for what Hawthorne, and we, understand intuitively, the significance of such forgetting. Earlier in the same paragraph we have been told something equally significant. Robin walks into the town "with as light a step as if his day's journey had not already exceeded thirty miles, and with as eager an eye as if he were entering London city, instead of the little metropolis of a New England colony." This though he has momentarily lost sight of the reason for his visit! As early as this we begin to suspect that the town attracts the youth for reasons which have nothing whatever to do with finding his influential relative. The intimation does not surprise us. Robin is eighteen. The ferryman has surmised that this is his first visit to town. In a general way we understand why his eye is "eager."

Robin makes his first inquiry for his kinsman with reasonable alacrity. But a considerable time appears to elapse before his second inquiry, at the tavern, and he is evidently spurred to enter it as much by the odor of food, which reminds him of his own hunger, as by any zeal to find the Major.

After his rebuff at the tavern it perhaps seems reasonable enough that Robin should drop his inquiries and simply walk through the streets looking for Major Molineux. If our critical faculties were not already somewhat relaxed, however, it might occur to us at once that this is a singularly inefficient way of looking for anyone. And Robin does not pursue his impractical plan with any ardor. He stares at the young men he encounters with as much interest as at the old ones; though he notices the jaunty gait of others, he never increases his pace; and there are many pauses "to examine the gorgeous display of goods in the shop windows."

Nor does his lack of success make him impatient. Only the approach of the elderly gentleman he had first accosted causes him to abandon his plan and turn down a side street. He is now so tired and hungry that he *considers* demanding guidance from the first solitary passerby he encounters. But while this resolution is, as Hawthorne puts it, "gaining strength," what he actually does is enter "a street of mean appearance, on either side of which a row of ill-built houses was straggling toward the harbor." It is of the utmost importance that Robin continues his "researches" on this less respectable street, although no one is visible along its entire extent. If we were not by now so completely immersed in the concealed story which is unfolding itself, we might begin to wonder consciously whether Robin is seriously searching for his kinsman.

The encounters with women which follow explain the attraction of the street. They show that unconsciously Robin is searching for sexual adventure. The strength of his desire is almost pathetically betrayed by his half-willingness to believe the cock-and-bull story of the pretty young "housekeeper." Here, if not before, we identify one of the specific forces which is inhibiting Robin in his search for his kinsman: he would like a greater measure of sexual freedom than it is reasonable to suppose he would enjoy in the home of a colonial official.

The encounter with the watchman furnishes additional evidence of Robin's ambivalence. The youth could scarcely hope to find a better person of whom to ask directions. It is likely that he is also held back in this case by guilt about what he has just been doing, but the ease with which he has permitted himself to be diverted from his search is probably one of the sources of that guilt.

After further wandering Robin finally detains the passerby who tells him that the Major will pass that very spot within the hour. In talking with the kindly gentleman who joins him to await the arrival of the Major, Robin is unable to restrain himself from boasting of his shrewdness and grown-upness. These boasts help us to understand another of the forces which has been holding him back: he wants to succeed through his own efforts and his own merit. His departure from home has evidently caused him to dream of achieving economic as well as sexual independence. When at the end of the story the gentleman suggests that Robin may decide to stay in town and may prosper without the help of his kinsman, he is simply giving expression to the youth's unvoiced but readily discernible desire.

The gentleman has an opportunity to observe how half-hearted Robin is about finding his kinsman. When the sounds of the approaching procession become more clearly audible, the youth comes to the conclusion that some kind of "prodigious merry-making" is going forward and suggests that he and his new-found friend step around the corner, to a point where he thinks everyone is hastening, and partake of their share of the fun. He has to be reminded by his companion that he is searching for his kinsman, who is supposed to pass by the place where they now are in a very short time. With insight and artistry Hawthorne spreads the evidence of Robin's irresoluteness of purpose from the very beginning of the story to the moment of Major Molineux's appearance; but so subtle is the evidence, so smoothly does it fit into the surface flow of the narrative, that its significance never obtrudes itself on our attention.

By this point in the story, furthermore, we unconsciously understand Robin's vacillation more completely than I have been able to suggest. We see that, unbeknown to himself, the youth has good reasons for *not* wanting to find Major Molineux: when he finds him, he will have to resubmit to the kind of authority from which, temporarily at least, he has just escaped. At some deep level the Major appears anything but a potential benefactor; he symbolizes just those aspects of the father from which the youth so urgently desires to be free. As an elderly relative of the father and an authority figure, he may be confused with the father. In any case, however undeservedly, he has now become the target of all the hostile and rebellious feelings which were originally directed against the father.

Hawthorne tells us these things, it is interesting to note, by means of just the kind of unconscious manifestations which twentieth century psychology has found so significant. While Robin sits on the steps of the church, fighting his desire to sleep, he has a fantasy in which he imagines that his kinsman is already dead! And his very next thought is of his father's household. He wonders how "that evening of ambiguity and weariness" has been spent at home, and has a second fantasy of such hallucinatory vividness that he wonders if he is "here or there." Nor is this an idle question. His father and Major Molineux are so inextricably linked in his mind that in a sense the drama in which he is involved is being played out "there"—at home—as well as in the town where bodily he happens to be.

The climax of this drama, so puzzling to the conscious intellect, is immediately comprehensible to that portion of the mind which has been following the hidden course of developments. It is comprehensible although Hawthorne describes Robin's feelings, as is right, in vague terms. Robin never understands those feelings and the reader would find it disturbing if they were too plainly labeled.

The feelings would probably never have secured open expression except under circumstances as out of the ordinary as those the story describes. But now everything conspires not simply to permit but to encourage Robin to give in to tendencies which as we know he was finding it difficult to control. To everyone present Major Molineux is overtly what he is to the youth on some dark and secret level—a symbol of restraint and unwelcome authority. He is this even to the elderly gentleman, the watchman, the man by his side—people whose disapproval of the crowd's behavior might have had a powerful effect upon him. Without a voice being raised in protest, the crowd is acting out the youth's repressed impulses and in effect urging him to act on them also. The joy the crowd takes in asserting its strength and the reappearance of the lady of the scarlet petticoat provide him with incentives for letting himself go.

And so Robin makes common cause with the crowd. He laughs—he laughs louder than anyone else. So long as he himself did not know how he would act he had reason to fear the crowd, and the relief he feels at the easing of the immediate situation is one of the sources of his laughter. But his decision resolves still deeper and more vexing conflicts. The relief he feels that he can vent his hostility for his kinsman and abandon his search for him is the ultimate source of his "riotous mirth." It is fueled by energy which until then was being expended in repression and inner conflict.

Although Hawthorne uses figurative language which may keep his meaning from being consciously noted, he is at pains to let us know that murderous hate underlies the merriment of the crowd of which Robin becomes a part. When the laughter momentarily dies down, the procession resumes its march.

On they went, like fiends that throng in mockery around some dead potentate, mighty no more, but majestic still in his agony. On they went, in counterfeited pomp, in senseless uproar, in frenzied merriment, trampling all on an old man's heart.

Symbolically and to some extent actually the crowd has carried out the fantasy Robin had on the steps of the church.

To the conscious mind "My Kinsman, Major Molineux" is a story of an ambitious youth's thwarted search for an influential relative he wants to find. To the unconscious, it is a story of the youth's hostile and rebellious feelings for the relative—and for the father—and his wish to be free of adult domination. To the conscious mind it is a story of a search which was unsuccessful because of external difficulties. To the unconscious—like *Hamlet,* with which it has more than one point in common—it is a story of a young man caught up in an enterprise for which he has no stomach and debarred from succeeding in it by internal inhibitions.

From one point of view the unacknowledged forces playing upon the apparently simple and candid central character of "My Kinsman, Major Molineux" are deeply abhorrent. Our sympathy for the character should tell us, however, that there is another side to the matter. The tendencies which assert themselves in Robin exist in all men. What he is doing, unwittingly but flamboyantly, is something which every young man does and must do, however gradually, prudently and inconspicuously: he is destroying an image of paternal authority so that, freed from its restraining influence, he can begin life as an adult.

"My Kinsman, Major Molineux" is one of a relatively small but distinguished group of stories which would be incomprehensible, in part or in their entirety, on the basis of what we understand consciously. In response to such stories it is evident that unconscious perception plays an indispensable role. Though it is less evident, I believe that the unconscious plays a role which is scarcely less important in response to many stories which are intelligible on some level to the conscious mind. For most, if not all fiction—and certainly the greatest fiction—has *additional* levels of meaning which must be communicated unconsciously. In many cases far more is communicated unconsciously than consciously. Even when this is not the case, the meanings grasped below the threshold of awareness may make a disproportionate contribution to the pleasure we receive from reading fiction.

It may be worthwhile to analyze a story which is perfectly comprehensible to the intellect but has many further levels of meaning. Let us glance, therefore, at Sherwood Anderson's story, "I Want to Know Why." It has many interesting points of similarity and contrast with "My Kinsman, Major Molineux." And as it happens, the story has been analyzed by Cleanth Brooks and Robert Penn Warren, so that once again we have a jumping-off point for our own explorations.

I shall assume that my readers are familiar with the story, and simply remind them of its chief events. It is narrated in the first person by its fifteen-year-old hero, whose name we never learn. A boy from Beckersville, Kentucky, a small town evidently in the blue-grass region, he is "crazy about thoroughbred horses"; to him they epitomize everything which is "lovely and clean and full of spunk and honest." A lump comes into his throat when he sees potential winners run. He knows he could capitalize on this physical reaction if he wanted to, but he has no desire to gamble; horses and racing represent something too important to him for that.

With three friends of about his own age, the boy runs away to attend the races at Saratoga. Bildad, a Negro from the same town who works at the tracks, feeds the boys, shows them a place to sleep and keeps still about them, which the hero seems to appreciate most of all.

The race the boys particularly want to see has two entries

that give the hero a lump in his throat, and the night before it is run he is so excited he cannot sleep. He aches to watch the two horses run, but he dreads it too, for he hates to see either one beaten. The day of the race he goes to the paddocks to look at the horses. As soon as he sees one of them, Sunstreak, a nervous and beautiful stallion, who is "like a girl you think about sometimes but never see," the boy knows that it is his day. Watching, he experiences a mystical communion with the horse and the horse's trainer, a man named Jerry Tillford, also from Beckersville, who has befriended him many times. The experience is so central to understanding the story that it must be quoted at considerable length.

I was standing looking at that horse and aching. In some way, I can't tell how, I knew just how Sunstreak felt inside. . . . That horse wasn't thinking about running. . . . He was just thinking about holding himself back 'til the time for the running came. . . . He wasn't bragging or letting on much or prancing or making a fuss, but just waiting. I knew it and Jerry Tillford his trainer knew. I looked up and then that man and I looked into each other's eyes. Something happened to me. I guess I loved the man as much as I did the horse because he knew what I knew. Seemed to me there wasn't anything in the world but that man and the horse and me. I cried and Jerry Tillford had a shine in his eyes. . . .

Sunstreak does win the race and the other Beckersville entry, a gelding named Middlestride, finishes second. The hero of the story was so confident that it would work out this way that he is scarcely excited. All through the race he thinks about Jerry Tillford and of how happy he must be. "I liked him that afternoon even more than I ever liked my own father." Jerry, he knows, has worked with Sunstreak since the horse was a baby colt, and he imagines that while watching the race the trainer must feel "like a mother seeing her child do something brave or wonderful."

That night the boy "cuts out" from his companions because he feels an impulse to be near Jerry. He walks along a road which leads to a "rummy-looking farmhouse" because he has seen "Jerry and some other men go that way in an automobile." He doesn't expect to find them, but shortly after he gets there an automobile arrives with Jerry and five other men, several of them from Beckersville and known to the boy. All of them except the father of one of the boys who has accompanied the hero to Saratoga, a gambler named Rieback who quarrels with the others, enter the farmhouse, which proves to be "a place for bad women to stay in."

The boy telling the story creeps to a window and peers in. What he sees sickens and disgusts him. The women are mean-looking and, except for one who a little resembles the gelding Middlestride, "but [is] not clean like him" and has "a hard ugly mouth," they are not even attractive. The place smells rotten, and the talk is rotten, "the kind a kid hears around a livery stable in a town like Beckersville in the winter but don't ever expect to hear talked when there are women around."

Jerry Tillford boasts like a fool, taking credit for Sunstreak's qualities and the victory the horse has won that afternoon. Then the trainer looks at the woman who somewhat resembles Middlestride and his eyes begin to shine as they had when he had looked at the teller of the story and Sunstreak that afternoon. As the man weaves toward the woman, the boy begins to hate him. "I wanted to scream and rush in the room and kill him . . . I was so mad . . . that I cried and my fists were doubled up so my fingernails cut my hands." When the man kisses the woman, the boy creeps away and returns to the tracks. That night he sleeps little. He tells his companions nothing of what he has seen, but the next morning he persuades them to start for home.

There he continues to live very much as before, but everything seems different.

At the tracks the air don't taste as good or smell as good. It's because a man like Jerry Tillford, who knows what he does, could see a horse like Sunstreak run, and

kiss a woman like that the same day. . . . I keep thinking
about it and it spoils looking at horses and smelling things
and hearing niggers laugh and everything. Sometimes I'm
so mad about it I want to fight someone. . . . What did
he do it for? I want to know why.

"I Want to Know Why" certainly means something to the
conscious intellect, and in *Understanding Fiction* Brooks and
Warren give one interpretation of the story's manifest content to which I should not wish to offer more than one or two
reservations. "I Want to Know Why," they declare, is an
initiation story in which a boy "discovers something about
the nature of evil, and tries to find some way of coming to
terms with his discovery."

The boy knows that evil exists in the world. According to
Brooks and Warren, what causes him to feel so much horror
and disgust at Saratoga is the realization—pointed up by the
parallelism of the scene at the paddocks and the scene at the
rummy-looking farmhouse—that good and evil may be so
closely linked, that they may coexist in the same person. He
discovers too that virtue is a human, not an animal, quality.
Unlike the horse, with which in other respects human beings
are frequently compared, man has the capacity for choice.
When he elects the bad, he is worse than the beasts.

It seems to me that the phrase "who knows what he does,"
on which Brooks and Warren base the last-mentioned observation, refers less to specific problems involving choice
than to the willingness of a creature like man to come to
terms with his predilection for evil. Nor can I assent to the
claim that the boy *discovers,* at the climax of the story, that
good and evil are closely joined. What he knows about Henry
Rieback's father has already taught him that, if nothing else
has. These are trifling qualifications, however. My real question is whether the interpretation offered by Brooks and
Warren goes far to explain the impact of the story, even
assuming the correctness of everything they say. They themselves seem a little uneasy on this score, for they write:

. . . having extracted what may seem to be a moral "message," one should remind oneself that the "message" is, as such, not the story. The story may be said to be the dramatization of the discovery. Now the message is something of which everyone is aware; it is a platitude. But the platitude ceases to be a platitude, it is revitalized and becomes meaningful again, when it is shown to be operating in terms of experience.

Here, again, there is little to which one can take exception. A very ordinary idea or event can be "revitalized" if dramatized successfully, and the fact that what we learn about Jerry Tillford is dramatized helps to account for its impact upon the boy at the farmhouse window and the reader looking over his shoulder. Even when dramatized, however, the knowledge that an adult is capable of good and evil is unlikely to have the powerful effect it has upon narrator and reader unless it has some special significance. Something about the nature of the narrator's relationship and experience with Jerry Tillford has eluded Brooks's and Warren's analysis. It has eluded it, I believe, in part because they are so preoccupied with the moral values of the story that they have not asked the most important questions which must be answered if we are to account for the story's appeal.

A central question, as I have indicated, is why the climactic scene can arouse such pain, disgust and bitter disillusionment in the boy who tells the story. His discovery of the underside of Jerry Tillford evidently frustrates some yearning he can scarcely bear to renounce. Once we have gone this far, it is not too difficult to identify this yearning: it is for an ideal relationship with a man who is like his father but better than his father—less fallible, more sympathetic with the boy's interests and, what is at first glance a curious requirement, devoid of sexuality. His disappointment is the keener because, on the very afternoon of the experience at the farmhouse, the consummation of his desire seemed within reach—for an ecstatic moment had actually been achieved.

That the unnamed narrator of "I Want to Know Why"

wanted to adopt Jerry Tillford as a kind of second father could not be more clear. Indeed, it could be maintained that the boy's feelings are sometimes too baldly revealed. They could be inferred from the few things he says about his father and various incidental remarks about the trainer. His father is "all right," and evidently extremely permissive but he doesn't make much money and so can't buy his son things. The boy says he doesn't care—he's too old for that—but since he has just listed the kind of presents Henry Rieback is always getting from his father we doubt his statement. At a deeper level, we sense, the boy is disappointed because his father does not satisfy an immaterial need: he evidently does not share his son's interest in thoroughbreds and racing. Jerry Tillford, of course, is not only interested in these subjects but an authority upon them, and his job puts him in a position to befriend the boy in terms of his interests. He has let the boy walk right into the stalls to examine horses, and so on. These favors may have made the boy think of Jerry Tillford as a kind of father. In any case, the language the boy uses to describe the trainer's treatment of Sunstreak shows that he attributes parental kindliness to him. ("I knew he had been watching and working with Sunstreak since the horse was a baby colt . . . I knew that for him it was like a mother seeing her child do something brave or wonderful.")

The various hints given us about the narrator's feelings for Jerry Tillford are confirmed by two explicit statements. The boy declares, it will be remembered, that on the afternoon of the race he liked the trainer even more than he ever liked his own father. He is equally frank about the feelings which prompted him to "ditch" his companions the night of the race in order to be near the trainer. "I was just lonesome to see Jerry, like wanting to see your father at night when you are a young kid."

What may require further explanation—although unconsciously we understand it very well—is why the boy's feelings are of such extraordinary strength and take the particular form they do. In part his hero worship of Jerry Tillford is a not uncommon outcome of an interrelated cluster of reac-

tions to the parents which arise in children of both sexes
during latency and early adolescence. The fuller knowledge
of reality children acquire at this stage of their development
and the resentment they feel for rebuffs, imaginary or real,
may cause them to become acutely aware of their parents'
circumstances and limitations. Though they continue to love
their parents, consciously or unconsciously they are likely to
feel dissatisfied with them or even ashamed of them. Frequently these feelings cause children to replace their parents
in fantasy—to imagine that their actual parents are mere pre-
tenders to that honor and that their "real" parents are per-
sonages who are powerful, famous or wealthy, or the
possessors of some other desired attribute. The children's
disaffection may also impel them to establish relationships
with adults who can easily be recognized as idealized replace-
ments of one or the other parent.

In boys these feelings are powerfully reinforced by the
changes which occur at puberty. The sudden upsurge of sexuality may reactivate the long-dormant Oedipus tendencies,
jeopardizing and in some cases at least temporarily upsetting
the still far from stable identification with the father. The
wish to protect this identification against the reawakened
competitiveness which threatens it is responsible for a curious
secondary development—an attempt to deny the sexuality of
the father and, by an inevitable chain of association, of the
mother also. Misguided as such an attempt may appear, it has
its own logic. Seen as a sexual being enjoying the favors of
the mother, the father again becomes a person who arouses
envy, hatred and fear. The knowledge of the sexual relations
of the parents is inherently painful and, as Freud has explained, is usually conveyed to the child in a way which tends
to belittle both his parents and himself. For this reason, too,
the information is usually resisted.

The secret of sexual life is revealed to [the growing boy]
in coarse language, undisguisedly derogatory and hostile in
intent, and the effect is to destroy the authority of adults,
which is irreconcilable with these revelations about their

sexual activities. The greatest impression on the child who is being initiated is made by the relation the information bears to his own parents, which is often instantly repudiated in some such words as these: "It may be true that your father and mother and other people do such things, but it is quite impossible that mine do." ("A Special Type of Choices of Object Made by Men.")

Now we are in a better position to approach the two contrasted scenes which do so much to make "I Want to Know Why" an impelling story. The scene at the paddocks depicts a fervently desired communion with an idealized and desexualized father, a father toward whom one need have no feelings of competitiveness and hostility. Moreover, it recalls just such a situation of innocence—it recalls the pre-Oedipal situation in which the feeling of father and son for the mother was a bond between them instead of the focus of rivalry, and father, mother and child were united in love. In this scene Sunstreak becomes the mother, and the boy and Jerry Tillford are brought together by their admiration and love for the stallion. (Sunstreak reminds the boy, it will be recalled, of "a girl you think about sometimes but never see.")

The scene at the rummy-looking farmhouse undoes the scene at the paddocks. Jerry's bragging, which is at the expense of Sunstreak, reveals that he has no real love for the stallion, and thus shows the boy that there was actually no foundation for the experience he thought he had had that afternoon. Because the boy identifies with the stallion, the trainer's boasts are also a blow to his self-esteem. Finally, the boasts show how unfit the trainer is to be the kind of parent the boy desired.

The disclosure of Jerry's sexuality wounds the boy still more deeply. Even more than his bragging, it disqualifies the trainer for the kind of relationship the boy had desired—a relationship which would be washed of all competitiveness and enmity. It is the source of a more encompassing disillusionment. It forces on the boy the unwelcome knowledge that this is a sexual, sinful world, in which he can nowhere hope to find the kind of communion he has sought or the perfection he once attributed to the parents and later hoped to find incarnated in others. The trainer's behavior, his very presence at the whorehouse, is also a particularly brutal and painful reminder of the sexuality of the parents—not only of the father, with whom Tillford is immediately associated, but of the mother as well. She is present in this scene also. She is the woman the trainer desires, the one, somewhat more attractive than the others, who resembles the gelding Middlestride. She is debased to a prostitute, a devaluation which almost always suggests itself—though of course it may be instantly repudiated—when an adolescent boy is compelled to take cognizance of the sexual relations of the parents. Freud describes the chain of reasoning in the same essay from which I have just quoted:

> Along with this piece of "sexual enlightenment" there seldom fails to go, as a corollary, a further one about the existence of certain women who practice sexual intercourse as a means of livelihood and are universally despised in consequence. To the boy himself this contempt is necessarily quite foreign; as soon as he realizes that he too can be initiated by these unfortunates into that sexual life which he has hitherto regarded as the exclusive prerogative of "grownups," his feeling for them is only a mixture of longing and shuddering. Then, when he cannot any longer maintain the doubt that claims exception for his own parents from the ugly sexual behavior of the rest of the world, he says to himself with cynical logic that the difference between his mother and a whore is after all not so very great, since at bottom they both do the same thing.

On one level Jerry Tillford's behavior is wounding because it punctures an attempt to idealize him, to deny his sexuality and the parents'. On still another level it is wounding because it has the character of a sexual rejection and betrayal. To some extent the boy's feelings are those of an outraged lover. Logically the two sets of reactions are incompatible with one another, but here, as is frequently the case, fiction is speaking to a part of the psyche not concerned with logic, a part which can simultaneously accommodate divergent and even contradictory feelings.

The scene at the farmhouse gains additional poignance by stirring feelings originally experienced at different periods of time. Like the scene at the paddocks, it recalls an earlier situation heavily charged with emotion: it condenses the infantile and the adolescent discoveries of sexuality. On the immediate, realistic level the scene depicts something which befalls a fifteen-year-old boy, but in every essential respect it duplicates the "primal scene," the original investigation of the parents' sexual relations. The looking, the secrecy, the mixture of fascination and horror, the ambivalence about whether one will "find anything," the feeling of being alone and betrayed when one does find what underneath one did expect—all the characteristics of the prototype experience are echoed here.

Although only the unconscious is likely to perceive it, in the last analysis both "My Kinsman, Major Molineux" and "I Want to Know Why" are stories of a boy's relationship with his father. Both describe more or less universal phases of the process of growing up, although, as in great fiction generally, the actual events are so altered that they may not be consciously recognizable, and so telescoped and heightened that they arouse even profounder affects than the less dramatic and more gradual experiences they draw upon and evoke. "My Kinsman, Major Molineux" concentrates on the young man's rebellious and hostile feelings toward an authoritative image of the father—an image which must be destroyed in the course of achieving independent adulthood. "I Want to Know Why" describes the frustration of two dear but unfulfillable wishes of the adolescent boy. The first wish is to deny the sexuality of the parents in order to avoid competition with the father. This wish is incompatible with what one inevitably learns in growing up and on some deep level already knows. The second wish is for a love relationship with the father which, though idealized in some respects, is still so heavily cathected with libido that its satisfaction would involve both continued dependence upon the father and a proprietary right to his affection.

Although both stories refer ultimately to emotions felt by sons for their fathers, it is interesting that in each case the feelings are displaced onto surrogates. In "My Kinsman, Major Molineux" the advantage of the alteration is evident: it facilitates the expression of hostility. "I Want to Know Why" is probably both more realistic and more moving because the immediate object of the hero's feelings is just such a man as Jerry Tillford. By the time a boy is fifteen the feelings of affection for the actual father are usually too admixed with other elements, the disillusionment too advanced, to permit the sharp contrasts of hopes raised and abruptly deflated upon which the structure and impact of the story depend.

THE SOCIOLOGICAL
APPROACH:

LITERATURE
AND SOCIAL IDEAS

Introduction

SOCIOLOGICAL CRITICISM starts with a conviction that art's relations to society are vitally important, and that the investigation of these relationships may organize and deepen one's aesthetic response to a work of art. Art is not created in a vacuum; it is the work not simply of a person, but of an author fixed in time and space, answering to a community of which he is an important, because articulate part. The sociological critic, therefore, is interested in understanding the social milieu and the extent to which and manner in which the artist responds to it.

Edmund Wilson traces sociological criticism to Vico's eighteenth century study of Homer's epics, which revealed the social conditions in which the Greek poet lived.[1] Herder in the nineteenth century continued with this approach, but it was the Frenchman Taine who brought it to fullest statement with his famous pronouncement that literature is the consequence of the moment, the race, and the milieu. Before that century ended, Marx and Engels had introduced a fourth factor, the methods of production, and thus made possible the development, in the thirties, of that special branch of the sociological approach—Marxist criticism.

The tendency to associate art and social values is natural, perhaps intrinsic, to the realistic movement. In America, Howells, Jack London, Hamlin Garland, and Frank Norris have all been concerned with the relation between literature and society. When the critic substituted social or political theory for the term "society," he found he had an integrating

[1] "The Historical Interpretation of Literature," added to *The Triple Thinkers* in 1948. Wilson's term is "historical criticism," but this involves the possibility of several confusions. A great deal of valuable historical investigation into the background of literature is not really critical or interpretive (it may, for instance, aim to establish a date of composition); and the social milieu investigated may not be sufficiently of the past to merit clearly the adjective "historical."

view of large masses of literature. Thus John Macy composed *The Spirit of American Literature* in 1908 from the viewpoint of Socialism, and the strength as well as the weakness of Parrington's *Main Currents in American Thought,* 1927-1930, came from his personal commitment to Jeffersonian liberalism. Of course the early debunkers of our period, Randolph Bourne and T. K. Whipple, for example, were at least implicitly thinking of the effects of society upon artists.

But with the economic depression writers began to add a powerful tool of judgment to their examination of literature as a mirror of society: the Marxist interpretation and evaluation of social forces. Both in England and America authors moved politically to the left. Witness the poetry of Auden, C. Day Lewis, Stephen Spender, and Archibald MacLeish. Journals were formed—for example, the *New Masses,* under Michael Gold's editorship, and the *Left Review,* under Edgell Rickword—which served as organs for Marxist criticism. Symposia were edited: Hicks' *Proletarian Literature in the United States,* 1935, C. Day Lewis' *The Mind in Chains,* 1937, Bernard Smith's *Forces in American Criticism,* 1939. And books by single authors argued the cause: V. F. Calverton's *The Liberation of American Literature,* 1931, John Strachey's *The Coming Struggle for Power,* 1933, and Ralph Fox's *The Novel and the People,* 1937.

The result was, first of all, an extraordinarily vigorous critical approach. The touchstone seemed clearly defined: dialectic materialism; the method of application seemed sure: how does the work contribute to the cause of this social truth? Consequently, the judgments could be made with an Old Testament force of conviction. So literature and its creators were sorted as being with or against the Truth; the single-minded critic, frequently unfazed by the complexities of art's relations to society, and strengthened by the mood of faith and the sense of revelation, demanded that writers share his creed, and that literature show its validity. There were exceptions: the vision was too narrow for some, notably Christopher Caudwell, whose profound knowledge of Marxism and mature taste for literature enabled him to resist the

gravitational pull toward the crude absolutism that characterized the approach of many lesser Marxists of the time.

But there was madness in the method. As the yardstick
became shorter and the applications more naïve, it became
uncomfortably apparent that the intensity of the vision was
achieved at the price of its breadth. James Farrell, in *A Note
on Literary Criticism*, 1936, took his fellow Marxists severely
to task for their benighted dilutions of the problem. Edmund
Wilson too, once he had abandoned the group (though Taine
as much as Marx had been his mentor) joined the attack with
his essay, "Marxism and Literature" in *The Triple Thinkers*,
1938. Finally, with the Russo-German pact and the outbreak
of World War II in 1939, and the consequent confusion and
defection of many votaries, the movement lost its central
strength and ceased to be a major force in literary criticism.

But the excesses of this critical aberration did not destroy
the validity of the sociological study of literature. If the
critic cannot reasonably hold an author or a work of art to
a particular creed, like Americanism, Proletarianism, Socialism, Capitalism, and so on, the fair-minded juxtaposition of
the work and social theory can strike sparks that are genuinely illuminating. The Achilles' heel of sociological criticism,
as of the moral in general, lies in the area of judgment—the
narrowing temptation to praise or condemn a piece according
to the extent to which its social or moral implications are
congruent with the convictions of the critic. We need not
condemn Restoration comedy for instance, as does L. C.
Knights,[2] for being so unrelated to the most important
thought of the period; but to view that body of writing with
the reminder that Isaac Newton, Sir Thomas Browne, and
John Bunyan also were forming, in their own ways, the cultural atmosphere, is to see the comic drama in a new light.
This is, in fact, what the best sociological critics do: place
the work of art in the social atmosphere, and define that rela-

[2] In "Restoration Comedy: The Reality and the Myth" from his
book *Explorations: Essays in Criticism Mainly on the Literature
of the Seventeenth Century*, 1946.

tionship. If too narrow an evaluation follows, this is likely to reveal the moral position of the critic, as much as the intrinsic merit of the work.

Scholars, of course, have long been interested in the ties between the art, the writer, and the social milieu, and very often their studies contain implicit judgments based on those associations. But the associations are not simple. Harry Levin has stated: ". . . the relations between literature and society are reciprocal. Literature is not only the effect of social causes; it is also the cause of social effects." [3] So we continue to have critics who are drawn to this complex association. Van Wyck Brooks has for a long time been writing a series of books devoted to the social atmosphere in which American writers worked; F. O. Matthiessen is the author of one of the most thoughtful of such studies, *American Renaissance,* 1941; L. C. Knights has pursued the same goal in *Drama and Society in the Age of Jonson,* 1937. It is clear that as long as literature maintains its bonds with society—and that cannot help but be forever—the sociological approach, with or without the persuasion of a particular theory, will continue to be a vigorous force in criticism.

[3] In "Literature as an Institution," *Accent,* (Spring, 1946).

Bibliographical Note

In addition to the works by Macy and Parrington already cited, an early sociological treatment of literature is T. K. Whipple's *Spokesmen*, 1928.

Other examples of the Marxist approach are V. F. Calverton, *The Newer Spirit*, 1925; Granville Hicks, *The Great Tradition*, 1933; Stephen Spender, *The Destructive Element*, 1935; Alick West, *Crisis and Criticism*, 1937; Philip Henderson, *The Poet and Society*, 1939; and George Thomson, *Marxism and Poetry*, 1945.

An interesting examination of Marxist parochialism is made by Auden in his essay, "The Public *v.* the Late Mr. William Butler Yeats" from *Partisan Review*, VI (Spring, 1939). Auden presents the cases for and against the poet in a lively and illuminating way.

Other general sociological approaches are taken by T. K. Whipple, *Study out the Land*, 1943; and James Farrell, *Literature and Morality*, 1947; F. W. Bateson in his *English Poetry; A Critical Introduction*, 1950, persuasively argues for the importance of "prose meaning" in poetry, and for the necessity of understanding the central interests of each poet's social milieu before critical evaluation. The *Scrutiny* writers are close students of texts, like the Formalist critics, but often their special leaning is sociological.

The Tragic Fallacy

By Joseph Wood Krutch

THROUGH THE LEGACY of their art the great ages have transmitted to us a dim image of their glorious vitality. When we turn the pages of a Sophoclean or a Shakespearean tragedy we participate faintly in the experience which created it and we sometimes presumptuously say that we "understand" the spirit of these works. But the truth is that we see them, even at best and in the moments when our souls expand most nearly to their dimensions, through a glass darkly.

It is so much easier to appreciate than to create that an age too feeble to reach the heights achieved by the members of a preceding one can still see those heights towering above its impotence, and so it is that, when we perceive a Sophocles or a Shakespeare soaring in an air which we can never hope to breathe, we say that we can "appreciate" them. But what we mean is that we are just able to wonder, and we can never hope to participate in the glorious vision of human life out of which they were created—not even to the extent of those humbler persons for whom they were written; for while to us the triumphant voices come from far away and tell of a heroic world which no longer exists, to them that spoke of immediate realities and revealed the inner meaning of events amidst which they still lived.

When the life has entirely gone out of a work of art come down to us from the past, when we read it without any emotional comprehension whatsoever and can no longer even imagine why the people for whom it was intended found it absorbing and satisfying, then, of course, it has ceased to be a work of art at all and has dwindled into one of those deceptive "documents" from which we get a false sense of comprehending through the intellect things which cannot be comprehended at all except by means of a kinship of feeling. And though all works from a past age have begun in this way to

fade there are some, like the great Greek or Elizabethan
tragedies, which are still halfway between the work of art and
the documents. They no longer can have for us the immediacy which they had for those to whom they originally belonged, but they have not yet eluded us entirely. We no
longer live in the world which they represent, but we can
half imagine it and we can measure the distance which we
have moved away. We write no tragedies today, but we can
still talk about the tragic spirit of which we would, perhaps,
have no conception were it not for the works in question.

An age which could really "appreciate" Shakespeare or
Sophocles would have something comparable to put beside
them—something like them, not necessarily in form, or spirit,
but at least in magnitude—some vision of life which would
be, however different, equally ample and passionate. But
when we move to put a modern masterpiece beside them,
when we seek to compare them with, let us say, a *Ghosts* or
a *Weavers,* we shrink as from the impulse to commit some
folly and we feel as though we were about to superimpose
Bowling Green upon the Great Prairies in order to ascertain
which is the larger. The question, we see, is not primarily one
of art but of the two worlds which two minds inhabited. No
increased powers of expression, no greater gift for words,
could have transformed Ibsen into Shakespeare. The materials
out of which the latter created his works—his conception of
human passions, his vision of the amplitude of human life—
simply did not and could not exist for Ibsen, as they did not
and could not exist for his contemporaries. God and Man
and Nature had all somehow dwindled in the course of the
intervening centuries, not because the realistic creed of modern art led us to seek out mean people, but because this
meanness of human life was somehow thrust upon us by the
operation of that same process which led to the development
of realistic theories of art by which our vision could be
justified.

Hence, though we still apply, sometimes, the adjective
"tragic" to one or another of those modern works of literature which describe human misery and which end more sadly

even than they begin, the term is a misnomer since it is obvious that the works in question have nothing in common with the classical examples of the genre and produce in the reader a sense of depression which is the exact opposite of that elation generated when the spirit of a Shakespeare rises joyously superior to the outward calamities which he recounts and celebrates the greatness of the human spirit whose travail he describes. Tragedies, in that only sense of the word which has any distinctive meaning, are no longer written in either the dramatic or any other form and the fact is not to be accounted for in any merely literary terms. It is not the result of any fashion in literature or of any deliberation to write about human nature or character under different aspects, any more than it is of either any greater sensitiveness of feeling which would make us shrink from the contemplation of the suffering of Medea or Othello or of any greater optimism which would make us more likely to see life in more cheerful terms. It is, on the contrary, the result of one of those enfeeblements of the human spirit not unlike that described in the previous chapter of this essay, and a further illustration of that gradual weakening of man's confidence in his ability to impose upon the phenomenon of life an interpretation acceptable to his desires which is the subject of the whole of the present discussion.

To explain that fact and to make clear how the creation of classical tragedy did consist in the successful effort to impose such a satisfactory interpretation will require, perhaps, the special section which follows, although the truth of the fact that it does impose such an interpretation must be evident to any one who has ever risen from the reading of *Oedipus* or *Lear* with that feeling of exultation which comes when we have been able, by rare good fortune, to enter into its spirit as completely as it is possible for us of a remoter and emotionally enfeebled age to enter it. Meanwhile one anticipatory remark may be ventured. If the plays and the novels of today deal with littler people and less mighty emotions it is not because we have become interested in commonplace souls and their unglamorous adventures but because we have come,

willy-nilly, to see the soul of man as commonplace and its
emotions as mean.

2

Tragedy, said Aristotle, is the "imitation of noble actions,"
and though it is some twenty-five hundred years since the
dictum was uttered there is only one respect in which we are
inclined to modify it. To us "imitation" seems a rather naïve
word to apply to that process by which observation is turned
into art, and we seek one which would define or at least
imply the nature of that interposition of the personality of
the artist between the object and the beholder which constitutes his function and by means of which he transmits a
modified version, rather than a mere imitation, of the thing
which he has contemplated.

In the search for this word the estheticians of romanticism
invented the term "expression" to describe the artistic purpose to which apparent imitation was subservient. Psycholo-
gists, on the other hand, feeling that the artistic process was
primarily one by which reality is modified in such a way as
to render it more acceptable to the desires of the artist, employed various terms in the effort to describe that distortion
which the wish may produce in vision. And though many of
the newer critics reject both romanticism and psychology, even
they insist upon the fundamental fact that in art we are
concerned, not with mere imitation, but with the imposition
of some form upon the material which it would not have if it
were merely copied as a camera copies.

Tragedy is not, then, as Aristotle said, the *imitation* of
noble actions, for, indeed, no one knows what a *noble* action
is or whether or not such a thing as nobility exists in nature
apart from the mind of man. Certainly the action of Achilles
in dragging the dead body of Hector around the walls of
Troy and under the eyes of Andromache, who had begged
to be allowed to give it decent burial, is not to us a noble action, though it was such to Homer, who made it the subject
of a noble passage in a noble poem. Certainly, too, the same

action might conceivably be made the subject of a tragedy and the subject of a farce, depending upon the way in which it was treated; so that to say that tragedy is the *imitation* of a *noble* action is to be guilty of assuming, first, that art and photography are the same, and, second, that there may be something inherently noble in an act as distinguished from the motives which prompted it or from the point of view from which it is regarded.

And yet, nevertheless, the idea of nobility is inseparable from the idea of tragedy, which cannot exist without it. If tragedy is not the imitation or even the modified representation of noble actions it is certainly a representation of actions *considered* as noble, and herein lies its essential nature, since no man can conceive it unless he is capable of believing in the greatness and importance of man. Its action is usually, if not always, calamitous, because it is only in calamity that the human spirit has the opportunity to reveal itself triumphant over the outward universe which fails to conquer it; but this calamity in tragedy is only a means to an end and the essential thing which distinguishes real tragedy from those distressing modern works sometimes called by its name is the fact that it is in the former alone that the artist has found himself capable of considering and of making us consider that his people and his actions have that amplitude and importance which make them noble. Tragedy arises then when, as in Periclean Greece or Elizabethan England, a people fully aware of the calamities of life is nevertheless serenely confident of the greatness of man, whose mighty passions and supreme fortitude are revealed when one of these calamities overtakes him.

To those who mistakenly think of it as something gloomy or depressing, who are incapable of recognizing the elation which its celebration of human greatness inspires, and who, therefore, confuse it with things merely miserable or pathetic, it must be a paradox that the happiest, most vigorous, and most confident ages which the world has ever known—the Periclean and the Elizabethan—should be exactly those which created and which most relished the mightiest tragedies; but the paradox is, of course, resolved by the fact that tragedy is essentially an expression, not of despair, but of the triumph over despair and of confidence in the value of human life. If Shakespeare himself ever had that "dark period" which his critics and biographers have imagined for him, it was at least no darkness like that bleak and arid despair which sometimes settles over modern spirits. In the midst of it he created both the elemental grandeur of Othello and the pensive majesty of Hamlet and, holding them up to his contemporaries, he said in the words of his own Miranda, "Oh, rare new world that hath *such* creatures in it."

All works of art which deserve their name have a happy end. This is indeed the thing which constitutes them art and through which they perform their function. Whatever the character of the events, fortunate or unfortunate, which they recount, they so mold or arrange or interpret them that we accept gladly the conclusion which they reach and would not have it otherwise. They may conduct us into the realm of pure fancy where wish and fact are identical and the world is remade exactly after the fashion of the heart's desire or they may yield some greater or less allegiance to fact; but they must always reconcile us in one way or another to the representation which they make and the distinctions between the genres are simply the distinctions between the means by which this reconciliation is effected.

Comedy laughs the minor mishaps of its characters away; drama solves all the difficulties which it allows to arise; and melodrama, separating good from evil by simple lines, distributes its rewards and punishments in accordance with the principles of a naïve justice which satisfies the simple souls of its audience, which are neither philosophical enough to question its primitive ethics nor critical enough to object to the way in which its neat events violate the laws of probability. Tragedy, the greatest and the most difficult of the arts, can adopt none of these methods; and yet it must reach its own happy end in its own way. Though its conclusion must be, by its premise, outwardly calamitous, though it must speak to those who know that the good man is cut off and that the fairest things are the first to perish, yet it must leave them, as *Othello* does, content that this is so. We must be and we are glad that Juliet dies and glad that Lear is turned out into the storm.

Milton set out, he said, to justify the ways of God to man, and his phrase, if it be interpreted broadly enough, may be taken as describing the function of all art, which must, in some way or other, make the life which it seems to represent satisfactory to those who see its reflection in the magic mirror, and it must gratify or at least reconcile the desires of the beholder, not necessarily, as the naïver exponents of Freudian psychology maintain, by gratifying individual and often eccentric wishes, but at least by satisfying the universally human desire to find in the world some justice, some meaning, or, at the very least, some recognizable order. Hence it is that every real tragedy, however tremendous it may be, is an affirmation of faith in life, a declaration that even if God is not in his Heaven, then at least Man is in his world.

We accept gladly the outward defeats which it describes for the sake of the inward victories which it reveals. Juliet died, but not before she had shown how great and resplendent a thing love could be; Othello plunged the dagger into his own breast, but not before he had revealed that greatness of soul which makes his death seem unimportant. Had he died in the instant when he struck the blow, had he perished still believing that the world was as completely black as he saw it before the innocence of Desdemona was revealed to him, then, for him at least, the world would have been merely damnable, but Shakespeare kept him alive long enough to allow him to learn his error and hence to die, not in despair, but in the full acceptance of the tragic reconciliation to life. Perhaps it would be pleasanter if men could believe what the child is taught—that the good are happy and that things turn out as they should—but it is far more important to be able to believe, as Shakespeare did, that however much things in the outward world may go awry, man has, nevertheless, splendors of his own and that, in a word, Love and Honor and Glory are not words but realities.

Thus for the great ages tragedy is not an expression of despair but the means by which they saved themselves from it. It is a profession of faith, and a sort of religion; a way of looking at life by virtue of which it is robbed of its pain. The sturdy soul of the tragic author seizes upon suffering and uses it only as a means by which joy may be wrung out of existence, but it is not to be forgotten that he is enabled to do so only because of his belief in the greatness of human nature and because, though he has lost the child's faith in life, he has not lost his far more important faith in human nature. A tragic writer does not have to believe in God, but he must believe in man.

And if, then, the Tragic Spirit is in reality the product of a religious faith in which, sometimes at least, faith in the greatness of God is replaced by faith in the greatness of man, it serves, of course, to perform the function of religion, to make life tolerable for those who participate in its beneficent illusion. It purges the souls of those who might otherwise despair and it makes endurable the realization that the events of the outward world do not correspond with the desires of the heart, and thus, in its own particular way, it does what all religions do, for it gives a rationality, a meaning, and a justification to the universe. But if it has the strength it has also the weakness of all faiths, since it may—nay, it must—be ultimately lost as reality, encroaching further and further into the realm of imagination, leaves less and less room in which that imagination can build its refuge.

3

It is, indeed, only at a certain stage in the development of the realistic intelligence of a people that the tragic faith can exist. A naïve people may have, as the ancient men of the north had, a body of legends which are essentially tragic, or it may have only (and need only) its happy and childlike mythology which arrives inevitably at its happy end, and where the only ones who suffer "deserve" to do so and in which, therefore, life is represented as directly and easily acceptable. A too sophisticated society on the other hand—one which, like ours, has outgrown not merely the simple optimism of the child but also that vigorous, one might almost say adolescent, faith in the nobility of man which marks a Sophocles or a Shakespeare, has neither fairy tales to assure it that all is always right in the end nor tragedies to make it believe that it rises superior in soul to the outward calamities which befall it.

Distrusting its thought, despising its passions, realizing its impotent unimportance in the universe, it can tell itself no stories except those which make it still more acutely aware of its trivial miseries. When its heroes (sad misnomer for the pitiful creatures who people contemporary fiction) are struck down it is not, like Oedipus, by the gods that they are struck but only, like Oswald Alving, by syphilis, for they know that the gods, even if they existed, would not trouble with them, and they cannot attribute to themselves in art an importance in which they do not believe. Their so-called tragedies do not and cannot end with one of those splendid calamities which in Shakespeare seem to reverberate through the universe, because they cannot believe that the universe trembles when their love is, like Romeo's, cut off or when the place where they (small as they are) have gathered up their trivial treasure is, like Othello's sanctuary, defiled. Instead, mean misery piles on mean misery, petty misfortune follows petty misfortune, and despair becomes intolerable because it is no longer even significant or important.

Ibsen once made one of his characters say that he did not read much because he found reading "irrelevant," and the adjective was brilliantly chosen because it held implications even beyond those of which Ibsen was consciously aware. What is it that made the classics irrelevant to him and to us? Is it not just exactly those to him impossible premises which make tragedy what it is, those assumptions that the soul of man is great, that the universe (together with whatever gods may be) concerns itself with him and that he is, in a word, noble? Ibsen turned to village politics for exactly the same reason that his contemporaries and his successors have, each in his own way, sought out some aspect of the common man and his common life—because, that is to say, here was at least something small enough for him to be able to believe.

Bearing this fact in mind, let us compare a modern "tragedy" with one of the great works of a happy age, not in order to judge of their relative technical merits but in order to determine to what extent the former deserves its name by achieving a tragic solution capable of purging the soul or of reconciling the emotions to the life which it pictures. And in order to make the comparison as fruitful as possible let us choose *Hamlet* on the one hand and on the other a play like *Ghosts,* which was not only written by perhaps the most powerful as well as the most typical of modern writers but which is, in addition, the one of his works which seems most nearly to escape that triviality which cannot be entirely escaped by any one who feels, as all contemporary minds do, that man is relatively trivial.

In *Hamlet* a prince ("in understanding, how like a god!") has thrust upon him from the unseen world a duty to redress a wrong which concerns not merely him, his mother, and his uncle, but the moral order of the universe. Erasing all trivial fond records from his mind, abandoning at once both his studies and his romance because it has been his good fortune to be called upon to take part in an action of cosmic importance, he plunges (at first) not into action but into thought, weighing the claims which are made upon him and contemplating the grandiose complexities of the universe. And when the time comes at last for him to die he dies, not as a failure, but as a success. Not only has the universe regained the balance which had been upset by what *seemed* the monstrous crime of the guilty pair ("there is nothing either good nor ill but thinking makes it so"), but in the process by which that readjustment is made a mighty mind has been given the opportunity, first to contemplate the magnificent scheme of which it is a part, and then to demonstrate the greatness of its spirit by playing a rôle in the grand style which it called for. We do not need to despair in *such* a world if it has *such* creatures in it.

Turn now to *Ghosts*—look upon this picture and upon that. A young man has inherited syphilis from his father. Struck by a to him mysterious malady he returns to his northern village, learns the hopeless truth about himself, and persuades his mother to poison him. The incidents prove, perhaps, that pastors should not endeavor to keep a husband and wife together unless they know what they are doing. But what a world is this in which a great writer can deduce nothing more than that from his greatest work and how are we to be purged or reconciled when we see it acted? Not only is the failure utter, but it is trivial and meaningless as well.

Yet the journey from Elsinore to Skien is precisely the journey which the human spirit has made, exchanging in the process princes for invalids and gods for disease. We say, as Ibsen would say, that the problems of Oswald Alving are more "relevant" to our life than the problems of Hamlet, that the play in which he appears is more "real" than the other more glamorous one, but it is exactly because we find it so that we are condemned. We can believe in Oswald but we cannot believe in Hamlet, and a light has gone out in the universe. Shakespeare justifies the ways of God to man, but in Ibsen there is no such happy end and with him tragedy, so called, has become merely an expression of our despair at finding that such justification is no longer possible.

Modern critics have sometimes been puzzled to account for the fact that the concern of ancient tragedy is almost exclusively with kings and courts. They have been tempted to accuse even Aristotle of a certain naïveté in assuming (as he seems to assume) that the "nobility" of which he speaks as necessary to a tragedy implies a nobility of rank as well as of soul, and they have sometimes regretted that Shakespeare did not devote himself more than he did to the serious consideration of those common woes of the common man which subsequent writers have exploited with increasing pertinacity. Yet the tendency to lay the scene of a tragedy at the court of a king is not the result of any arbitrary convention but of the fact that the tragic writers believed easily in greatness just as we believe easily in meanness. To Shakespeare, robes and crowns and jewels are the garments most appropriate to man because they are the fitting outward manifestation of his inward majesty, but to us they seem absurd because the man who bears them has, in our estimation, so pitifully shrunk. We do not write about kings because we do not believe that any man is worthy to be one and we do not write about courts because hovels seem to us to be dwellings more appropriate to the creatures who inhabit them. Any modern attempt to dress characters in robes ends only by making us aware of a comic incongruity and any modern attempt to furnish them with a language resplendent like Shakespeare's ends only in bombast.

True tragedy capable of performing its function and of purging the soul by reconciling man to his woes can exist only by virtue of a certain pathetic fallacy far more inclusive than that to which the name is commonly given. The romantics, feeble descendants of the tragic writers to whom they are linked by their effort to see life and nature in grandiose terms, loved to imagine that the sea or the sky had a way of according itself with their moods, of storming when they stormed and smiling when they smiled. But the tragic spirit sustains itself by an assumption much more far-reaching and no more justified. Man as it sees him lives in a world which he may not dominate but which is always aware of him. Occupying the exact center of a universe which would have no meaning except for him and being so little below the angels that, if he believes in God, he has no hesitation in imagining Him formed as he is formed and crowned with a crown like that which he or one of his fellows wears, he assumes that each of his acts reverberates through the universe. His passions are important to him because he believes them important throughout all time and all space; the very fact that he can sin (no modern can) means that this universe is watching his acts; and though he may perish, a God leans out from infinity to strike him down. And it is exactly because an Ibsen cannot think of man in any such terms as these that his persons have so shrunk and that his "tragedy" has lost that power which real tragedy always has of making that infinitely ambitious creature called man content to accept his misery if only he can be made to feel great enough and important enough. An Oswald is not a Hamlet chiefly because he has lost that tie with the natural and supernatural world which the latter had. No ghost will leave the other world to warn or encourage him, there is no virtue and no vice which he can possibly have which can be really important, and when he dies neither his death nor the manner of it will be, outside the circle of two or three people as unnecessary as himself, any more important than that of a rat behind the arras.

Perhaps we may dub the illusion upon which the tragic spirit is nourished the Tragic, as opposed to the Pathetic, Fallacy, but fallacy though it is, upon its existence depends not merely the writing of tragedy but the existence of that religious feeling of which tragedy is an expression and by means of which a people aware of the dissonances of life manages nevertheless to hear them as harmony. Without it neither man nor his passions can seem great enough or important enough to justify the sufferings which they entail, and literature, expressing the mood of a people, begins to despair where once it had exulted. Like the belief in love and like most of the other mighty illusions by means of which human life has been given a value, the Tragic Fallacy depends ultimately upon the assumption which man so readily makes that something outside his own being, some "spirit not himself"— be it God, Nature, or that still vaguer thing called a Moral Order—joins him in the emphasis which he places upon this or that and confirms him in his feeling that his passions and his opinions are important. When his instinctive faith in that correspondence between the outer and the inner world fades, his grasp upon the faith that sustained him fades also, and Love or Tragedy or what not ceases to be the reality which it was because he is never strong enough in his own insignificant self to stand alone in a universe which snubs him with its indifference.

In both the modern and the ancient worlds tragedy was dead long before writers were aware of the fact. Seneca wrote his frigid melodramas under the impression that he was

following in the footsteps of Sophocles, and Dryden probably thought that his *All for Love* was an improvement upon
Shakespeare, but in time we awoke to the fact that no amount
of rhetorical bombast could conceal the fact that grandeur
was not to be counterfeited when the belief in its possibility
was dead, and turning from the hero to the common man, we
inaugurated the era of realism. For us no choice remains except that between mere rhetoric and the frank consideration
of our fellow men, who may be the highest of the anthropoids
but who are certainly too far below the angels to imagine
either that these angels can concern themselves with them or
that they can catch any glimpse of even the soles of angelic
feet. We can no longer tell tales of the fall of noble men
because we do not believe that noble men exist. The best that
we can achieve is pathos and the most that we can do is to
feel sorry for ourselves. Man has put off his royal robes and
it is only in sceptered pomp that tragedy can come sweeping
by.

4

Nietzsche was the last of the great philosophers to attempt
a tragic justification of life. His central and famous dogma—
"Life is good *because* it is painful"—sums up in a few words
the desperate and almost meaningless paradox to which he
was driven in his effort to reduce to rational terms the far
more imaginative conception which is everywhere present but
everywhere unanalyzed in a Sophocles or a Shakespeare and
by means of which they rise triumphant over the manifold
miseries of life. But the very fact that Nietzsche could not
even attempt to state in any except intellectual terms an attitude which is primarily unintellectual and to which, indeed,
intellectual analysis is inevitably fatal, is proof of the distance
which he had been carried (by the rationalizing tendencies of
the human mind) from the possibility of the tragic solution
which he sought; and the confused, half-insane violence of his
work will reveal, by the contrast which it affords with the
serenity of the tragic writers whom he admired, how great
was his failure.

Fundamentally this failure was, moreover, conditioned by exactly the same thing which has conditioned the failure of all modern attempts to achieve what he attempted—by the fact, that is to say, that tragedy must have a hero if it is not to be merely an accusation against, instead of a justification of, the world in which it occurs. Tragedy is, as Aristotle said, an imitation of noble actions, and Nietzsche, for all his enthusiasm for the Greek tragic writers, was palsied by the universally modern incapacity to conceive man as noble. Out of this dilemma, out of his need to find a hero who could give to life as he saw it the only possible justification, was born the idea of the Superman, but the Superman is, after all, only a hypothetical being, destined to become what man actually was in the eyes of the great tragic writers—a creature (as Hamlet said) "how infinite in capacities, in understanding how like a god." Thus Nietzsche lived half in the past through his literary enthusiasms and half in the future through his grandiose dreams, but for all his professed determination to justify existence he was no more able than the rest of us to find the present acceptable. Life, he said in effect, is not a Tragedy now but perhaps it will be when the Ape-man has been transformed into a hero (the *Uebermensch*), and trying to find that sufficient, he went mad.

He failed, as all moderns must fail when they attempt, like him, to embrace the tragic spirit as a religious faith, because the resurgence of that faith is not an intellectual but a vital phenomenon, something not achieved by taking thought but born, on the contrary, out of an instinctive confidence in life which is nearer to the animal's unquestioning allegiance to the scheme of nature than it is to that critical intelligence characteristic of a fully developed humanism. And like other faiths it is not to be recaptured merely by reaching an intellectual conviction that it would be desirable to do so.

Modern psychology has discovered (or at least strongly emphasized) the fact that under certain conditions desire produces belief, and having discovered also that the more primitive a given mentality the more completely are its opinions determined by its wishes, modern psychology has concluded that the best mind is that which most resists the tendency to believe a thing simply because it would be pleasant or advantageous to do so. But justified as this conclusion may be from the intellectual point of view, it fails to take into account the fact that in a universe as badly adapted as this one to human as distinguished from animal needs this ability to will a belief may bestow an enormous vital advantage as it did, for instance, in the case at present under discussion where it made possible for Shakespeare the compensations of a tragic faith completely inaccessible to Nietzsche. Pure intelligence, incapable of being influenced by desire and therefore also incapable of choosing one opinion rather than another simply because the one chosen is the more fruitful or beneficent, is doubtless a relatively perfect instrument for the pursuit of truth, but the question (likely, it would seem, to be answered in the negative) is simply whether or not the spirit of man can endure the literal and inhuman truth.

Certain ages and simple people have conceived of the action which passes upon the stage of the universe as of something in the nature of a Divine Comedy, as something, that is to say, which will reach its end with the words "and they lived happily ever after." Others, less naïve and therefore more aware of those maladjustments whose reality, at least so far as outward events are concerned, they could not escape, have imposed upon it another artistic form and called it a Divine Tragedy, accepting its catastrophe as we accept the catastrophe of an *Othello,* because of its grandeur. But a Tragedy, Divine or otherwise, must, it may again be repeated, have a hero, and from the universe as we see it both the Glory of God and the Glory of Man have departed. Our cosmos may be farcical or it may be pathetic but it has not the dignity of tragedy and we cannot accept it as such.

Yet our need for the consolations of tragedy has not passed with the passing of our ability to conceive it. Indeed, the dissonances which it was tragedy's function to resolve grow more insistent instead of diminishing. Our passions, our disappointments, and our sufferings remain important to us though important to nothing else and they thrust themselves upon us with an urgency which makes it impossible for us to dismiss them as the mere trivialities which, so our intellects tell us, they are. And yet, in the absence of tragic faith or the possibility of achieving it, we have no way in which we may succeed in giving them the dignity which would not only render them tolerable but transform them as they were transformed by the great ages into joys. The death of tragedy is, like the death of love, one of those emotional fatalities as the result of which the human as distinguished from the natural world grows more and more a desert.

Poetry, said Santayana in his famous phrase, is "religion which is no longer believed," but it depends, nevertheless, upon its power to revive in us a sort of temporary or provisional credence and the nearer it can come to producing an illusion of belief the greater is its power as poetry. Once the Tragic Spirit was a living faith and out of it tragedies were written. Today these great expressions of a great faith have declined, not merely into poetry, but into a kind of poetry whose premises are so far from any we can really accept that we can only partially and dimly grasp its meaning.

We read but we do not write tragedies. The tragic solution of the problem of existence, the reconciliation to life by means of the tragic spirit is, that is to say, now only a fiction surviving in art. When that art itself has become, as it probably will, completely meaningless, when we have ceased not only to write but to *read* tragic works, then it will be lost and in all real senses forgotten, since the devolution from Religion to Art to Document will be complete.

George Bernard Shaw: A Study of the Bourgeois Superman

"A good man fallen among Fabians." LENIN

By CHRISTOPHER CAUDWELL

SHAW IN HIS LIFE acquired general recognition among the ordinary members of the "middle class" both here and in America, as representative of Socialist thought. The case of Shaw is in many ways interesting and significant; is a proof of how stubborn is the bourgeois illusion. The bourgeois may be familiar with Marxism and keenly critical of the social system, and anxious to change it, and yet all this leads only to an ineffectual beating of the air because he believes that man is in himself free.

Shaw is an ex-anarchist, a vegetarian, a Fabian, and, of late years, a Social Fascist: he is inevitably a *Utopian* socialist. His idea of Utopia was expounded in *Back to Methuselah,* a paradise of Ancients who spend their days in *thought* and despite the butterfly young who engage in the *active* work of artistic creation and science.

Shaw then exposed the weakness as well as the essence of his characteristically bourgeois brand of socialism. It represents the primacy of pure contemplation. In pure contemplation man is alone, is apparently exempt from cooperation, is wrapped in a private world; and he is then believed, by bourgeois thought, to be wholly free. Is not this the illusion of the scientist? No, for science is not *pure* thought, it is thought allied to action, testing all its cogitations at the bar of reality. It is thought as thought ought to be, passing always in dialectic movement between knowing and being, between dream and outer reality. Shaw abhors this kind of thought. He abhors modern science not as he might do for its human weaknesses, but hating it for its essence, for its social qualities, for all that is good in its active creative rôle.

147

This is a familiar spectacle: the intellectual attempting to dominate hostile reality by "pure" thought. It is a human weakness to believe that by retiring into his imagination man can elicit categories or magical spells which will enable him to subjugate reality contemplatively. It is the error of the "theoretical" man, of the prophet, of the mystic, of the metaphysician, in its pathological form the error of the neurotic. It is the trace of the primitive believer in magic that remains in us all. In Shaw it takes a characteristically bourgeois form. He sees that truth brings freedom, but he refuses to see that this understanding is a social product and not a thing that one clever man can find alone. Shaw still believes that out of his Platonic soul man can extract pure wisdom in the form of world-dominating Ideas, and out of debate and ratiocination, without social action, beat out a new and higher consciousness.

It is notable that the real artist, like the real scientist, never makes this mistake. Both find themselves repeatedly pushed into contact with reality; they desire and seek reality outside them.

Reality is a large, tough, and—as man gets to know it—increasingly complex substance. To know it requires the socially pooled labors of generations of men. So complex has science already grown that a man can only hope to grasp completely a small corner of it. The old dream of all-knowledge for one mind has vanished. Men must be content to cooperate by giving a few stitches in the vast tapestry, and even these few stitches may be as complex as the earlier large design of a Newton or a Darwin.

Now Shaw with his bourgeois individualism is impatient at the restriction science sets on the domination of reality by one acute intellect. Shaw cannot hope to master the apparatus of science, therefore he sweeps it all away as mumbo-jumbo. It is nonsense, Shaw says, that the sun is ninety million miles away from the earth. Natural Selection is preposterous. And so instead of these concepts reached with so much labor, Shaw puts forward ideas drawn purely from his desires like those of any Hindu mystic theorizing about the world. Sweeping aside all science as nonsense, he rewrites the history of reality in terms of a witch-doctor's "life-force" and a jam-tomorrow God. Shavian cosmology is barbarous; it is idealistic. Shaw dominates this tough, distressing, gritty environment by the familiar neurotic method, by imposing on it a series of fictional delusions of a wish-fulfillment type. This is not because Shaw is foolish but precisely because he is possessed of a naturally acute intellect. Its very acuteness has given him a pride which makes him feel he ought to be able to dominate all knowledge without social aid, by pure cerebration. He will not recognize, except cursorily, the social nature of knowledge. So we get in his cosmology an effect like that of an exceptionally brilliant medicine man theorizing about life. Since the average intellectual is still infected with similarly barbaric theorizing, it is not surprising that he does not detect the essential crudity of all Shaw's philosophy. Bourgeois speaks to bourgeois.

It is barbarous to believe in action without thought, that is the Fascist heresy. But it is equally barbarous to believe in thought without action, the bourgeois intellectual heresy. Thought is immobilized—or rather races like a machine with nothing to bite on—once it is declutched from action, for thought is an aid to action. Thought guides action, but it learns *how* to guide *from* action. Being must historically and always proceed knowing, for knowing evolves as an extension of being.

Shaw's instinctive bourgeois belief in the primacy of lonely thought is of course evidenced not only in his ludicrous cosmology and repulsive Utopia, but also in his Butlerian biology, in which the various animals decide whether they want long necks and so forth, and by concentrating their minds on this aim, succeed in growing them. Ludicrous as this Butlerian neo-Lamarckianism is, it has enormous emotional influence on the bourgeois mind. It appeals to it so powerfully that sober scientists, even while admitting that no atom of evidence can be found for this hypothesis and all kinds of evidence for the opposite standpoint, yet insist on giving it a provisional approval, because it seems so "nice" to them. To a mind obsessed with bourgeois concepts of liberty and the autonomy of the individual mind, such a conception seems to promise a kind of substitute for the paradise which determinism denies him.

This would be unimportant if Shaw's Fabianism did not pervade all his work, robbing it of artistic as well as of political value. Believing in the solitary primacy of thought, all his plays are devoid of humanity, because they represent human beings as walking intellects. Fortunately they are not, or the human race would long ago have perished in some dreamfantasy of logic and metaphysics. Human beings are mountains of unconscious being, walking the old grooves of instinct and simple life, with a kind of occasional phosphorescence of consciousness at the summit. And this conscious phosphorescence derives its value and its power from the emotions, from the instincts; only its form is derived from the intellectual shapes of thought. Age by age man strives to make this consciousness more intense, the artist by subtilizing and intensifying the emotions, the scientist by making fuller and more real the thought form, and in both cases this is done by burning more being in the thin flame. Shaw, however, is obsessed with the "pure" flame, phosphorescence separate from being. The ideas thus abstracted become empty and petty and strike with a remote tinkling sound in the ears. Shaw's plays become an "unearthly ballet of bloodless categories."

This mixed thought and feeling of consciousness is not the source of social power, only a component of it. Society with its workshops, its buildings, its material solidity, is always present below real being and is a kind of vast reservoir of the unknown, unconscious and irrational in every man, so that of everyone we can say his conscious life is only a fitful gleam on the mass of his whole existence. Moreover, there is a kind of carapacious toughness about the conscious part of society which resists change, even while, below these generalizations, changes in material and technique and real detailed being are going on. This gives rise in every man to a tension which is a real dynamic force in society, producing artists, poets, prophets, madmen, neurotics and all the little uncertainties, irra-

tionalities, impulses, sudden unreasoning emotions, all the
delights and horrors, everything that makes life the thing it is,
enrapturing the artist and terrifying the neurotic. It is the
sum of the uneasy, the anticonservative, the revolutionary. It
is everything which cannot be content with the present but
causes lovers to tire of love, children to flee their happy parental circle, men to waste themselves in apparently useless
effort.

This source of all happiness and woe is the disparity between man's being and man's consciousness, which drives on
society and makes life vital. Now all this tension, everything
below the dead intellectual sphere, is blotted out in Shaw.
The Life Love, which is his crude theological substitute for
this real active being, is itself intellectually conceived. Thus
his characters are inhuman; all their conflicts occur on the
rational plane, and none of their conflicts are ever resolved—
for how can logic ever resolve its eternal antinomies, which
can only be synthesized in action? This tension creates
"heroes" like Cæsar and Joan of Arc, who, in response to the
unformulated guidance of experience, call into existence tremendous talent forces of whose nature they can know nothing,
yet history itself seems to obey them. Such heroes are inconceivable to Shaw. He is bound to suppose that all they
brought about they consciously willed. Hence these heroes
appear to him as the neat little figures of a bourgeois history
book, quite inhuman, and regarding their lives as calmly as
if they were examination papers on the "currents of social
change." These plays are not dramas. This is not art, it is
mere debate and just as unresolved, just as lacking in tragic
finality, temporal progress or artistic unity as is all debate.

For this reason, too, Shaw is a kind of intellectual aristo-
crat, and no one who is not capable of declaring his motives
rationally and with the utmost acuity on instant demand
appears in his plays, except as a ludicrous or second-rate
figure. The actors are nothing; the thinkers are everything.
Even a man who in real life would be powerful, formidable
and quite brainless—the "armorer" of *Major Barbara*—has
to be transformed into a brilliant theoretician before (as Shaw

thinks) he can be made impressive on the stage. But we all know and admire characters devoid of the ability for intellectual formulation who yet seem in their influence upon reality nobler, grander, more powerful and effective than any of our intellectual friends. We know well enough in life at all events, that thought alone does not suffice to drive on the world, and recognize this in our homage to "illusory" "irrational" art, art that speaks to the mere experience of us, stirring it into a fleeting and purely emotional consciousness. None of these characters, who in war, art, statesmanship and ethics have been of significance in the world's history, appear in Shaw's plays. He is incapable of drawing a character who is impressive without being a good arguer in bourgeois dialectic. This weakness naturally shows itself in his proletarians. Like the proletarians in the Army hostel of *Major Barbara*, they are simply caricatures. Only by being "educated," like the chauffeur in *Man and Superman*, can they become respectable.

It therefore follows that Shaw's ideal world is a world not of communism, but like Wells's is a world ruled by intellectual Samurai guiding the poor muddled workers; a world of Fascism. For bourgeois intellectuals obsessed with a false notion of the nature of liberty are by the inherent contradictions of their notion at length driven to liberty's opposite, Fascism. Shaw's Utopia is a planned world imposed from above in which the organization is in the hands of a bureaucracy of intellectuals. Such a world is negated by the world of communism, in which all participate in ruling and active intellectuals, no longer divorced from being, learn from the conscious worker just as much as the workers demand guidance from thought. The fatal class gap between thought and action is bridged. This world, with its replaceable officials not specially trained for the task, is the opposite of the old Fabian dream or nightmare, the class Utopia in which the ruling class now takes the form of a permanent, intellectual, trained bureaucracy, wielding the powers of State for the "good" of the proletariat. This world was a pleasant dream of the middle class, which neither owned the world, like the capitalist, nor had the certainty of one day owning it like the proletariat.

It is an unrealizable dream which yet holds the intellectual away from the proletariat and makes him a bulwark of reaction and Fascism. Shaw is still obsessed with the idea of liberty as a kind of medicine which a man of goodwill can impose on the "ignorant" worker from without. That liberty would be medicine for the bourgeois, not the worker. He does not see that neither intellectual nor worker possesses as yet this priceless freedom to give, both are confined within the categories of their time, and communism is the active creation of true liberty which cannot yet be given by anybody to anybody. It is a voyage of discovery, but we are certain of one thing. The liberty which the Roman, the feudal lord and the bourgeois achieved, proved illusory, simply because they believed that a ruling class could find it, and impose it on society. But we can see that they failed and man is still everywhere in chains, because they did not share the pursuit of liberty with their slaves, their serfs, or the exploited proletariat; and they did not do so because to have done so would have been to cease to be a ruling class, a thing impossible until productive forces had developed to a stage where ruling classes were no longer necessary. Therefore, before the well meaning intellectual, such as Shaw, seeks this difficult liberty, he must first help to change the system of social relations to one in which all men and not a class have the reins of society in their hands. To achieve liberty a man must govern himself; but since he lives in society, and society lives by and in its productive relations, this means that for men to achieve liberty society must govern its productive relations. For a man to rule himself presupposes that society is not ruled by a class from which he himself is excluded. The search for liberty only begins in the classless state, when society, being completely self-governing, can learn the difficult ways of freedom. But how can this be achieved when its destiny is planned by a class, or controlled by the higgling of a market, or even arranged by a company of elegant Samurai? How can the intellectual Samurai ever agree, since no two philosophers have ever agreed about absolute truth and justice? Only one referee has ever been found for the interminable *sic et non* of thought—action. But in a world where thought rules and action must hold its tongue, how can the issue ever be resolved? Action permeates every pore of society: its life is the action of every man. Society is torn apart as soon as its form is determined by the thought of a few which is privileged and separate from the action of the many.

Since Shaw implicitly denies the elementary truth that thought flows from being, and that man changes his consciousness by changing his social relations, which change is the result of the pressure of real being below those relations, Shaw must necessarily deny the efficacy of revolutionary action as compared with the activities of propaganda. Like Wells he believes that preaching alone will move the world. But the world moves, and though it moves through and with preaching, it does not follow that all preaching moves it, but only that that preaching moves it which moves with the law of motion of the world, which marches along the line of action, and cuts down the grain of events. Yet a bourgeois intellectual always believes that whatever he conceives as absolute truth and justice—vegetarianism or equal incomes or antivaccination—can be imposed on the world by successful argument. Hence Shaw's plays.

But here Shaw is faced with a dilemma. He is to impose his absolute truths on the world by the process of logical debate. But the world of non-thinkers or half-thinkers on which he imposes it are necessarily an inferior race of creatures—the mere laborers, the nit-wit aggregation of the non-intellectuals, the plastic amorphous mass whom the intellectual lords of creation save from disaster by their godlike commands. How can one drill sense into these creatures? What will appeal to their infantile frivolous minds? One must of course treat them as one treats children, one must sugar the pill of reason with paradox, humor, with lively and preposterous incident.

Thus Shaw, whom a belief in the primacy of intellectual consciousness prevented from becoming an artist, was by this same belief prevented from becoming a serious thinker or a real force in contemporary consciousness. He became the world's buffoon; because his messages were always wrapped in the sugar of humor, they were taken as always laughable. The British bourgeois, who ignored Marx, vilified Lenin and threw its Tom Manns into prison, regarded Shaw with a tolerant good humor as a kind of court jester. The people he had depreciated depreciated him. The sugar he put on his pill prevented the pill from acting.

Marx by contrast did not attempt to make *Das Kapital* appealing to the tired brains of the British bourgeoisie. He did not attempt to become a best seller, or veil his views in West End successes. He did not give humorous interviews to the contemporary press. His name was known only to a few Englishmen of his time, while that of Shaw is known to millions. But because he gave his message seriously, treating the race of men as his equals, his message was received seriously and well. Because he did not believe that thought rules the world, but that thought must follow the grain of action, his thought has been more world-creating than that of any single man. Not only has it called into existence a new civilization over a sixth of the world's surface, but in all other countries all revolutionary elements are oriented round Marx's thought; all contemporary politics are of significance only in so far as they are with Marx or against him.

It is no answer to say that Marx's is a greater intellect than Shaw's. Doubtless if Shaw had been Marx he would have been Marx. No one has devised a standard for measuring intellects in themselves, since intellects do not exist in themselves, but only in their overt mentation. Shaw and Marx were both men of keen intellect, as evidenced in their writings, and both were aware, from experience, of the breakdown of greedy bourgeois social relations; but the mind of one was able to leap forward to the future, the other is prisoned always in the categories of the bourgeoisdom it despises. Because Shaw gave his message condescendingly and flippantly, treating the race of men as his inferiors, his message has been much read and little noted, and the message itself betrays all the falsehood and unreality of the attitude which settled its delivery.

Shaw read Marx early in life, and he was given therefore the alternative of being a dangerous revolutionary instead of a popular reformist who would dream of a world saved by a converted middle class. He decided that although Marx had shown him the shame and falsities of bourgeois life, he would refuse to recognize the necessity for the overthrow of this decaying class by the class of the future. From that moment Shaw was divided against himself.

This decision is explained by his personal history. Born into a middle-class family that had fallen from affluence and social position to embarrassment, the ambitious young Shaw, impressed from childhood with the necessity for retrieving the former Shavian status, came to London to gain success. Here he existed for a time by writing, as poor as any worker. But thanks to the possession of a dress suit and a gift for playing on the piano, he was still able to mix in refined Kensington circles. Faced with proletarianization, he clung to the bourgeois class. In the same way, faced with the problem of ideological proletarianization in his reading of Marx, he resisted it, and adhered to Fabianism, with its bourgeois traditions and its social respectability.

This problem and his answer to it decided his ideology and also his art. His knowledge of Marx enabled him to attack destructively all bourgeois institutions. But he was never able to give any answer to the question: *What shall we do here and now to improve them besides talking?* This problem, in the veiled form of "tainted money," comes up in his work repeatedly—in *Widowers' Houses, Major Barbara, Mrs. Warren's Profession*—and always it is *patched up*. We must accept things as they are until the system is changed. But no immediate steps besides talking are ever to be taken to change the system. Major Barbara, horrified at first by finding the Christ she believes in has sold out to capital, ends all the same by marrying the manager of the armament factory whose proprietor has bought Him. Shaw himself, who discovered the ruling class was rotten to the core, and built on the exploitation of the workers, yet ends by marrying ideologically money, respectability, fame, peaceful reformism and ultimately even

Mussolini. He who takes no active steps to change the system, helps to maintain the system.

Yet just because Shaw has read Marx, he understands the essential contradictions of this solution. For this reason his plays are full of deliberately forced conversions, unconvincing *dénouements,* and a general escape from reality through the medium of fantasy and humor. Shaw dealt quite simply in his life with the problem of tainted goods that arose from the sufferings of animals. Meat and sera, one resulting from the slaughter and the other from the vivisection of animals, must not be used, even though in spite of one's abstention the wicked business goes merrily on. But he cannot make that renouncement in the case of money and of all the intangibles of bourgeois respectability—fame as a Fabian intellectual instead of suppression as a dangerous revolutionary. Meat and sera are not essential to the life of society, and therefore it is possible to abstain from them. In bourgeois society money is what holds society together: no one can ever eat without it; therefore it is impossible to "abstain" from it. But this in itself exposes the futility of Shaw's bourgeois abstaining approach to the problem, like that of the pacifist who will not fight but continues to be fed at the expense of the community. Shaw's ambivalent attitude to social evils reveals his cowardice before the prime evil, the very hinge of society, which he will accept, while he abstains from the lesser evils. Thus his vegetarianism acts as a kind of compensation for his betrayal on the larger issue, and a symbol of his whole reformist approach. He will abstain; he will criticize; but he will not act. This last refusal infects his criticism and makes his abstention an active weapon of reaction. And so, all through his plays and prefaces, money is the god, without which we are nothing, are powerless and helpless. "Get money, and you can be virtuous; without it you cannot even start to be good." Shaw repeats this so often and so loudly that he seems anxious to convince himself as well as others. "Renounce it," he asks, "and what help is your altruism? Even if you throw it in the gutter, some scoundrel will pick it up. Wait till the system is changed."

But how is it to be changed? Shaw has no convincing

answer. There is no need to accuse Shaw of conscious dishonesty. Shaw is helplessly imprisoned in the categories of bourgeois thought. He could not see that because being conditions knowing, the bourgeois class for all their "cleverness" are doomed to collapse and the workers for all their "stupidity" are able to play an active creative rôle in building a new civilization on the wreckage of the old. Faced with this choice—*worker or bourgeois*—the bourgeois—with all the brilliance of bourgeois culture behind him—seemed to Shaw preferable to the other, ignorant, "irrational" and "brutalized" by poverty. Hence arose his life problem, how to persuade this bourgeois class to renounce its sins. He had to convert them, or fold his hands in despair; and yet in his heart he did not believe in their future, for he had read Marx.

This decision, conditioned by his class and his experience, led to all his difficulties. He could never really bring himself to believe in a bourgeois class regenerated by Fabianism, and events made still clearer its hopelessness and its decay. Hence, more and more, his plays become futile and unresolved. Civilization is driven "On the Rocks" or is in the "Apple Cart." Relief is found in the faith of a Life Force making inevitably for a Utopia (*Back to Methuselah*). Or as in *St. Joan* he tries to comfort himself by turning to a period when this class he has committed himself to, this bourgeois class, played an active creative part: he draws St. Joan as the heroine and prophet of bourgeois individuality, amid a dying medievalism. In *Heartbreak House* he records simply a Chekhovian detachment and disillusion. Evidently all Shaw's failing, all the things that prevented him from fulfilling the artistic and intellectual promise of his native gifts, arise in a most direct fashion from his fatal choice of the bourgeois class at a period of history when the choice was wrong. From this choice springs the unreality of his plays, their lack of dramatic resolutions, the substitution of debate for dialectic, the belief in life forces and thought Utopias, the bungling treatment of human beings in love, the lack of scientific knowledge, and the queer strain of mountebank in all Shaw says, as of a man who in mocking others is also mocking himself because he despises himself but despises others more.

Shaw performed a useful function in exposing the weakness of the bourgeois class. He exposes the rottenness of its culture and at the same time commits the future to its hands, but neither he nor his readers can believe in the success of that; and so he represents symbolically bourgeois intelligence as it is today, shamefaced and losing confidence in itself. He plays this active part, that he is one of the forces of defeatism and despair which help the decay of a world that has had its day. This disintegration is no more than pathological without the active forces of revolution which can shatter the rotten structure and build it anew. This confidence Shaw has never achieved, nor the insight that is needed for it. He stands by the side of Wells, Lawrence, Proust, Huxley, Russell, Forster, Wassermann, Hemingway, and Galsworthy as typical of their age, men who proclaim the disillusionment of bourgeois culture with itself, men themselves disillusioned and yet not able to wish for anything better or gain any closer grasp of this bourgeois culture whose pursuit of liberty and individualism led men into the mire. Always it is their freedom they are defending. This makes them pathetic rather than tragic figures, for they are helpless, not because of overwhelming circumstances but because of their own illusion.

Rudyard Kipling

By George Orwell

It was a pity that Mr. Eliot should be so much on the defensive in the long essay with which he prefaces this selection of Kipling's poetry,[1] but it was not to be avoided, because before one can even speak about Kipling one has to clear away a legend that has been created by two sets of people who have not read his works. Kipling is in the peculiar position of having been a byword for fifty years. During five literary generations every enlightened person has despised him, and at the end of that time nine-tenths of those enlightened persons are forgotten and Kipling is in some sense still there. Mr. Eliot never satisfactorily explains this fact, because in answering the shallow and familiar charge that Kipling is a "Fascist," he falls into the opposite error of defending him where he is not defensible. It is no use pretending that Kipling's view of life, as a whole, can be accepted or even forgiven by any civilized person. It is no use claiming, for instance, that when Kipling describes a British soldier beating a "nigger" with a cleaning rod in order to get money out of him, he is acting merely as a reporter and does not necessarily approve what he describes. There is not the slightest sign anywhere in Kipling's work that he disapproves of that kind of conduct—on the contrary, there is a definite strain of sadism in him, over and above the brutality which a writer of that type has to have. Kipling *is* a jingo imperialist, he *is* morally insensitive and æsthetically disgusting. It is better to start by admitting that, and then to try to find out why it is that he survives while the refined people who have sniggered at him seem to wear so badly.

And yet the "Fascist" charge has to be answered, because the first clue to any understanding of Kipling, morally or

[1] *A Choice of Kipling's Verse,* made by T. S. Eliot (Faber & Faber, London).

politically, is the fact that he was *not* a Fascist. He was further from being one than the most humane or the most "progressive" person is able to be nowadays. An interesting instance of the way in which quotations are parroted to and fro without any attempt to look up their context or discover their meaning is the line from "Recessional," "Lesser breeds without the Law." This line is always good for a snigger in pansy-left circles. It is assumed as a matter of course that the "lesser breed" are "natives," and a mental picture is called up of some pukka sahib in a pith helmet kicking a coolie. In its context the sense of the line is almost the exact opposite of this. The phrase "lesser breeds" refers almost certainly to the Germans, and especially the pan-German writers, who are "without the Law" in the sense of being lawless, not in the sense of being powerless. The whole poem, conventionally thought of as an orgy of boasting, is a denunciation of power politics, British as well as German. Two stanzas are worth quoting (I am quoting this as politics, not as poetry):

> *If, drunk with sight of power, we loose*
> *Wild tongues that have not Thee in awe,*
> *Such boastings as the Gentiles use,*
> *Or lesser breeds without the Law—*
> *Lord God of hosts, be with us yet,*
> *Lest we forget—lest we forget!*
>
> *For heathen heart that puts her trust*
> *In reeking tube and iron shard,*
> *All valiant dust that builds on dust,*
> *And guarding, calls not Thee to guard,*
> *For frantic boast and foolish word—*
> *Thy mercy on Thy People, Lord!*

Much of Kipling's phraseology is taken from the Bible, and no doubt in the second stanza he had in mind the text from Psalm cxxvii.: "Except the Lord build the house, they labour in vain that build it; except the Lord keep the city, the watchman waketh but in vain." It is not a text that makes much impression on the post-Hitler mind. No one, in our time, believes in any sanction greater than military power; no one believes that it is possible to overcome force except by greater force. There is no "law," there is only power. I am not saying that that is a true belief, merely that it is the belief which all modern men do actually hold. Those who pretend otherwise are either intellectual cowards, or power-worshipers under a thin disguise, or have simply not caught up with the age they are living in. Kipling's outlook is pre-Fascist. He still believes that pride comes before a fall and that the gods punish *hubris*. He does not foresee the tank, the bombing plane, the radio and the secret police, or their psychological results.

But in saying this, does not one unsay what I said above about Kipling's jingoism and brutality? No, one is merely saying that the nineteenth century imperialist outlook and the modern gangster outlook are two different things. Kipling belongs very definitely to the period 1885-1902. The Great War and its aftermath embittered him, but he shows little sign of having learned anything from any event later than the Boer War. He was the prophet of British Imperialism in its expansionist phase (even more than his poems, his solitary novel, *The Light That Failed*, gives you the atmosphere of that time) and also the unofficial historian of the British Army, the old mercenary army which began to change its shape in 1914. All his confidence, his bouncing vulgar vitality, sprang out of limitations which no Fascist or near-Fascist shares.

Kipling spent the later part of his life in sulking, and no doubt it was political disappointment rather than literary vanity that accounted for this. Somehow history had not gone according to plan. After the greatest victory she had ever known, Britain was a lesser world power than before, and Kipling was quite acute enough to see this. The virtue had gone out of the classes he idealized, the young were hedonistic or disaffected, the desire to paint the map red had evaporated. He could not understand what was happening, because he had never had any grasp of the economic forces underlying imperial expansion. It is notable that Kipling does not seem to realize, any more than the average soldier or colonial administrator, that an empire is primarily a money-making concern. Imperialism as he sees it is a sort of forcible evangelizing. You turn a Gatling gun on a mob of unarmed "natives," and then you establish "the Law," which includes roads, railways and a courthouse. He could not foresee, therefore, that the same motives which brought the Empire into existence would end by destroying it. It was the same motive, for example, that caused the Malayan jungles to be cleared for rubber estates, and which now causes those estates to be handed over intact to the Japanese. The modern totalitarians know what they are doing, and the nineteenth century English did not know what they were doing. Both attitudes have their advantages, but Kipling was never able to move forward from one into the other. His outlook, allowing for the fact that after all he was an artist, was that of the salaried bureaucrat who despises the "box-wallah" and often lives a lifetime without realizing that the "box-wallah" calls the tune.

But because he identifies himself with the official class, he does possess one thing which "enlightened" people seldom or never possess, and that is a sense of responsibility. The middle-class Left hate him for this quite as much as for his cruelty and vulgarity. All left-wing parties in the highly industrialized countries are at bottom a sham, because they make it their business to fight against something which they do not really wish to destroy. They have internationalist aims, and at the same time they struggle to keep up a standard of life with which those aims are incompatible. We all live by robbing Asiatic coolies, and those of us who are "enlightened" all maintain that those coolies ought to be set free; but our standard of living, and hence our "enlightenment," demands that the robbery shall continue. A humanitarian is always a hypocrite, and Kipling's understanding of this is perhaps the central secret of his power to create telling phrases. It would be difficult to hit off the one-eyed pacifism of the English in fewer words than in the phrase, "making mock of uniforms that guard you while you sleep." It is true that Kipling does not understand the economic aspect of the relationship between the highbrow and the blimp. He does not see that the map is painted red chiefly in order that the coolie may be exploited. Instead of the coolie he sees the Indian Civil Servant; but even on that plane his grasp of function, of who protects whom, is very sound. He sees clearly that men can only be highly civilized while other men, inevitably less civilized, are there to guard and feed them.

How far does Kipling really identify himself with the administrators, soldiers and engineers whose praises he sings? Not so completely as is sometimes assumed. He had traveled very widely while he was still a young man, he had grown up with a brilliant mind in mainly philistine surroundings, and some streak in him that may have been partly neurotic led him to prefer the active man to the sensitive man. The nineteenth century Anglo-Indians, to name the least sympathetic of his idols, were at any rate people who did things. It may be that all that they did was evil, but they changed the face of the earth (it is instructive to look at a map of Asia and compare the railway system of India with that of the surrounding countries), whereas they could have achieved nothing, could not have maintained themselves in power for a single week, if the normal Anglo-Indian outlook had been that of, say, E. M. Forster. Tawdry and shallow though it is, Kipling's is the only literary picture that we possess of nineteenth century Anglo-India, and he could only make it because he was just coarse enough to be able to exist and keep his mouth shut in clubs and regimental messes. But he did not greatly resemble the people he admired. I know from several private sources that many of the Anglo-Indians who were Kipling's contemporaries did not like or approve of him. They said, no doubt truly, that he knew nothing about India, and on the other hand, he was from their point of view too much of a highbrow. While in India he tended to mix with "the wrong" people, and because of his dark complexion he was wrongly suspected of having a streak of Asiatic blood. Much in his development is traceable to his having been born in India and having left school early. With a slightly different background he might have been a good novelist or a superlative writer of music-hall songs. But how true is it that he was a vulgar flag-waver, a sort of publicity agent for Cecil Rhodes? It is true, but it is not true that he was a yes-man or a time-server. After his early days, if then, he never courted public opinion. Mr. Eliot says that what is held against him is that he expressed unpopular views in a popular style. This narrows the issue by assuming that "unpopular" means unpopular with the intelligentsia, but it is a fact that Kipling's "message" was one that the big public did not want, and, indeed, has never accepted. The mass of the people, in the nineties as now, were antimilitarist, bored by the Empire, and only unconsciously patriotic. Kipling's official admirers are and were the "service" middle class, the people who read *Blackwood's.* In the stupid early years of this century, the blimps, having at last discovered someone who could be called a poet and who was on their side, set Kipling on a pedestal, and some of his more sententious poems, such as "If," were given almost Biblical status. But it is doubtful whether the blimps have ever read him with attention, any more than they have read the Bible. Much of what he says they could not possibly approve. Few people who have criticized England from the inside have said bitterer things about her than this gutter patriot. As a rule it is the British working class that he is attacking, but not always. That phrase about "the flannelled fools at the wicket and the muddied oafs at the goal" sticks like an arrow to this day, and it is aimed at the Eton and Harrow match as well as the Cup-Tie Final. Some of the verses he wrote about the Boer War have a curiously modern ring, so far as their subject matter goes. "Stellenbosch," which must have been written about 1902, sums up what every intelligent infantry officer was saying in 1918, or is saying now, for that matter.

Kipling's romantic ideas about England and the Empire might not have mattered if he could have held them without having the class prejudices which at that time went with them. If one examines his best and most representative work, his soldier poems, especially *Barrack-Room Ballads,* one notices that what more than anything else spoils them is an underlying air of patronage. Kipling idealizes the army officer, especially the junior officer, and that to an idiotic extent, but the private soldier, though lovable and romantic, has to be a comic. He is always made to speak in a sort of stylized Cockney, not very broad but with all the aitches and final "g's" carefully omitted. Very often the result is as embarrassing as the humorous recitation at a church social. And this accounts for the curious fact that one can often improve Kipling's poems, make them less facetious and less blatant, by simply going through them and transplanting them from Cockney into standard speech. This is especially true of his refrains, which often have a truly lyrical quality. Two examples will do (one is about a funeral and the other about a wedding):

> *So it's knock out your pipes and follow me!*
> *And it's finish up your swipes and follow me!*
> *Oh, hark to the big drum calling,*
> *Follow me—follow me home!*

and again:

> *Cheer for the Sergeant's wedding—*
> *Give them one cheer more!*
> *Grey gun-horses in the lando,*
> *And a rogue is married to a whore!*

Here I have restored the aitches, etc. Kipling ought to have known better. He ought to have seen that the two closing lines of the first of these stanzas are very beautiful lines, and that ought to have overridden his impulse to make fun of a working man's accent. In the ancient ballads the lord and the peasant speak the same language. This is impossible to Kipling, who is looking down a distorting class-perspective, and by a piece of poetic justice one of his best lines is spoiled—for "follow me 'ome" is much uglier than "follow me home." But even where it makes no difference musically the facetiousness of his stage Cockney dialect is irritating. However, he is more often quoted aloud than read on the printed page, and most people instinctively make the necessary alterations when they quote him.

Can one imagine any private soldier, in the nineties or now, reading *Barrack-Room Ballads* and feeling that here was a writer who spoke for him? It is very hard to do so. Any soldier capable of reading a book of verse would notice at once that Kipling is almost unconscious of the class war that goes on in an army as much as elsewhere. It is not only that he thinks the soldier comic, but that he thinks him patriotic, feudal, a ready admirer of his officers and proud to be a soldier of the Queen. Of course that is partly true, or battles could not be fought, but "What have I done for thee, England, my England?" is essentially a middle-class query. Almost any working man would follow it up immediately with "What has England done for me?" In so far as Kipling grasps this, he simply sets it down to "the intense selfishness of the lower classes" (his own phrase). When he is writing not of British but of "loyal" Indians he carries the "Salaam, sahib" motif to sometimes disgusting lengths. Yet it remains true that he has far more interest in the common soldier, far more anxiety that he shall get a fair deal, than most of the "liberals" of his day or our own. He sees that the soldier is neglected, meanly underpaid and hypocritically despised by the people whose incomes he safeguards. "I came to realise," he says in his posthumous memoirs, "the bare horrors of the private's life, and the unnecessary torments he endured." He is accused of glorifying war, and perhaps he does so, but not in the usual manner, by pretending that war is a sort of football match. Like most people capable of writing battle poetry, Kipling had never been in battle, but his vision of war is realistic. He knows that bullets hurt, that under fire everyone is terrified, that the ordinary soldier never knows what the war is about or what is happening except in his own corner of the battlefield, and that British troops, like other troops, frequently run away:

I 'eard the knives be'ind me, but I dursn't face my man,
Nor I don't know where I went to, 'cause I didn't stop to see,
Till I 'eard a beggar squealin' out for quarter as 'e ran,
An' I thought I knew the voice an'—it was me!

Modernize the style of this, and it might have come out of one of the debunking war books of the nineteen twenties. Or again:

An' now the hugly bullets come peckin' through the dust,
An' no one wants to face 'em, but every beggar must;
So, like a man in irons, which isn't glad to go,
They moves 'em off by companies uncommon stiff an' slow.

Compare this with:

> *Forward the Light Brigade!*
> *Was there a man dismayed?*
> *No! though the soldier knew*
> *Someone had blundered.*

If anything, Kipling overdoes the horrors, for the wars of his youth were hardly wars at all by our standards. Perhaps that is due to the neurotic strain in him, the hunger for cruelty. But at least he knows that men ordered to attack impossible objectives *are* dismayed, and also that fourpence a day is not a generous pension.

How complete or truthful a picture has Kipling left us of the long-service, mercenary army of the late nineteenth century? One must say of this, as of what Kipling wrote about nineteenth century Anglo-India, that it is not only the best but almost the only literary picture we have. He has put on record an immense amount of stuff that one could otherwise only gather from verbal tradition or from unreadable regimental histories. Perhaps his picture of army life seems fuller and more accurate than it is because any middle-class English person is likely to know enough to fill up the gaps. At any rate, reading the essay on Kipling that Mr. Edmund Wilson has just published,[2] I was struck by the number of things that are boringly familiar to us and seem to be barely intelligible to an American. But from the body of Kipling's early work there does seem to emerge a vivid and not seriously misleading picture of the old pre-machine-gun army—the sweltering barracks in Gibraltar or Lucknow, the red coats, the pipe-clayed belts and the pillbox hats, the beer, the fights, the floggings, hangings and crucifixions, the bugle calls, the smell of oats and horse piss, the bellowing sergeants with foot-long moustaches, the bloody skirmishes, invariably misman-aged, the crowded troopships, the cholera-stricken camps, the "native" concubines, the ultimate death in the workhouse. It is a crude, vulgar picture, in which a patriotic music-hall term seems to have got mixed up with one of Zola's gorier passages, but from it future generations will be able to gather some idea of what a long-term volunteer army was like. On about the same level they will be able to learn something of British India in the days when motorcars and refrigerators were unheard of. It is an error to imagine that we might have had better books on these subjects if, for example, George Moore, or Gissing, or Thomas Hardy, had had Kipling's opportunities. That is the kind of accident that cannot happen. It was not possible that nineteenth century England should produce a book like *War and Peace,* or like Tolstoy's minor stories of army life, such as "Sebastopol" or "The Cossacks," not because the talent was necessarily lacking but because no one with sufficient sensitiveness to write such books would ever have made the appropriate contacts. Tolstoy lived in a great military empire in which it seemed natural for almost any young man of family to spend a few years in the army, whereas the British Empire was and still is demilitarized to a degree which continental observers find almost incredible. Civilized men do not readily move away from the centers of civilization, and in most languages there is a great dearth of what one might call colonial literature. It took a very

[2] Published in a volume of essays, *The Wound and the Bow* (Houghton Mifflin, 1941).

improbable combination of circumstances to produce Kipling's gaudy tableau, in which Private Ortheris and Mrs. Hauksbee pose against a background of palm trees to the sound of temple bells, and one necessary circumstance was that Kipling himself was only half civilized.

Kipling is the only English writer of our time who has added phrases to the language. The phrases and neologisms which we take over and use without remembering their origin do not always come from writers we admire. It is strange, for instance, to hear the Nazi broadcasters referring to the Russian soldiers as "robots," thus unconsciously borrowing a word from a Czech democrat whom they would have killed if they could have laid hands on him. Here are half a dozen phrases coined by Kipling which one sees quoted in leader-ettes in the gutter press or overhears in saloon bars from people who have barely heard his name. It will be seen that they all have a certain characteristic in common:

East is East, and West is West.
The white man's Burden.
What do they know of England who only England know?
The female of the species is more deadly than the male.
Somewhere East of Suez.
Paying the Dane-geld.

There are various others, including some that have outlived their context by many years. The phrase "killing Kruger with your mouth," for instance, was current till very recently. It is also possible that it was Kipling who first let loose the use of the word "Huns" for Germans; at any rate he began using it as soon as the guns opened fire in 1914. But what the phrases I have listed above have in common is that they are all of them phrases which one utters semiderisively (as it might be "For I'm to be Queen o' the May, mother, I'm to be Queen o' the May"), but which one is bound to make use of sooner or later. Nothing could exceed the contempt of the *New Statesman*, for instance, for Kipling, but how many times during the Munich period did the *New Statesman* find itself

quoting that phrase about paying the Dane-geld? [3] The fact is
that Kipling, apart from his snack-bar wisdom and his gift
for packing much cheap picturesqueness into a few words
("Palm and Pine"—"East of Suez"—"The Road to Mandalay"), is generally talking about things that are of urgent
interest. It does not matter, from this point of view, that
thinking and decent people generally find themselves on the
other side of the fence from him. "White man's burden" instantly conjures up a real problem, even if one feels that it
ought to be altered to "black man's burden." One may disagree to the middle of one's bones with the political attitude
implied in "The Islanders," but one cannot say that it is a
frivolous attitude. Kipling deals in thoughts which are both
vulgar and permanent. This raises the question of his special
status as a poet, or verse-writer.

Mr. Eliot describes Kipling's metrical work as "verse" and
not "poetry," but adds that it is *"great* verse," and further
qualifies this by saying that a writer can only be described as
a "great verse-writer" if there is some of his work "of which
we cannot say whether it is verse or poetry." Apparently
Kipling was a versifier who occasionally wrote poems, in
which case it was a pity that Mr. Eliot did not specify these
poems by name. The trouble is that whenever an æsthetic
judgment on Kipling's work seems to be called for, Mr. Eliot
is too much on the defensive to be able to speak plainly. What
he does not say, and what I think one ought to start by saying
in any discussion of Kipling, is that most of Kipling's verse is
so horribly vulgar that it gives one the same sensation as one
gets from watching a third-rate music-hall performer recite

[3] 1945. On the first page of his recent book, *Adam and Eve,* Mr.
Middleton Murry quoted the well known lines:

> There are nine and fifty ways
> Of constructing tribal lays,
> And every single one of them is right.

He attributes these lines to Thackeray. This is probably what is
known as a "Freudian error." A civilized person would prefer not
to quote Kipling—i.e., would prefer not to feel that it was Kipling
who had expressed his thought for him.

"The Pigtail of Wu Fang Fu" with the purple limelight on his face, *and yet* there is much of it that is capable of giving pleasure to people who know what poetry means. At his worst, and also his most vital, in poems like "Gunga Din" or "Danny Deever," Kipling is almost a shameful pleasure, like the taste for cheap sweets that some people secretly carry into middle life. But even with his best passages one has the same sense of being seduced by something spurious, and yet unquestionably seduced. Unless one is merely a snob and a liar it is impossible to say that no one who cares for poetry could get any pleasure out of such lines as:

For the wind is in the palm trees, and the temple bells they say,
"Come you back, you British soldier, come you back to Mandalay!"

and yet those lines are not poetry in the same sense as "Felix Randal" or "When icicles hang by the wall" are poetry. One can, perhaps, place Kipling more satisfactorily than by juggling with the words "verse" and "poetry," if one describes him simply as a good bad poet. He is as a poet what Harriet Beecher Stowe was as a novelist. And the mere existence of work of this kind, which is perceived by generation after generation to be vulgar and yet goes on being read, tells one something about the age we live in.

There is a great deal of good bad poetry in English, all of it, I should say, subsequent to 1790. Examples of good bad poems—I am deliberately choosing diverse ones—are "The Bridge of Sighs," "When All the World Is Young, Lad," "The Charge of the Light Brigade," Bret Harte's "Dickens in Camp," "The Burial of Sir John Moore," "Jenny Kissed Me," "Keith of Ravelston," "Casabianca." All of these reek of sentimentality, and yet—not these particular poems, perhaps, but poems of this kind, are capable of giving true pleasure to people who can see clearly what is wrong with them. One could fill a fair-sized anthology with good bad poems, if it were not for the significant fact that good bad poetry is usually too well known to be worth reprinting. It is no use pretending that in an age like our own, "good" poetry can have any genuine popularity. It is, and must be, the cult of a very few people, the least tolerated of the arts. Perhaps that statement needs a certain amount of qualification. True poetry can sometimes be acceptable to the mass of the people when it disguises itself as something else. One can see an example of this in the folk poetry that England still possesses, certain nursery rhymes and mnemonic rhymes, for instance, and the songs that soldiers make up, including the words that go to some of the bugle calls. But in general ours is a civilization in which the very word "poetry" evokes a hostile snigger or, at best, the sort of frozen disgust that most people feel when they hear the word "God." If you are good at playing the concertina you could probably go into the nearest public bar and get yourself an appreciative audience within five minutes. But what would be the attitude of that same audience if you suggested reading them Shakespeare's sonnets, for instance? Good bad poetry, however, can get across to the most unpromising audiences if the right atmosphere has been worked up beforehand. Some months back Churchill produced a great effect by quoting Clough's "Endeavour" in one of his broadcast speeches. I listened to this speech among people who could certainly not be accused of caring for poetry, and I am convinced that the lapse into verse impressed them and did not embarrass them. But not even Churchill could have got away with it if he had quoted anything much better than this.

In so far as a writer of verse can be popular, Kipling has been and probably still is popular. In his own lifetime some of his poems traveled far beyond the bounds of the reading public, beyond the world of school prize days, Boy Scout singsongs, limp-leather editions, poker-work and calendars, and out into the yet vaster world of the music halls. Nevertheless, Mr. Eliot thinks it worth while to edit him, thus confessing to a taste which others share but are not always honest enough to mention. The fact that such a thing as good bad poetry can exist is a sign of the emotional overlap between the intellectual and the ordinary man. The intellectual *is*

THE FORMALISTIC
APPROACH:

LITERATURE
AS AESTHETIC STRUCTURE

Introduction

WITHOUT QUESTION, the most influential critical method of our time is the formalistic.[1] It has commanded the zeal of most of our leading critics; has established its unofficial organs of journalism—the *Kenyon Review,* the *Sewannee Review, Accent,* and the *Hudson Review;* is, in fact, the method one almost automatically thinks of when speaking of contemporary criticism.

There is some reason to trace the seeds to Coleridge's view that a literary piece exists in its own way, with its own kind of life. His concept of organic unity—the whole being the harmonious involvement of all the parts—surely calls for a critical approach that would attend to the efficiency of the various elements as they work together to form a unified total meaning. In this respect, Poe's principle of the unified effect of a work of literature may be listed in the ancestry of the modern movement, although Poe seems to have had little direct influence upon contemporary critics. And Henry James's scrupulous attention to the matters of his own craft, shown in his numerous prefaces, has probably given direction to Eliot and Blackmur.

T. S. Eliot is a major figure in the development of formalistic criticism. Under the influence of Pound and Hulme, he announced the high place of art as art, rather than as an expression of social, religious, ethical, or political ideas, and advocated the close study of the texts of the works themselves. In numerous essays he applied his view of poetry as an independent organism, and his attention, in Blackmur's words, to "the facts in the work under consideration as they are relevant to literature as such." [2] His dictum, pronounced in "Tradition and the Individual Talent," that the poet escapes

---

[1] Other names are frequently used: aesthetic, textual, ontological, or most frequently, the "new criticism."
[2] In "T. S. Eliot," *Hound and Horn,* I, Nos. 3 and 4 (1928).

into the poem from emotion and personality, encouraged critics to move away from biographical study into the scrutiny of the craft of the poem. He was, in short, concerned to formulate a kind of criticism that would be free of the pursuit of extrinsically historic, moral, psychological, and sociological interpretations, and free to concentrate on the æsthetic quality of the work.

Less directly, the poetry of Eliot and Pound (and that of numerous followers) with its complicated techniques developed from the French Symbolists of the nineteenth century and the English Metaphysicals of the seventeenth, demanded the closest of examinations and gave occasion for the sharpening of critical tools.

A second great guide is I. A. Richards. Just as his *Principles of Literary Criticism,* 1924, with its analysis of the poem-audience relationship was to give impetus to the psychological approach, so his work with Ogden in *The Meaning of Meaning,* 1923, offered a vocabulary for discussing and analyzing the kinds of meaning that occur in the response to verbal stimuli; and laid the foundations of the semantic approach in literary criticism. *The Science of Poetry,* 1926, studied the fallen place of poetry in our age when most beliefs have been demonstrated, according to Richards, to be "pseudo-statements." Although he later abandoned this degrading evaluation, the book obviously has a place in the growing search for the *intrinsic* merit of poetry. *Practical Criticism,* 1929, classified and analyzed certain misinterpretations of thirteen poems, most of them of kinds later invalidated by ontological critics. In all these matters, Richards cleared the arena for later occupation by the "new" critics; but probably his fundamental contribution was in his investigation of meaning, which led on the one hand into semantics, the science of signs and sign interpretation, and on the other into the scrupulous explications of poems as illustrated by the work, for example, of Empson and Blackmur.

Besides the important contributions of Eliot and Richards, a factor in the development of formalistic criticism was the reaction against the Victorian and Neo-humanist emphasis on the moral uses of literature, the academic interest in historical and literary tradition and the biography of the author, and the willingness of impressionists to make of each literary experience an odyssey of the critic's personality. It is also likely that there was some reaction against the Marxist's stress on social values, and the psychological stress on the neuroses of writers. In any case, the atmosphere of the thirties was ripe for just such an approach as the formalistic critics then began to practice.

Though there are considerable differences among these "new" critics, they are best defined by their common beliefs, attitudes, and practices. Primarily they regard poetry as a valid source of knowledge that cannot be communicated in terms other than its own. This leads them to shun all material such as the personal or social conditions behind the composition, the moral implications, and so on, so long as these are "extrinsic"—that is, tangential to an understanding of the poem, and to concentrate on the structure of each poem, or on elements of that structure as they relate to the total poetic experience. Robert Penn Warren puts it this way: "Poetry does not inhere in any particular element but depends upon the set of relationships, the structure, which we call the poem." [3] The critic, then, examines these elements in their interconnections, assuming that the meaning is made up of matters of form (meter, image, diction, and so forth) and matters of content (tone, theme, and so forth) working not separately but together. The closeness of reading required by such a method has existed before, wherever an analytic reader has approached literature, but it has come to seem the signature of the "new" criticism. The central position and many particular applications are to be found in Brooks and Warren's *Understanding Poetry*, 1938. Although many ontological critics have disagreed with one or more of their dicta,[4] the introduction gathers forcefully and clearly all the essential elements of the formalistic approach.

[3] "Pure and Impure Poetry," *Kenyon Review* V (Spring, 1943).
[4] E.g., Ransom has argued for the value of paraphrase, while Brooks and Warren disclaim its validity.

So vigorous a movement was bound to be attacked and surely some of the attacks validly reflect its limitations. The most tangential disapprobation is by Kazin, who deplores the cliquishness of the tactics and their tendency to develop a terminology that approaches jargon, thereby excluding those who are not initiated members of the society. Perhaps, too, the special vocabulary has permitted some with insufficient imagination or taste to ride the bandwagon. R. S. Crane has protested the establishment of Brooks' "paradox" (or of Ransom's "texture," Tate's "tension," or Empson's "ambiguities") as the sole principle of poetry. This goes along with L. C. Knights's and F. R. Leavis' accusation that Empson and Richards have isolated one part of the work of art for examination, forgetting the poem as a totality. Even John Crowe Ransom, the Dean of the group, has protested, in commenting on Brooks' *Well Wrought Urn*, the use of analysis to such an extreme that the sense of the whole is lost in the study of a part. R. P. Blackmur, himself an insider, writes that the method deals chiefly with "the executive technique of poetry (and only with a part of that) or with the general verbal techniques of language," and that it works best with the Yeats-Eliot school of modern poetry, and less effectively with other sorts. Finally there is the charge that the values of literature to man as more than an æsthetic being have been neglected in favor of the analysis of form. T. S. Eliot has to some extent met this stricture by asserting that the ontological approach can establish the literary quality of a work, but that other methods are necessary to determine its greatness. Since his religious conversion, he himself has been concerned with the formal aspects of art when he writes closely of particular pieces, and with the philosophic values of art in his more general essays.

The mention of R. S. Crane's censure prompts some attention to the dissidence between the formalists and the "Chicago" School. The public nature of the debate suggests they are irreconcilable antagonists; actually theirs is a family quarrel. Both are chiefly concerned with "internal" analysis of the work of art, eschewing social, moral, philosophical,

and personal material as irrelevant; both insist on close
textual study. But the Chicago critic makes a strong plea for
a basic æsthetic, of an Aristotelian sort, in order to differentiate between *species* of works of art, and to deduce the
rules for each particular kind accordingly. Crane describes
the method as one which

> seeks to appraise a writer's performance in a given work
> in relation to the nature and requirements of the particular
> task he has set himself, the assumed end being the perfec-
> tion of the work as an artistic whole of the special kind he
> decided it should be.[5]

From this point of view, the formalistic critic examines the
total poem without proper regard for the species of which it
is an example, thus failing to distinguish between the broad
genres (drama, novel, lyric, epic) or, still less, between subspecies (one kind of tragedy, perhaps mimetic, as opposed to
another, perhaps didactic).

A second point of disagreement is that the Chicago critic
charges the ontological writer with monism. He himself is
prepared to welcome social, moral, historical aspects of the
work—*after* the analysis of the parts and their propriety according to the rules of the species—as of value in recognizing
the supra-æsthetic significance of the experience.

W. K. Wimsatt, Jr., in rebuttal disputes the value of dealing
with species, genres, and subspecies.[6] Such categories are too
rigid, and tend to blind the critic to elements that are actually
operating in the literary work, when such elements are not
required by the species. He also arraigns the "Neo-Aris-
totelians" for going outside the poem—not to history, psychology, or morality, but to a theory of the genre by which
to judge the particular instance. This leads to the fallacy of
evaluating a work according to the intention of the author.

[5] R. S. Crane, "The Concept of Plot and the Plot of 'Tom Jones,'"
in *Critics and Criticism Ancient and Modern*, 1952.
[6] In "The Chicago Critics" in *Comparative Literature*, V, No. 1
(Winter, 1953).

Both sides, being seriously devoted to the problems of criticism, toss charges of dogmatism and narrowness at each other. But the quarrel is really between Saul and David; the differences between themselves are not nearly so great as those between them and other kinds of critics. The kinship can be seen when the exposition of theory is abandoned, and the critical performance begins; compare, for example, the study of "Sailing to Byzantium" by Elder Olson (Chicago) with that of "Among School Children" by Brooks (Formalistic), in *The Well Wrought Urn.*

Probably no approach can boast so many brilliant practitioners as the Formalistic. Empson, Blackmur, Tate, Ransom, Cleanth Brooks, and Robert Penn Warren are only the best known; there are many others who have contributed essays to periodicals, with equal rigor and insight.

Bibliographical Note

Many of the best examples of formalistic criticism are to be found in the following works. Various chapters deal with the theory of criticism, while others illustrate the practice: R. P. Blackmur, *The Double Agent,* 1935, *The Expense of Greatness,* 1940, *Language as Gesture,* 1952, and *The Lion and the Honeycomb,* 1955; Cleanth Brooks, *The Well Wrought Urn,* 1947, *Understanding Poetry* (with Robert Penn Warren), 1938, *Understanding Fiction* (with Warren), 1943, and *Understanding Drama* (with Robert Heilman), 1945; Brooks's exposition of the theory behind Formalistic criticism appears in *Kenyon Review* XIII (Winter, 1951); T. S. Eliot, *The Sacred Wood,* 1920; William Empson, *Seven Types of Ambiguity,* 1930, and *Some Versions of Pastoral,* 1935 (reprinted as *English Pastoral Poetry,* 1938); John Crowe Ransom, *The World's Body,* 1938, and *The New Criticism,* 1941; Allen Tate, *Reactionary Essays,* 1936, *Reason in Madness,* 1941, *On the Limits of Poetry,* 1948, and *The Forlorn Demon,* 1953; Robert Penn Warren's excellent essay, "Pure and Impure Poetry" appears in *Kenyon Review* V (Spring, 1943).

Attacks upon and modifications of the approach may be found in Alfred Kazin, *On Native Grounds* (section 4 of Chapter 14), 1942; R. S. Crane, "Cleanth Brooks: or, the Bankruptcy of Critical Monism," *Modern Philology* XLV (May, 1948); John Crowe Ransom, "Poetry: The Formal Analysis," *Kenyon Review* IX (Summer, 1947); Elder Olson, "William Empson, Contemporary Criticism, and Poetic Diction" in *Critics and Criticism Ancient and Modern,* 1952; and R. P. Blackmur, "A Burden for Critics," most recently reprinted in *The Lion and the Honeycomb,* 1955.

The Explicator is a magazine which devotes itself to the publication of short formalistic pieces.

As You Like It

By James Smith

It is a commonplace that Jaques and Hamlet are akin. But it is also a commonplace that Jaques is an intruder into *As You Like It,* so that in spite of the kinship the plays are not usually held to have much connection. I have begun to doubt whether not only *As You Like It* and *Hamlet,* but almost all the comedies and the tragedies as a whole are not closely connected, and in a way which may be quite important.

Recent criticism of Shakespeare has directed itself with profit upon the tragedies, the "problem plays," and certain of the histories. The early comedies, on the other hand, have either been disparaged or entirely overlooked. Yet the same criticism owes part of its success to a notion of what it calls Shakespeare's "integrity"; his manifold interests, it has maintained, being coordinated so as rarely to thwart, regularly to strengthen one another. Hence he was alert and active as few have been, while his writing commanded not part but the whole of his resources.

Such a notion seems sound and proves useful. Belief in an author's integrity, however, ought to forbid the dismissal of any part of his work, at least its hasty dismissal. The comedies, to which he gave a number of years of his life, are no insignificant part of Shakespeare's. If it is true that they shed no light on the tragedies nor the tragedies on them, it would seem he deserves credit for a unique dissipation rather than concentration of his powers.

It is of course comprehensible that the comedies should be shunned. To some readers they are less inviting than the tragedies, to all they are more wearisome when their study is begun. Not only are the texts in a state of comparative impurity; the form itself is impure. Being less serious than tragedy—this, I am sure, is disputed, but would suggest that the word has a number of meanings—being less serious than

187

tragedy, comedy admits of interludes and sideshows; further, the material for the sideshows is not infrequently such that it might be material for the comedy itself. Decision is important, but not always easy whether or not it should be disregarded.

The desultory nature of the following notes may, I hope, be forgiven, partly because of complications such as these, partly because of contemporary distractions which leave no time for elaboration. I start with Jaques's melancholy, in respect of which alone he has been likened to Hamlet.

It is, I think, most accessible to study in his encounter with Rosalind at the beginning of Act IV. Having abundant leisure he needs a companion to while it away. "I prethee, pretty youth," he says, "let me be better acquainted with thee." But Rosalind, who has heard unfavorable reports, is by no means eager to comply: "They say you are a melancholy fellow." As for that, replies Jaques, his melancholy is at least sincere, for it is as pleasing to him as jollity to other men: "I doe love it better then laughing." But sincerity is irrelevant unless to deepen his offense. As there is an excess of laughter so there is of sadness which should not be pleasing to anybody:

Those that are in extremity of either, are abhominable fellowes, and betray themselves to every moderne censure, worse than drunkards.

The rebuke is no more than a rebuke of common sense. Your melancholy, objects Rosalind, is not justifiable merely because it is your melancholy, for it may be one of the things which, though they exist, ought not to do so. But the rebuke is none the less pertinent, common sense implying a minimum of alertness and Jaques being afflicted with languor. Either as cause or as consequence of his state he is blind and fails to see, or is stupid and fails to ponder obvious truths.

The force of the rebuke is to be noticed. From Shakespeare, medieval rather than modern in this as other matters, drunkards receive no more than temporary tolerance: Falstaff is in the end cast off, Sir Toby beat about the coxcomb. And the respect which they receive is not even temporary. Wine and wassail make

. . . Memorie, the Warder of the Braine
. . . a Fume, and the Receit of Reason
A Lymbeck only;

the sleep they produce is "swinish," by them nature is "drenched." A drunkard as such forfeits not only his manhood but his humanity. Nor does Rosalind's "modern" mean what the word does now, "modish" or what has been invented of late. Rather it is that which has always been the mode, and which stands plain to reason so that there never was need to invent it. In this play, for example, the justice is described as

Full of wise sawes and moderne instances

—of instances which belong to proverbial wisdom, apt and sound so that they have become trite. What Rosalind is saying is that Jaques by his melancholy is turned into a beast, and that an old woman would be less ignorant, less pitiable, than he.

Taken aback for the moment, he can think of nothing to reaffirm his liking: "Why, 'tis good to be sad and say nothing." Crudely, however, so that he lays himself open to the crude retort: "Why, then, 'tis good to be a poste." And it would seem to be this which finally rouses him to a defense.

His melancholy, he begins, is not like others Rosalind has heard of:

I have neither the Schollers melancholy, which is emulation; nor the Musitians, which is fantasticall; nor the Courtiers, which is proud; nor the Souldiers, which is ambitious . . .

and so on. Jaques's melancholy has its source not in private hopes, anxieties, and disappointments, but in what is of wider importance, as it is in the world outside. "It is a melancholy," he continues, "of mine owne"—one, that is, which he is the first to discover—"compounded of many simples, extracted from many objects." Or, in other words, it is "the sundrie contemplation of my travells, in which [m]y often rumination wraps me in a most humorous sadnesse."

Jaques's meaning may not be quite clear, and I do not think it is or can be, but his intention would seem to be so. By boasting of originality, breadth, and freshness of information he hopes to impress, perhaps to intimidate, the youthful Rosalind. But she mistakes, and I suspect purposely, his drift: as she is intelligent enough to distrust originality, she is subtle enough to challenge it in this way. Seizing on the word "travels" she exclaims:

A traveller: by my faith you have great reason to be sad; I feare you have sold your owne lands, to see other mens; then to have seene much, and to have nothing, is to have rich eyes and poore hands.

She ventures after all, that is, to assimilate his melancholy to other people's, suggesting that it may be due to poverty, which is a private anxiety. But Jaques rejects with scorn the notion that his travels have on a balance brought him anything but profit: "I have gain'd," he insists, "my experience." Once more he is implying that something, because it exists, has a title to do so; that his experience, as it has been gained, was necessarily worth the gaining. Once more therefore, and if possible more vigorously this time, she appeals to common sense for his condemnation. Whatever profit he imagines he has brought back from his travels, there is something which the merest stay-at-home could tell him is a loss:

JAQUES: I have gain'd my experience.
ROSALIND: And your experience makes you sad: I had rather have a foole to make me merrie, then experience to make me sad, and to travaile for it too.

Whether or not Rosalind is aware of it, this second rebuke is of peculiar force as addressed to Jaques. Of all characters it is he alone who, in previous scenes, has expressed complete satisfaction in the company of Touchstone, the fool. He has gone even further, and claimed that nowhere but in folly ought satisfaction to be found:

> . . . *Oh noble foole,*
> *A worthy foole: Motley's the onely weare . . .*
> *. . . O that I were a foole,*
> *I am ambitious for a motley coat.*

Yet now he has to be reminded that there is an office which fools can perform. About his conduct it seems there is a grave inconsistency, for at one time he countenances factitious gaiety, at another equally factitious gloom.

If it stood alone, such an inconsistency might be puzzling; but it has a companion, which also serves to explain it. In claiming in his interchange with Rosalind that all experience is worthwhile, Jaques is claiming in effect that no experience is worth anything at all. In asserting that, in the present, there are no reasons why he should do one thing rather than another—why, for example, he should be merry rather than mope—he is shutting his eyes to reasons why, in the future, one thing rather than another should be done. In other words he is posing as a skeptic, and skepticism is an inconsistent doctrine. Though a belief itself, it denies the possibility of belief; it denies to man the possibility of action, though by his nature he cannot refrain from acting. And it is because Jaques, in his more alert moments, is aware of this second inconsistency that he commits the first. He seeks shelter in the motley to persuade himself that, though he acts and cannot help doing so, he nevertheless does nothing. For if his actions are mere folly they are of no account and as good as nothing at all.

It is, however, only at rare moments, as, for example, when stirred by a first meeting with Touchstone, that Jaques is alert. For the greater part of his time he is characterized by the languor already referred to: which keeps him from making sustained efforts, even that which (as he is not wholly unintelligent) being a fool requires. Instead of concerning himself to justify his skepticism, he quietly submits to it; and his submission is his melancholy, his "sadness." A man in whose eyes the world contains nothing of value cannot be spurred to action either by the sight of objects he wishes to obtain or by the thought of ideals he hopes to realize. The only action open to him—and as he is human, he cannot remain wholly inert—no more than half deserves the name, for in it he is as much passive as active. He needs, so to speak, to be betrayed into action—to be propelled into it from behind, by agencies of which he is not completely aware. Such agencies are the mechanism of habit, or a conspiracy of circumstance. In comedy, where characters are not relentlessly harassed by circumstance, they are able continually to yield to habit.

The travels to which Jaques refers the origin of his skepticism are equally likely to have been its consequence, for travel and exploration degenerate into habit. When the senses are dazzled by a ceaseless and rapid change of objects, the intellect has no time to discriminate between them, the will no occasion for choice, so that in the end a man becomes capable of neither. The habit is then a necessity to life, which at the same time and to the same extent has slackened, becomes languid. It concerns itself only with the surface of objects, while their substance is neglected. Jaques's decision in Act V proceeds from a habit of this kind:

> *The Duke hath put on a Religious life . . .*
> *To him will I.*

His pretext is that

> *. . . out of these convertites*
> *There is much matter to be heard, and learn'd.*

But his reason, rather than to learn, is to avoid learning. He quits the court for the monastery much as amateur students, threatened with the labor of mastering a subject, abandon it for the preliminaries of another—usually as different as possible. If during the course of the play, Jaques does not engage on travel, it should be remembered that he frequently changes, not his surroundings, but his interlocutor. He indulges the habit of gossip, which is that of a traveler immobilized. That he has abundant leisure for gossip is only natural: time hangs heavy on a skeptic's hands, for whom the world contains nothing that can take it off.

It hangs heavy on Hamlet's, and this is the most obvious point of resemblance between him and Jaques. "I have of late," Hamlet complains, "lost all my mirth, forgone all custome of exercise"; and he goes on to give general reasons. They imply skepticism of a kind: the earth and sky, he says, seem but a "foule and pestilent congregation of vapours," such as do not encourage enterprise: man himself has come to appear but the "Quintessence of dust," with whom he would not willingly have commerce. In the same way, to refer to another tragedy, time hangs heavy on Macbeth's hands, at least as he draws near his end. Neither sight nor sound can rouse his interest, nor could it be roused by any conceivable sight or sound. He finds himself incapable of believing in the reality even of his wife's death: the report of it, he suggests, should be kept from him until tomorrow. But at the same time he knows that tomorrow will find him as insensible, as incredulous, as today.

Skepticism of a kind: but it is immediately obvious that Hamlet speaks with a disgust or an impatience, Macbeth with a weariness, which to Jaques are unknown. Even in this matter in which alone they are similar, their dissimilarity is yet greater. Anticipating a little, it might be said that Macbeth and Hamlet lead a fuller, a more complete life than Jaques; they are, that is, more conscious of themselves, and rather than languid are continuously, perhaps, feverishly alert.

One consequence is that they cannot easily be betrayed into action. Whereas Jaques looks back without regret, even with complacency, on his travels, it is only with reluctance that Macbeth lapses into the habit of fighting for fighting's sake:

> Why should I play the Roman Foole, and dye
> On mine owne sword? whiles I see lives, the gashes
> Do better upon them.

Sentiment and rhythm are flat to extinction, Macbeth is speaking sullenly. What he is about to do may be better than nothing; it is all he can do; nevertheless, it is no more than might be done by a common bully, by an animal. For them it might be a full life; for himself, Macbeth admits, it can be no more than the slackened half-life of habit. Similarly the "custome of exercise" and all custom have lost their hold on Hamlet; for him to act he needs to be surprised by extraordinary circumstance.

Nevertheless, as has been said, neither he nor Macbeth is idle. The energy which their state of mind forbids they should employ on the world, they employ on the state of mind itself; so that not only the inconsistency, the evil (what Rosalind meant by the "beastliness") of skepticism is continually before them. They see it is not the solution to a problem, but rather a problem which presses to be solved; not the tempering of feeling and the invigoration of thought, but the denial of both. They not only reject Jaques's flight into folly, which was to preserve skepticism; they agonize over the sort of reflection with which, in both languid and alert moments, Jaques is lulled. "And all our yesterdayes," exclaims Macbeth in despair at what forces itself upon him as the nothingness of man,

> And all our yesterdayes have lighted Fooles
> The way to dusty death;

" 'tis but an hour agoe," observes Jaques with satisfaction,

> 'Tis but an hour agoe, since it was nine,
> And after one houre more, 'twill be eleven,
> And so from houre to houre, we ripe, and ripe,
> And then from houre to houre, we rot, and rot . . .

or rather Touchstone observes this, from whom Jaques is quoting. Touchstone is by profession and conviction a fool, the seriousness of whose statements will come up for consideration later; Jaques is as little serious as, in a quotation, it is possible to be. He is echoing more sound than sense; the

latter he has not plumbed (the movement, the rhythm, show
it), and the statement he has made no more than half his
own—fitting accompaniment and expression of a half-life of
habit. Elsewhere he compares human life to a theatrical performance as though, in harmony with his skepticism, to stress
its unreality; but very soon, in harmony with his languor, the
theater begins to appear a substantial, for all he cares, a
permanent structure. Performances in it last a long time, so
that it is possible to make a full display of talent:

> . . . one man in his time playes many parts,
> His Acts being seven ages.

And then Jaques recites the ages, diverting himself with objects separated on this occasion not in space but in time.
When the same comparison occurs to Macbeth he is so over-
whelmed with the notion of unreality that he does not allow
even the actor to act: the latter "struts and frets . . . upon
the Stage," struts and frets not for a full performance but
only for "his houre . . . and then is heard no more." In
Macbeth's verse the comparison flares up and extinguishes
itself in indignation at what it implies of man's lot:

> . . . It is a Tale
> Told by an Ideot, full of sound and fury
> Signifying nothing.

That of Jaques continues to demean itself elegantly even
when describing in detail man's end:

> Sans teeth, sans eyes, sans taste, sans everything.

Once again the rhythm and the movement show that Jaques
is meaning little of what he says; that, a true traveler once
more, he is occupied with the surface only, not the substance
of objects before him.

If I may look aside or ahead for a moment, I would venture to suggest that the essential difference between comedy

and tragedy may perhaps be this sort of difference: not one of kind, I mean, but of degree. As far as I can see, it is possible and even probable that tragedy and comedy—Shakespearean comedy, at any rate—treat of the same problems, comedy doing so (to repeat the word) less seriously. And by "less seriously," I may now explain, I mean that the problems are not forced to an issue: a lucky happening, a lucky trait of character (or what for the purposes of the play appears lucky), allowing them to be evaded. As, for example, conditions in Arden and conditions of his own temper preserve Jaques from fully realizing the nature and consequences of his skepticism: to Rosalind, to the reader, it is obvious that his interests are restricted, his vigor lessened, but he is never put to the test. Hamlet, on the other hand, in a similar spiritual state, is called upon to avenge a father, foil an uncle, and govern a kingdom. And when at last chance forces him into action it is not only that he may slaughter, but also that he may be slaughtered: in other words, not that in spite of his disability he may achieve his end, but that because of it he may fail. In *Othello* hardly an accident happens which does not lend plausibility to Iago's deceit, so that the problem posed by human malice on the one hand, human ignorance on the other, cannot but be faced; in *Much Ado* there is a final accident—and a very obvious one, for its name is Dogberry—which unmasks Don John. In *Lear* accident of the wildest form unites with malice and with the elements to convince a human being of his imbecility; in *The Winter's Tale* accident equally wild serves to hide that imbecility, if not from Leontes (who is, however, encouraged to forget it), at least from Florizel. In comedy the materials for tragedy are procured, in some cases heaped up; but they are not, so to speak, attended to, certainly not closely examined. And so what might have caused grief causes only a smile, or at worst a grimace.

I apologize for speculations of this kind, which can only remain gratuitous until it is known more exactly what comedy, more especially what *As You Like It,* is about. At least one other resemblance, possibly an important one, between it and the tragedies, calls, I think, for attention. As

Hamlet's melancholy is caused by the sin of others and Macbeth's by sins of his own, so Jaques—if the Duke is to be trusted—has not only traveled, but been

> . . . *a Libertine,*
> *As sensuall as the brutish sting itself.*

And the cure for all three, according to each of the three plays, is very much the same. Fortinbras reproaches Hamlet, and Hamlet reproaches himself, with lacking a "hue of resolution," which, as it is "native," is a defect he should not possess; Macbeth contrasts the division of counsels within him, suspending activity, with the strong monarchy or "single state" enjoyed in the healthy man by the reason. Similarly, Rosalind confronts Jaques with the desirability of what she calls merriment or mirth: from her remark already quoted it is obvious she does not mean laughter, not at any rate laughter without measure, and therefore not laughter in the first place. For the confusion of Jaques it is necessary she should speak emphatically; in a conversation which irks her she is to be excused if she is brief. Were the occasion other, or were she given to reflection, she might perhaps describe this "mirth" more closely—as something similar to her own "alertness," which has already drawn attention: the prerequisite of common sense, and what in more recent times, according to the sympathies and perspicacity of the speaker, has been known either as "vitality" or "faith." The meaning of "mirth" in fifteenth and sixteenth century devotional books should be borne in mind, and its meaning on the lips of, say, Saint Thomas More. Hamlet, it will be remembered, noted as first among his distressing symptoms that he had "lost all his mirth."

This scene at the beginning of Act IV sheds light, I do not think it would be too much to claim, on all that Jaques says or does. If so, it is important to a not inconsiderable part of the play, and in that at least Jaques cannot be an intruder. For his quips and monologues, however loose in their immediate context, have a dependence on this dialogue, to which he is indispensable. He is so not only by what he says, but also by what he causes to be said to him. I am going to suggest that, in spite of the familiar verdict, he is no more of an intruder anywhere. For the rest of the play consists largely of situations which, if he is taken as primary melancholic, might be described as modeled on that in which he finds himself with Rosalind. Either she or a temporary ally or deputy of hers—frequently Corin the Old Shepherd—faces and condemns a succession of characters who, like Jaques, are incapable of or indisposed to action. Silvius, Touchstone, Orlando, the Duke, each has a melancholy of his own; and so too has Rosalind, in so far as she is in love with Orlando. But not even that escapes her judgment, since she can judge it disguised as someone other than herself. Add that the minor characters occasionally condemn or at least reprove one another, and it is possible to gain some notion of the pattern which Shakespeare seems to have intended for *As You Like It*. A single motif is repeated, giving unity to the whole; but at the same time it varies continually, so that the whole is complex.

Such, I think, was Shakespeare's intended pattern: unfortunately it has been either obscured by revision, or incomplete revision has failed to impress it clearly on the play. The theory of the New Cambridge editors must no doubt be accepted, that there are at least two strata of text, an early and a late. This is a difficulty of the kind referred to, that a student must expect from textual impurities in a comedy. But certain portions of the pattern are sufficiently clear to give, to a careful reader, some idea of the whole.

Take, for example, the relations obtaining between the Old Shepherd, on the one hand, and Jaques and Touchstone, on the other. Touchstone has been much sentimentalized, partly because of his wit, partly because of a supposed loyalty to Celia. But his wit has been treated as though it were a mere interlude, a diversion for the reader as well as for the Duke; whereas little else would seem more closely knit into the play. And as will be suggested, this is the reverse of sentimental. As for Touchstone's loyalty, it would seem to be mentioned only in Celia's line,

He'll go along o'er the wide world with mee.

It may have had importance in an earlier version, but in that which has survived Shakespeare is no more concerned with how the characters arrive in Arden—whether under Touchstone's convoy or not—than how they are extricated from it. Touchstone's loyalty is about as interesting to him, and should be as interesting to the reader, as Oliver's green and gold snake.

What is interesting is a disingenuous reply which Touchstone gives to the question: "And how like you this shepherds life?" He pretends to make distinctions where it is impossible there should be any:

Truely . . . in respect of it selfe, it is a good life; but in respect that it is a shepherds life, it is naught. In respect that it is solitary, I like it verie well: but in respect that it is private, it is a very vile life . . .

A shepherd's life, no more than other things, can be distinguished from itself, nor can what is solitary be other than private. What Touchstone is saying is that he neither likes nor dislikes the shepherd's life, while at the same time he does both; or, in other words, that towards the shepherd's life he has no feelings whatever. And, in truth, towards all things, if not quite all, Touchstone is as apathetic as Jaques. He too has his melancholy, as has been said: and naturally resembling Jaques more than Hamlet or Macbeth, he too accepts distraction from a habit. It is not the ceaseless search for novelty or gossip, but what he calls "philosophy" or the barren intercourse of a mind with itself. He multiplies distinction like the above, or pursues similarities based solely on sound or letter, neglecting the meaning of a word. The result is skepticism in a very practical sense, such as unchecked would destroy language and all possibility of thought. Even the old Shepherd is not slow to realize this, for his sole reply to the blunt question, "Has't any Philosophie in thee . . . ?" is to recite a number of obvious truths:

I know the more one sickens, the worse at ease he is: and
that hee that wants money, meanes, and content, is without three good friends. That the propertie of raine is to
wet, and fire to burne . . .

and so on. However obvious, they are at least truths, at least
significant; and he concludes:

hee that hath learned no wit by Nature, nor Art, may com-
plaine of dull breeding, or comes of a very dull kindred.

In other words: he who cannot behave in a more responsible
way than Touchstone is an idiot. But "idiot is what I mean
by a philosopher"—

Such a one is a naturall philosopher

rejoins Touchstone, indifferent enough to his diversion not to
claim that it is more than it is.

He proceeds to indulge in it at length. The Shepherd, he
says, is damned because he has not been to court, court
manners being good and what is not good being wicked. Too
patiently the Shepherd replies with a distinction which, as it
is he and not Touchstone who makes it, is of primary importance:

those that are good manners at the Court, are as ridiculous
in the Countrey, as the behaviour of the Countrie is most
mockeable at the Court.

But this is brushed aside, and Touchstone emphasizes his
perversity by changing the order in which court and country
are ranked. Henceforward, he decrees, they shall be on a
level, or rather the court shall be the more wicked. In despair
the Shepherd retires from a conversation in which words, as
they have so variable a meaning, have as good as no meaning
at all:

You have too Courtly a wit, for mee, Ile rest.

Had he said "too philosophical a wit" his point might have been more immediately clear; but for him, no doubt as for Touchstone, court and "philosophy" are closely allied.

To justify himself he adds the following description:

> Sir, I am a true Labourer, I earne that I eate: get that I weare; owe no man hate, envie no mans happinesse; glad of other mens good[,] content with my harme: and the greatest of my pride, is to see my Ewes graze, and my Lambes sucke.

Of himself, that is, he claims to go about his own affairs, and to go about them with the mirth or minimum of serenity demanded by Rosalind. He has no need of "incision"—whatever that may mean—or of any other remedy to conduct himself like an adult being: whereas Touchstone, who suggests the remedy, has at the moment no affairs, appears to be able to conceive of no affairs to go about at all.

For Shepherd and audience the conversation is over. To them it seems that Touchstone is defeated beyond recovery; not, however, to Touchstone himself. He insists on adding a last word, and in doing so hints at one of the things to which he is not yet wholly indifferent, in respect of which therefore he parts company with Jaques. Mention of ewes and sucking lambs spurs him on to the following:

> That is another simple sinne in you, to bring the Ewes and the Rammes together, and to offer to get our living by the copulation of Cattle, to be bawd to a Belwether, and to betray a shee-Lambe of a twelvemonth to a crooked-pated olde Cuckoldly Ramme, out of all reasonable match. If thou bee'st not damn'd for this, the divell himselfe will have no shepherds, I cannot see how else thou shouldst escape.

About this there are two things to be noticed: first, that it is nasty, and, secondly, that it is the nastier because it falls outside the conversation. Touchstone is no longer endeavoring to prove anything about country and court, whether sound or fantastic: he assimilates the sexual life of men to that of beasts solely because it seems of itself worth while to do so. Yet this should not cause surprise: if in this passage he appears to exalt the latter, elsewhere in deeds as well as words he is diligent to degrade the former.

Upon their first arrival in Arden, when he and Rosalind overhear Silvius's complaint, Rosalind sighs:

> *Jove, Jove, this Shepherds passion*
> *Is much upon my fashion.*

"And mine," exclaims Touchstone, adding, however, immediately, "but it growes somewhat stale with mee." That is, he is impatient of the elaborations and accretions received by the sexual desire, when a persistent subject in an otherwise healthy mind. His next appearance is as the wooer of Audrey, a country wench who thanks the gods that she is "foul," and whom no elaborations have been necessary to win. Her desire to be a "woman of the world," in other words a married woman, is ingenuous and no more a secret from Touchstone than from anyone else.

It is by no means to her discredit, nor would it be to Touchstone's, if, gratifying her desire, he thereby eased his own and was thankful. But the opposite is true. He is neither eased, nor does he spare an occasion, public or private, of pouring ridicule on the ingenuousness of which he has taken advantage. It is as though, aware that he can no longer hope for desire to be restrained, he sought to humiliate it with the least attractive object, then proceeded to revenge himself upon the object for his own lack of restraint. Audrey protests that she is "honest" or chaste; but that, he answers, has had no share in drawing his attentions:

AUDREY: Would you not have me honest?
TOUCH: No truly, unless thou wert hard favour'd . . .
AUDREY: Well, I am not faire, and therefore I pray the
    Gods make me honest.

TOUCH: Truly, to cast away honesty upon a foule slut, were to put good meate in an uncleane dish . . . But be it, as it may bee, I will marrie thee . . .

To a large extent this conversation, like most of Touchstone's, is mere playing with words; but in so far as it has any meaning, it is that the word "honesty" deserves only to be played with. And when at last he brings himself to mention honesty with an air of seriousness, it is not that she but that he himself may be praised:

. . . a poore virgin sir, an il-favor'd thing sir, but mine owne, a poore humour of mine sir, to take that that no man else will: rich honestie dwels like a miser sir, in a poore house, as your Pearle in your foule oyster.

He is presenting her to the Duke as his intended: and, since her exterior has nothing to explain his choice, hints that an explanation is to be found within. That is, he is claiming for himself the credit due to perspicacity.

Unfortunately he put forward at the same time a claim to modesty, thus showing with how little seriousness he is continuing to speak. Did he value honesty at all, he would not represent the choice of it as a sacrifice; nor would he describe Audrey, its exemplar, as a "poor thing." His modesty, it should further be noticed, itself suggests confusion or deceit, for not only does it permit of advertisement, it is advertised not at Touchstone's expense but at someone else's. He does not in one respect decry himself so that he may be exalted in another; rather in order to exalt himself he decries his future wife. The first would in any case be tiresome, as is all inverted vanity; but the second, as a hypocritical form of selfishness, is contemptible.

Given that Touchstone is a man of sense, a performance like this can be due only to his attempting two things at once, and two things not very compatible one with another. As usual he is seeking to ridicule Audrey; but at the same time, I think, to recommend himself to the Duke. While sharing all Jaques's objections to purposeful activity, he is without Jaques's income: he must provide himself with a living or must starve. And skepticism and melancholy being essentially unnatural, no one starves for their sake. At Touchstone's entry on the stage it was hinted that the Duke might be willing to appoint a jester:

> Good my Lord, bid him welcome: This is the Motley-minded Gentleman, that I have so often met in the Forrest: he hath bin a Courtier he sweares. . . . Good my Lord, like this fellow.

And the Duke is well known to be, in Jaques's word, "disputatious." It is solely to please him that Touchstone, among his other preoccupations, does what he can to handle the notions "honesty" and "modesty"; were he speaking to a crony or to himself they would not enter his head, no more than the euphuistic apologue about oysters with which he ends.

A similar reason is to be advanced for his string of court witticisms which follow, about the causes of a quarrel and the degree of a lie. So long as to be tiresome, the modern reader is tempted to dismiss it as an interlude; it is not, however, wholly without dramatic excuse. At the stage reached by his candidature, Touchstone thinks it proper to give an exhibition of professional skill. And that, too, he makes subserve his sexual passion: having drawn all eyes to himself, for a moment he directs them to Audrey:

> Upon a lye, seven times removed: (beare your bodie more seeming Audrey) . . .

and so she is ridiculed once more.

It seems likely he obtains his appointment: at any rate he makes the impression he desires. "He is very swift and sententious," says the Duke.

> He uses his folly like a stalking-horse, and under the presentation of that he shoots his wit.

Which of course is just what the real Touchstone never does, in spite of what the critics say. The judgment of the Old Shepherd is sounder, that Touchstone's folly has no purpose at all, or, if any, that of discrediting and ruining purpose. And so is Jaques sounder, when he recognizes in Touchstone's folly the cover for his skepticism.

It is interesting, and significant of the subtle pattern which Shakespeare intends to weave—a pattern not only of intrigue but of ideas—that the Duke, who is thus easily gulled when Touchstone assumes a virtue, protests immediately when required to accept as a virtue Touchstone's vice. Jaques describes to him, and asks for himself, the liberty of railing which Touchstone enjoys:

> . . . weed your better jujements
> Of all opinion that grows ranke in them,
> That I am wise. I must have liberty
> Withall, as large a Charter as the winde,
> To blow on whom I please, for so fooles have. . . .
> Invest me in my motley: Give me leave
> To speake my mind.

Such impunity, the Duke sees, can have no results of the kind Jaques promises:

> . . . I will through and through
> Cleanse the foule bodie of the' infected world . . .

but only evil for himself and others:

> Fie on thee. I can tell what thou wouldst do. . . .
> Most mischeevous foule sin.

And he proceeds to diagnose it correctly. Only a man ruined by evil, he suggests, confines himself to the correction of evil; for this implies not that evil finds him peculiarly sensitive, but that he is insensitive both to evil and to good. To good, because he neglects and therefore runs the risk of destroying it; to evil, because he seeks no relief from what should stifle and nauseate. Brutalized to this degree, Jaques can see no reason why others should not be brutalized too:

> . . . all the' imbossed sores, and headed evils,
> That thou with license of free foot hast caught,
> Would'st thou disgorge into the generall world.

The portrait is drawn in high color, but Hamlet would recognize it. Jaques presumably does not, being, as has been said, less alert and therefore less perspicacious; but here unfortunately there is a cut in the text of *As You Like It*.

Further instances of this Shakespearean subtlety are two scenes in which Jaques and Touchstone, usually allies, are brought, if not into conflict, into contrast. As Touchstone is as acutely sensitive to the brutish sting as ever Jaques may have been in the past, in the present he can on occasion be resolute as Jaques is not. In response to the sting he can make conquest of Audrey, browbeat William for her possession:

> . . . abandon the society of this Female, or Clowne thou perishest . . . I will kill thee a hundred and fifty wayes, therefore tremble and depart.

William obediently trembles. But it is Jaques of all characters whom Shakespeare chooses to administer a rebuke to Touchstone for this; as though to make it clear that if he condemns inertia he does not, with a crudeness familiar in more recent times, advocate precipitancy; if he deplores apathy, he does not commend brute appetite. When Touchstone contemplates a hedge-marriage so that he might have "a good excuse hereafter" to leave his wife, it is Jaques who prevents him:

> And will you (being a man of your breeding) be married under a bush like a beggar? Get you to church. . . .

And at the final leave-taking it is Jaques who foretells to Touchstone a future of wrangling, a "loving voyage . . . but for two moneths victuall'd."

At the opposite pole to the characters hitherto considered, tolerating no elaboration in love, stand Silvius and Phebe, who seek to conform their lives to the pastoral convention, one of the fullest elaborations known. The scenes in which they appear are perhaps too short to have the effect intended, now that the convention, if not forgotten, is no longer familiar. But to an Elizabethan the sentiments and the verse— the former largely echoes, external as well as internal, to the play: the latter easy yet mannered—would suffice to evoke a wealthy tradition. A modern judges of this perhaps most readily by the apostrophe to Marlowe:

> *Dead Shepherd, now I [f]ind thy saw of might,*
> *Who ever lov'd that lov'd not at first sight?*

No incongruity is intended or feared from his introduction with fleece and crook: the tradition being rich enough to absorb him, vigorous enough to assert even beside him its actuality.

And also the apostrophe may serve to dispel some of the mist which has hung about pastoral in England since the seventeenth century, and notably since the attack of Johnson. Though actual, pastoral need not be realistic; and to apply to it realistic canons as he did is to misconceive it entirely. It is not an attempt to portray a shepherd's life: but in its purity—though frequently, of course, it is impure—to portray a life in which physical misery is reduced to a minimum or has disappeared. Traditionally such a life is called a shepherd's: in which, therefore, man is held to enjoy every happiness, if only his desires will let him. But as becomes clear with the progress of the pastoral, his desires will not. Removed from the danger of physical pain those of the intellect and the imagination become the acuter; in particular the passion of love, with neither social pressure nor economic necessity inclining it in any direction, becomes incalculable in its vagaries. It remains an ever open source of calamity. A tragic note of undertone is thus inseparable from pastoral, and if subdued is only the more insistent. It is in permanent contrast with the composure or gaiety of the rest of the score.

By their share in a tradition of this kind, the Silvius and Phebe scenes have a claim to be effective out of all proportion to their length; and the effect they are intended to produce is in the first place a serious, not a comic one. That there is a close connection between Shakespearean tragedy and comedy, I have already stated, is one of my assumptions in this paper.

As the Old Shepherd is contrasted with Touchstone, so he is with Silvius. When the latter pours out his complaints, Corin's attitude is far from one of incomprehension:

> *Oh Corin, that thou knew'st how I do love her.*
> *—I partly guesse; for I have lov'd ere now.*

Far also from impatience, for the complaints are not of the briefest, far, however, from approval. To put the matter at its crudest, Silvius is not prudent in his conduct:

> *That is the way to make her scorne you still.*

And however charitably Corin listens to the recital of another's extravagances, he has no regret that now he is rid of his own:

> *How many actions most ridiculous*
> *Hast thou been drawne to by thy fantasie?*
> *—Into a thousand that I have forgotten.*

His attitude seems to be that Silvius's extravagances will pass with time as his own have passed; meanwhile they may at least be tolerated, for they are decent.

Touchstone's reaction to the meeting with Silvius has already been noticed. Rosalind's is somewhat more complicated:

> *Alas poor Shepherd searching of [thy wound],*
> *I have by hard adventure found my own.*

She approves of the premises on which the pastoral convention is based, both that the wound of love is genuine and that it is sharp and serious. But the assumption that therefore it is deserving of sole attention, or that by receiving such attention it can in any way be cured, she criticizes as does Corin, and less patiently. It conflicts with the common sense, for which she is everywhere advocate, and which requires either as condition or as symptom of health a wide awareness of opportunity, a generous assumption of responsibility. By confining his attention to love, Silvius is restricting both, frustrating his energies like the other melancholics. That Rosalind should be less patient than Corin is natural, as she is younger: she cannot trust the action of time upon Silvius, when as yet she is not certain what it will be upon herself.

For she too is tempted by love, and in danger of the pastoral convention. Though she rebukes Silvius and Phebe from the outset, she does so in language more nearly approaching theirs than ever she approached Jaques's. But the luck of comedy, which (it has been suggested) stifles problems, is on her side, causing Phebe to fall in love with her. She needs only to reveal herself as a woman, and the folly of pastoralism—as a convention which allows freedom to fancy or desire—comes crashing to the ground. Taught by such an example and by it teaching others, she pronounces the judgment that if Silvius and Phebe persist in love yet would remain rational creatures, they must get married.

It is the same judgment she pronounced on all lovers in the play. Of the four who are left, two only call for separate consideration: herself and Orlando.

Orlando has achieved an extravagance but, unlike Silvius, not a decent one; his verse, even in Touchstone's ears, is the "right Butter-womans ranke to Market." As Touchstone is concerned only to destroy he finds criticism easy, but specimens of the verse prove he is not wholly unreliable. And therefore Rosalind chooses to deal with Orlando in prose:

> These are all lies, men have died from time to time, and wormes have eaten them, but not for love.

—I would not have my right *Rosalind* of this mind, for I protest her frowne might kill me.
—By this hand, it will not kill a flie.

Her purpose once again is to disabuse her interlocutor about the supposed supreme importance of love. And to do so effectively she makes use at times of a coarseness almost rivaling Touchstone's:

What would you say to me now, and I were your verie, verie Rosalind?
—I would kisse before I spoke.
—Nay, you were better speak first, and when you were gravel'd, for lacke of matter, you might take occasion to kisse: verie good Orators when they are out, they will spit, and for lovers, lacking (God warne us) matter, the cleanliest shift is to kisse.

Not that she agrees with Touchstone, except materially. She may say very much the same as he says, but her purpose is different. It is not to deny that desire, no more than other things, has value; but to assess its proper value, by no means so high as Orlando thinks.

She can undertake to do so with some sureness, and command some confidence from the reader, because she herself has firsthand acquaintance with desire. All criticisms passed on others are also criticisms on herself, and she is aware of this (or if not, as on one occasion, Celia is at hand to remind her). The consequences for the play are manifold. First the criticisms, which as applying to other persons might seem scattered, are bound together as applying to her; over the pattern of the repeating motif, such as has been already described, she superposes as it were another pattern, or encloses it in a frame. Then the final criticism, or judgment which resumes them all, is seen to issue from the body of the play itself, not to be imposed on it by author or authority from without. Finally a breadth and a sanity in the judgment are guaranteed. If Rosalind freely acknowledges in herself the absurdities she rebukes in others—"Ile tell thee *Aliena*," she says, "I cannot be out of sight of Orlando: Ile goe find a shadow and sigh till he come"—in return she transfers to others her own seriousness and suffering:

O coz, coz, coz; my pretty little coz, that thou didst know how many fathom deepe I am in love: but it cannot bee sounded: my affection hath an unknowne bottome, like the Bay of Portugall.

Or in a phrase which has a foretaste or reminiscence of Donne:

One inche of delay more, is a South-sea of discoverie. I pre-thee tell me, who it is quickely, and speake apace.

The final judgment would seem to run somewhat as follows. As Rosalind says to Orlando at their first meeting: "Love is purely a madnesse, and I tel you, deserves wel a darke house, and a whip, as madmen do"; it is, however, a madness which, owing to the number of victims, there are only two ways of controlling. One is to "forsweare the ful stream of the world, and to live in a nooke merely Monasticke"—and this way does not generally recommend itself. The second, then, must be adopted, which is marriage. Above all, whines and cries such as combine to a chorus in Act V must be prevented:

> . . . tell this youth what 'tis to love.
> —It is to be all made of sighes and teares,
> And so am I for Phebe.
> —And I for Ganimed.
> —And I for Rosalind.
> —And I for no woman.
> —It is to be all made of faith and service,
> And so am I for Phebe . . .

da capo three times. Rosalind, though as lover she joined in, as critic and judge rejects it as "the howling of Irish wolves against the Moone." To it the alacrity of Oliver and Celia are to be preferred: "They are in the verie wrath of love, and they will together. Clubbes cannot part them."

If once again this seems reminiscent of Touchstone, and of Touchstone at his worst, the distinction already drawn should be remembered. The same words can mean different things on Touchstone's lips and on Rosalind's. She is not inciting her fellow characters to marriages which shall hold only until the "blood breaks," but to "high wedlock," which is "great Juno's crown," and a "blessed bond"—the masquing song, though possibly not by Shakespeare, aptly summarizes certain of the play's sentiments. Further, that Rosalind and Touchstone agree on a single topic, even a topic so important as the qualities of desire, does not mean that one of them is not superior to the other. Rosalind is very obviously the superior: not, however, in respect of the topic on which she and Touchstone agree. She is distinguished and privileged beyond him, not because she knows desire—rather that confounds both him and her—but because she is, whereas he is not, at the same time many things besides. She is not only a capable manager of her own life, but a powerful influence for good on the lives of others. And finally a word may be put in for Touchstone himself. If Shakespeare, as has been said, does not condemn apathy in order to commend lust, neither does he disapprove of lust in order to advocate Puritanism. Touchstone is on the way to tragedy because he has allowed desire to get out of control; had he controlled it, he would have built up a life more satisfactory than do those who, while living in the world, neglect desire altogether or overmuch. And therefore he remains a positive critic even in his failure and to some extent because of it; it is proper not only that he himself should rebuke Orlando, but also that Rosalind, taking, it would seem, words from his lips, should rebuke large groups of people.

If *As You Like It* is planned at all in the way I have suggested, the least title it deserves is, I think, "unsentimental." But for common practice I would go further and call it "unromantic"; and suggest that, to get the measure of its unromanticism, no more is necessary than to read it alongside its source, Lodge's *Rosalynde*. And the title "unromantic" would possibly be confirmed by an investigation of the Duke's melancholy, which in this paper it has not been possible to investigate.

There is little time to return to the topic from which the paper started, the relation namely between the tragedies and the comedies. But perhaps it is obvious that, conceived as unromantic, the early comedies are a fitting preparation for the "problem plays," while from these to the tragedies is but a step.

"Sailing to Byzantium": Prolegomena to a Poetics of the Lyric

By Elder Olson

THE CRITIC who seeks to discuss and the poet who seeks to construct a lyric poem are apt to discover all too quickly that in this particular province of literature, extensive and important as it is, little has been said which affords them any real guidance. At first sight, critical discussion of the lyric appears abundant, even though scarcely commensurate with the importance of the lyric itself; but closer examination readily reveals this abundance to be one of bons mots on the character of the lyric poet, of startling analogies to the psychological or physiological effects of lyric poetry, of "dull receipts how poems may be made," of oracular statement in which the tradition of ambiguous if portentous declamation is usually preserved by the oracle, and finally, in very considerable part, of mere *loci* within a general discussion of literature which is concerned with the lyric only because the lyric possesses some characteristic in common with other forms. In the last quarter of a century, to be sure, literary magazines have often been clamorous with disputations concerning the nature of the lyric; but perhaps without exception these have been declarations of purely individual predilections, or, as in the case of Ezra Pound's famous ten precepts for Imagists, definitions of a doctrine or of a convention rather than of a lyric poem. One might be tempted to conclude that a subject so persistently slighted is perhaps not worth discussion, were it not for the fact that, more than frequently, the critical statements suggest abortive attempts at precisely that.

What has been so often attempted unsuccessfully must be approached with caution. To rectify all errors, to supply all deficiencies, to strike out a poetics for the lyric at a single blow would be a noble and ambitious project, but the causes that make it so also operate to make it improbable of achievement. It is only prudent to propose something at once less striking and more feasible; to propose an attempt to discover —through the analysis of a particular poem—some index as to how, eventually, a poetics of the lyric might be framed.

It should go without saying that any attempt to furnish indices toward a poetics of the lyric can be significant only in a philosophy in which the arts and sciences are held distinct from each other; for, unless that is the case, the inquiry into principles peculiar to poetics would turn on a nonsense question: if, in any sense whatever, all knowledge is one, then it must follow that the objects of knowledge must also be one in that same sense, and the question of peculiarities appears as a meaningless one. Further, it should be clear that poetics in such a system cannot deal with every question which may possibly be raised about a work of art, but only with those raised concerning it *qua* work of art; it is not merely conceivably but actually the case that questions about works of art may fall under many sciences, according to the manner of consideration. For instance, a question relevant to a poem as an existent thing falls under metaphysics, a question relevant to it as productive of, say, social consciousness, falls under politics; lacking the proper peculiarity to poetry neither of these questions would be poetic questions in the sense in which I propose to employ the term *poetic,* for *being* and *political instrumentality* are predicable of things other than poems, and whatever answers could be found to such questions would turn, not on the nature of poetry, but on a community between poetry and something else. Further, poetics in the present conception would be analytical and inductive, since the work is the object of consideration, and therefore, like any object of knowledge, must exist prior to any knowledge of it.

The scrutiny of particular poems would thus be the beginning of the critical enterprise; but the principles eventually reached, as disclosed by analysis, would not be rules governing the operations involved in the construction of any further poem, nor would the enumeration of poetic parts and poetic devices suffer extension beyond those objects to which analysis had been turned. In other words, poetics as conceived here would not afford a series of recipes for making poems, nor a set of rules according to which they must be made, for the very character of poetics is such that it must be subsequent to the inventive utilizations of the medium by the artist. Obviously, anything which should constrain invention would be detrimental to rather than productive of art. Properly taken, poetic questions would be concerning the poetic structure of a particular work, in the sense of inquiring what form has been imposed upon the medium of words. Such an inquiry, properly prosecuted, would terminate in a discovery of the parts of a work and of the interrelations through which the parts are parts of a whole.

The philosophic criticism of literature has provided us richly with instruments for almost every other mode of consideration; but with respect to this one mode, only one treatise —the *Poetics* of Aristotle— is relevant; and while that treatise serves both to differentiate and to illustrate the manner of working of that mode, generally, its specific concern is only with such species of poetry as have for their principle a tissue of incidents, a plot. To attempt to find a plot in the lyric, however, would be a profitless if not impossible task; to attempt on the other hand to find in the lyric some analogue of plot in the drama and in epic, for the mere sake of imitating Aristotle, would be to run counter to the broader indications of his very method—a method involving the distinction of diverse departments of inquiry diversely prosecuted. In the absence of any specific formal treatment of the lyric, then, its analyst must not only fulfill his proper function, but find his own warrant for his operation as well. Complex as his task is, however, it is by no means hopeless; the procedure reduces to an attempt to discover some principle in the work which is the principle of its unity and order—a principle which, it goes without saying, will have to be a purely poetic principle, i.e., a formal principle of the poem, and not something extrinsic to it such as the differentiation either of authors, audiences, subject matters, or orders of diction would afford. Since in a formal consideration the form is the end, and since the end renders everything else intelligible, a mark of the discovery of the formal principle would be that everything else in the poem would be found to be explicable in terms of it.

We may take as the subject of our analysis the lyric "Sailing to Byzantium" by Yeats.

> That is no country for old men. The young
> In one another's arms, birds in the trees,
> —Those dying generations—at their song,
> The salmon-falls, the mackerel-crowded seas,
> Fish, flesh, or fowl, commend all summer long
> Whatever is begotten, born, and dies.
> Caught in that sensual music all neglect
> Monuments of unageing intellect.
>
> An aged man is but a paltry thing,
> A tattered coat upon a stick, unless
> Soul clap its hands and sing, and louder sing
> For every tatter in its mortal dress,
> Nor is there singing school but studying
> Monuments of its own magnificence;
> And therefore I have sailed the seas and come
> To the holy city of Byzantium.
>
> O sages standing in God's holy fire
> As in the gold mosaic of a wall,
> Come from the holy fire, perne in a gyre,
> And be the singing-masters of my soul.
> Consume my heart away; sick with desire
> And fastened to a dying animal
> It knows not what it is; and gather me
> Into the artifice of eternity.
>
> Once out of nature I shall never take
> My bodily form from any natural thing,
> But such a form as Grecian goldsmiths make
> Of hammered gold and gold enamelling

> To keep a drowsy Emperor awake;
> Or set upon a golden bough to sing
> To lords and ladies of Byzantium
> Of what is past, or passing, or to come.

In "Sailing to Byzantium" an old man faces the problem of old age, of death, and of regeneration, and gives his decision. Old age, he tells us, excludes a man from the sensual joys of youth; the world appears to belong completely to the young, it is no place for the old; indeed, an old man is scarcely a man at all—he is an empty artifice, an effigy merely, of a man; he is a tattered coat upon a stick. This would be very bad, except that the young also are excluded from something; rapt in their sensuality, they are ignorant utterly of the world of the spirit. Hence if old age frees a man from sensual passion, he may rejoice in the liberation of the soul; he is admitted into the realm of the spirit; and his rejoicing will increase according as he realizes the magnificence of the soul. But the soul can best learn its own greatness from the great works of art; hence he turns to those great works, but in turning to them, he finds that these are by no means mere effigies, or monuments, but things which have souls also; these live in the noblest element of God's fire, free from all corruption; hence he prays for death, for release from his mortal body; and since the insouled monuments exhibit the possibility of the soul's existence in some other matter than flesh, he wishes reincarnation, not now in a mortal body, but in the immortal and changeless embodiment of art.

There are thus the following terms, one might say, from which the poem suspends: the condition of the young, who are spiritually passive although sensually active; the condition of the merely old, who are spiritually and physically impotent; the condition of the old, who, although physically impotent, are capable of spiritual activity; the condition of art considered as inanimate—that is, the condition of things which are merely monuments; and finally the condition of art considered as animate—as of such things as artificial birds which have a human soul. The second term, impotent and unspiritual old age, is a privative, a repugnant state which causes the progression through the other various alternative terms, until its contrary is encountered. The first and third terms are clearly contraries of each other; taken together as animate nature they are further contrary to the fourth term, inanimate art. None of these terms represent a wholly desirable mode of existence; but the fifth term, which represents such a mode, amalgamates the positive elements and eliminates the negative elements of both nature and art, and effects thus a resolution of the whole, for now the soul is present, as it would not be in art, nor is it passive, as it would be in the young and sensual mortal body, nor is it lodged in a "dying animal," as it would be in the body of the aged man; the soul is now free to act in its own supremacy and in full cognizance of its own excellence, and its embodiment is now incorruptible and secure from all the ills of flesh.

About these several oppositions the poem forms. The whole turns on the old man's realization, now that he is in the presence of the images of Byzantium, that these images have souls; there are consequently two major divisions which divide the poem precisely in half, the first two stanzas presenting art as inanimate, the second two, as animate; and that this is the case can be seen from such signs as that in the first half of the poem the images are stated as passive objects—they are twice called "monuments," they are merely objects of contemplation, they may be neglected or studied, visited or not visited, whereas in stanzas III and IV they are treated as gods which can be prayed to for life or death, as beings capable of motion from sphere to sphere, as instructors of the soul, as sages possessed of wisdom; and the curious shift in the manner of consideration is signalized by the subtle phrasing of the first two lines of stanza III: "O sages standing in God's holy fire/As in the gold mosaic of a wall." According to the first part, the images at Byzantium were images, and one should have expected at most some figurative apostrophe to them: "O images set in the gold mosaic of a wall, much as the sages stand in God's holy fire"; but here the similitude is reversed, and lest there should be any error, the sages are besought to come from the holy fire and begin the tuition of the soul, the destruction of the flesh.

Within these two halves of the poem, further divisions may be found, coincident with the stanzaic divisions. Stanza I presents a rejection of passion, stanza II an acceptance of intellection; then, turning on the realization that art is insouled, stanza III presents a rejection of the corruptible embodiment, and stanza IV, an acceptance of the incorruptible. There is an alternation, thus, of negative and affirmative; out of passion into intellection, out of corruption into permanence, in clear balance, the proportion being I: II: III: IV; and what orders these sections is their dialectical sequence. That is, passion must be condemned before the intellect can be esteemed; the intellect must operate before the images can be known to be insouled; the realization that the images are insouled precedes the realization that the body may be dispensed with; and the reincarnation of the soul in some changeless medium can be recognized as a possibility only through the prior recognition that the flesh is not the necessary matter of the soul. The parallel opposition of contraries constitutes a sharp demarcation: in stanza I a mortal bird of nature amid natural trees sings a brief song of sensual joy in praise of mortal things, of "whatever is begotten, born, and dies"; in stanza IV an immortal and artificial bird set in an artificial tree sings an eternal song of spiritual joy in praise of eternal things, of "what is past, or passing, or to come"; and similarly, in stanza II a living thing is found to be an inanimate artifice, "a tattered coat upon a stick," incapable of motion, speech, sense or knowledge, whereas in stanza III what had appeared to be inanimate artifice is found to possess a soul, and hence to be capable of all these. A certain artificial symmetry in the argument serves to distinguish these parts even further: stanzas I and IV begin with the conclusions, and I is dependent upon II for the substantiation of its premises, as IV is dependent upon III.

This much indication of the principal organization of the work permits the explication, in terms of this, of the more elementary proportions. The first line of stanza I presents immediately, in its most simple statement, the condition which is the genesis of the whole structure: "That is no country for old men"; old men are shut out from something, and the remainder of the first six lines indicates precisely what it is from which they are excluded. The young are given over to sensual delight, in which old men can no longer participate. But a wall, if it shuts out, also shuts in; if the old are excluded from something, so are the young; lines 7 and 8, consequently, exhibit a second sense in which "That is no country for old men," for the young neglect all intellectual things. Further, the use of "that" implies a possible "this"; that is, there is a country for the old as for the young; and, again, the use of "that" implies that the separation from the country of the young is already complete. The occupation of the young is shrewdly stated: at first sight the human lovers "in one another's arms" have, like the birds at their song, apparently a romantic and sentimental aura; but the curious interpolation of "Those dying generations" in the description of the birds foreshadows the significance they are soon to have; and the phrases immediately following remove all sentimentality: "the salmon-falls, the mackerel-crowded seas" intend the ascent of salmon to the headwaters, the descent of mackerel to the deep seas in the spawning season, and the ironic intention is clear: all—the human lovers, the birds, the fish, do but spawn, but copulate, and this is their whole being; and if the parallel statement does not make this sufficiently evident, the summation of all in terms merely of animal genera—"fish, flesh, or fowl"—is unmistakable. The country of the young, then, is in its air, in its waters, and on its earth, from headwaters to ocean, wholly given over to sensuality; its inhabitants "commend all summer long" anything whatsoever, so long as it be mortal and animal—they commend "whatever is begotten, born, and dies"; and while they "commend" because they have great joy, that which they praise, they who praise, and their praise itself are ephemeral, for these mortals praise the things of mortality, and their commendation, like their joy, lasts but a summer, a mating season. The concluding lines of the stanza remove all ambiguity, and cancel all possibility of

a return to such a country; even if the old man could, he would not return to a land where "Caught in that sensual music, all neglect/Monuments of unageing intellect." The young are "caught," they are really passive and incapable of free action; and they neglect those things which are unageing.

Merely to end here, however, with a condemnation of youthful sensuality would be unsatisfactory; as the second stanza expounds, old age itself is no solution; the old man cannot justly say, like Sophocles when he was asked whether he regretted the loss of youth and love, "Peace; most gladly have I escaped the thing of which you speak; I feel as if I had escaped from a mad and furious master"; for merely to be old is merely to be in a state of privation, it is to be "a paltry thing/A tattered coat upon a stick," it is to be the merest scarecrow, the merest fiction and semblance of a man, an inanimate rag upon a dead stick. A man merely old, then, is worse off than youth; if the souls of the young are captive, the old have, in this sense at least, no souls at all. Something positive must be added; and if the soul can wax and grow strong as the body wanes, then every step in the dissolution of the body—"every tatter in its mortal dress"—is cause for a further augmentation of joy. But this can occur only if the soul can rejoice in its own power and magnificence. The soul of the aged must be strong to seek that which youth neglects. Hence the old must seek Byzantium; that is the country of the old; it is reached by sailing the seas, by breaking utterly with the country of the young; all passion must be left behind, the soul must be free to study the emblems of unchanging things.

Here the soul should be filled with joy; it should, by merely "studying," commend changeless things with song, as youth commends the changing with song; it would seem that the problem has been resolved, and the poem hence must end; but the contemplation of the monuments teaches first of all that these are no mere monuments but living things, and that the soul cannot grow into likeness with these beings of immortal embodiment unless it cast off its mortal body utterly. Nor is joy possible until the body be dissolved; the heart is still sick with the impossible desires of the flesh, it is still ignorant of its circumstances, and no song is possible to the soul while even a remnant of passion remains. Hence the old man prays to the sages who really stand in God's holy fire and have merely the semblance of images in gold mosaic; let them descend, "perning in a gyre," that is, moving in the circular motion which alone is possible to eternal things, let them consume with holy fire the heart which is the last seat of passion and ignorance, let them instruct the soul, let them gather it into the artifice of eternity and make the old man like themselves; even Byzantium, so long as the flesh be present, is no country for old men.

What it is to be like these, the soul, as yet uninstructed, can only conjecture; at any rate, with the destruction of the flesh it will be free of its ills; and if, as in Plato's myth of Er, the soul after death is free to choose some new embodiment, it will never again elect the flesh which is so quickly corruptible and which enslaves it to passion; it will choose some such form of art as that of the artificial birds in Theophilus' garden;[1] it will be of incorruptible and passionless gold; and it will dwell among leaves and boughs which are also of incorruptible and passionless metal. And now all sources of conflict are resolved in this last: the old has become the ageless; impotency has been exchanged for a higher power; the soul is free of passion and free for its joy, and it sings as youth once sang, but now of "What is past, and passing, and to come"—of the divisions of Eternity—rather than of

---

[1] In his note to the poem (*Collected Poems*, New York, 1933, p. 450) Yeats remarks: "I have read somewhere that in the Emperor's palace at Byzantium was a tree made of gold and silver, and artificial birds that sang." Undoubtedly the Emperor was Theophilus (829–842), and the birds conform to the descriptions of certain automata constructed for him by Leo Mathematicus and John Hlylilas. Cf. *Hist. Byzan. Script post Theoph.*, Anon. Cont. Theoph., 107; Constantini Manassis, *Brev. Hist.*, 107; and Michaeli Glycae, *Annales*, 292. See also Gibbon, *Decline and Fall*, Chapter LIII, and George Finlay, *History of the Byzantine Empire* (London, 1906), pp. 140, 148, where further references are given.

"Whatever is begotten, born, and dies"—of the divisions of mortal time. And it has here its country, its proper and permanent habitation.

Although the argument as we have stated it clearly underlies the poem, it would be erroneous to suppose that this in itself constitutes the poem, for in that case there would be no difference between our paraphrase and the poem itself. The poem itself comprehends the argument and collocates with it many terms which, although they could scarcely be formulated into some order approximating the pattern of the argument, nevertheless qualify the argument and determine its course. The basic analogies of the poem—of the natural world to a country, of the aged man to a scarecrow, of the world of art to Byzantium, and of artificial to natural generation—all these function as do the definitions of terms in actual argument; they serve to delimit the sphere of discourse and to make the argument intelligible.

This point is worth some discussion. The criticism of poetry has often turned chiefly on the so-called psychological connotations of readers with single words or phrases; but one may doubt whether the reader is at liberty to intrude such irrelevancies as the accidents of personal experience or the inevitable ambiguities of language would necessarily afford. Surely the ultimate consequence of such assumptions must be either that the poem becomes a mere stimulus to independent poetic activities on the part of the reader—that is, the reader becomes the true poet, his reading the true poem—or, on the other hand, that the reader becomes the matter or medium of art, in which case all the arts would have a common medium, the soul of the spectator. Neither of these consequences, it need scarcely be said, complies with the stipulations which initiated this discussion.

If the basic terms of a lyric poem do not receive their meanings from the chance associations of the reader, neither do they have their dictionary meanings; like terms in most discourse, they take their significance from their context, through juxtaposition to other terms with which they are equated, contrasted, correlated, or combined. In the present poem, for instance, the term "singing" is explicitly extended beyond its usual meaning to cover two kinds of jubilation, the rejoicing of the natural creature and that of the artificial; as a consequence, all the terms which relate to jubilation and song are affected; for example, "commend," "music," "singing-school," and "singing-masters" suffer an extension commensurate with that of singing. Similarly, the term "intellect" and all the terms associated with it suffer extension; and the monuments here are not ordinary monuments, but changeless embodiments of the changeless soul—by no means effigies, but truly living creatures, capable of will, of desire, of jubilation, of local motion, of intellection and instruction. Nor is Byzantium the historical city; the tourist is not invited to recall that here once he was overcharged, nor is the historian invited to contribute such information as that this was a city visited by Hugh of Vermandois; Byzantium is not a place upon a map, but a term in the poem; a term signifying a stage of contemplation wherein the soul studies itself and so learns both what it is and in what consists true and eternal joy.

Furthermore, if the words of a poem have meanings which the poet may arbitrarily determine, the "objects" in poetry are also given whatever "properties" the poet sees fit to assign to them. That is, whereas the physical thing has its determinate nature and is subject to physical laws such as Newton's laws, the "things" of a poem—the artificial and natural creatures here, for instance—have only such properties as statement within the poem affords them. Poetic statements must not be confused, however, with propositions; since they are not statements about things which exist outside the poem, it would be meaningless to evaluate them as true or false; they have rather the status of definitions or resolutions; and while in certain poems the coordination is dialectical, as in this poem, no criteria of dialectic could be significantly applied to them, for a dialectic is necessarily regulated by the natures of things external to the dialectic and must ultimately be evaluated, whereas the coordination of elements in a poem cannot involve reference to anything outside the poem. Even when poetic statements are incidentally true propositions, even when their coordination is also cogent argument, these coincidences would not affect their poetic status. Thus, "To His Coy Mistress" is an excellent poem, whether the lover's argument is valid or not. In a sense, every poem is a microcosmos, a discrete and independent universe with its laws provided by the poet; his decision is absolute; he can make things good or bad, great or small, powerful or weak, just as he wills; he may make men taller than mountains or smaller than atoms, he may suspend whole cities in the air, he may destroy creation or re-form it; within his universe the impossible becomes the possible, the necessary the contingent— if he but says they do.

I have said that the bare argument of "Sailing to Byzantium" is not the poem; but I should argue that the argument (considered not as a real argument, but, according to what I have said, as a certain collocation of terms) is the *principle* of this poem, in a sense analogous to that in which, for Aristotle, plot is the principle of tragedy. For if the principle is that for the sake of which all other things in the poem exist, and that, consequently, in terms of which all are intelligible, what could be the principle, other than the thing we have supposed? There is here no plot, no ordered tissue of incidents, for, first of all, the whole poem is of a moment— the moment in which the old man confronts the monuments and addresses them—whereas a tissue of incidents, a plot, must extend over a span of time. And second, there can be no plot because there are no incidents; the "events" in a lyric poem are never incidents as such, connected by necessity or probability, but devices for making poetic statements. Again, since there is no action, there is no agent, that is, *character*, in the sense in which there are differentiated agents in drama or epic, each duly discriminated for his distinct part in the action; rather, the character in the sense in which character may be said to exist here is almost completely universalized. Hence, if plot does not constitute the principle of the poem, neither does character; for not all the parts of the poem would be explicable in terms of character, nor are we presented with any precise depiction of character here, as we should be if it were the end. On the merely verbal level, again, we can account for nothing; the words must be explained in terms of something else, not the poem in terms of the words; and further, a principle must be a principle of something other than itself; hence the words cannot be a principle of their own arrangements.

Rather, it is clear as we look at the poem, that a certain problem orders the whole—the problem of finding a suitable compensation for the losses suffered in old age; the poem begins with exclusion from the pleasures of youth, develops among ordered dialectical alternatives, and ends when the problem is permanently solved. As the problem determines the limits of the poem, so it determines all else; the character is determined by it, for example, because—according to the very nature of the problem—a young man could not have conceived of the problem as it is stated, nor could a raging and sensual old man, nor could an old man who was contented with age, like Sophocles; since an ideal and permanent solution was to be given to the problem, a character conscious of loss, and capable of conceiving an ideal solution, was necessitated. Nothing beside this is indicated with respect to the speaker. Again, the words themselves are determined by the problem; while the choice of metaphors of a "country," or "song," and of modes of embodiment was initially arbitrary, once the metaphors have been stated they must be carried out according to the dictates of the problem; indeed, it is possible to trace variations in diction precisely proportional to the stages of the dialectic. For example, the stages are verbally signalized by the succession "flesh," "stick," "dying animal," "gold," in terms of expressions of embodiment, or "no country," "Byzantium," "the artifice of eternity," which is amid "holy fire," in terms of habitation; and the metaphor of the artificial bird in the fourth stanza bears such relation—in terms of setting, song, character of joy, object of joy, and "bodily form"—to the real birds—"those dying generations"—in stanza I as the solution of the problem bears to the element the negation of which generated the dialectic.

In a similar manner the presence of nearly every word in the poem might be justified if space permitted.

On the basis of our examination, then, we may say that there exists a kind of poem (since we have here one instance of it) which has argument, in the sense we have stipulated, as its principle; not, let us remember, a dialectic referable to externals, but a certain formal collocation of terms which is referable to nothing outside itself and which may be called the soul of the poem in the sense in which Aristotle calls plot the soul of tragedy. This kind of poetry has the same means as tragedy, epic, and comedy, but whereas the latter are imitations of human action, so that their principle is a certain collocation of incidents organized by necessity and probability—whereas, that is, these are dynamic, for they imitate change—the kind which we have been scrutinizing is static; it abstracts from motion and change, and though it sometimes appears to recount events, these are not events as parts of a plot connected by probability or necessity, but events in the sense in which we speak of events in a philosophical dialogue—they are only dialectically separable stages in the treatment of a problem, and are reducible to statements within the problem. Whereas in the Aristotelian treatment of poems which have a plot as their principle, certain qualitative parts of the various species resulted from an analysis of the object of imitation, that is, the action, a different procedure is necessary here; the principle is a tissue not of events but of ideas, and the ordering of the poem will not be by necessity and probability, by the antecedents and consequents of action, but by dialectical priority and posteriority. Lastly, while character will be necessitated here as where a plot is the principle, it will be determined, not by its share in an action, but by its role in a drama, not of action, but of thought. That is, it is determined, as the characters in a Platonic dialogue are determined, by the nature of the discourse which they are to utter.

It would be a mistake, however, to assume that all lyrics are of the order considered here. The term lyric itself has been given an extraordinary variety of applications, and the scrupulous analyst and critic will attempt to keep the variety of critical approaches almost commensurate with these, on the assumption that great art—however familiar the pattern in which it is apparently laid—is always in the last analysis *sui generis*.

Keats's Sylvan Historian: History without Footnotes*

BY CLEANTH BROOKS

THERE IS MUCH in the poetry of Keats which suggests that he would have approved of Archibald MacLeish's dictum, "A poem should not mean/But be." There is even some warrant for thinking that the Grecian urn (real or imagined) which inspired the famous ode was, for Keats, just such a poem, "palpable and mute," a poem in stone. Hence it is the more remarkable that the "Ode" itself differs from Keats's other odes by culminating in a statement—a statement even of some sententiousness in which the urn itself is made to say that beauty is truth, and—more sententious still—that this bit of wisdom sums up the whole of mortal knowledge.

This is "to mean" with a vengeance—to violate the doctrine of the objective correlative, not only by stating truths, but by defining the limits of truth. Small wonder that some critics have felt that the unravished bride of quietness protests too much.

T. S. Eliot, for example, says that "this line ["Beauty is

* This essay had been finished some months before I came upon Kenneth Burke's brilliant essay on Keats's "Ode" ("Symbolic Action in a Poem by Keats," *Accent,* Autumn, 1943). I have decided not to make any alterations, though I have been tempted to adopt some of Burke's insights, and, in at least one case, his essay has convinced me of a point which I had considered but rejected—the pun on "breed" and "Brede."

I am happy to find that two critics with methods and purposes so different should agree so thoroughly as we do on the poem. I am pleased, for my part, therefore, to acknowledge the amount of duplication which exists between the two essays, counting it as rather important corroboration of a view of the poem which will probably seem to some critics overingenious. In spite of the common elements, however, I feel that the emphasis of my essay is sufficiently different from Burke's to justify my going on with its publication.

231

truth," etc.] strikes me as a serious blemish on a beautiful poem; and the reason must be either that I fail to understand it, or that it is a statement which is untrue." But even for persons who feel that they do understand it, the line may still constitute a blemish. Middleton Murry, who, after a discussion of Keats's other poems and his letters, feels that he knows what Keats meant by "beauty" and what he meant by "truth," and that Keats used them in senses which allowed them to be properly bracketed together, still, is forced to conclude: "My own opinion concerning the value of these two lines *in the context of the poem itself* is not very different from Mr. T. S. Eliot's." The troubling assertion is apparently an intrusion upon the poem—does not grow out of it—is not dramatically accommodated to it.

This is essentially Garrod's objection, and the fact that Garrod does object indicates that a distaste for the ending of the "Ode" is by no means limited to critics of notoriously "modern" sympathies.

But the question of real importance is not whether Eliot, Murry, and Garrod are right in thinking that "Beauty is truth, truth beauty" injures the poem. The question of real importance concerns beauty and truth in a much more general way: what is the relation of the beauty (the goodness, the perfection) of a poem to the truth or falsity of what it seems to assert? It is a question which has particularly vexed our own generation—to give it I. A. Richards' phrasing, it is the problem of belief.

The "Ode," by its bold equation of beauty and truth, raises this question in its sharpest form—the more so when it becomes apparent that the poem itself is obviously intended to be a parable on the nature of poetry, and of art in general. The "Ode" has apparently been an enigmatic parable, to be sure: one can emphasize *beauty* is truth and throw Keats into the pure-art camp, the usual procedure. But it is only fair to point out that one could stress *truth* is beauty, and argue with the Marxist critics of the thirties for a propaganda art. The very ambiguity of the statement, "Beauty is truth, truth beauty" ought to warn us against insisting very much on the statement in isolation, and to drive us back to a consideration of the context in which the statement is set.

It will not be sufficient, however, if it merely drives us back to a study of Keats's reading, his conversation, his letters. We shall not find our answer there even if scholarship does prefer on principle investigations of Browning's ironic question, "What porridge had John Keats?" For even if we knew just what porridge he had, physical and mental, we should still not be able to settle the problem of the "Ode." The reason should be clear: our specific question is not what did Keats the man perhaps want to assert here about the relation of beauty and truth; it is rather: was Keats the poet able to exemplify that relation in this particular poem? Middleton Murry is right: the relation of the final statement in the poem to the total context is all-important.

Indeed, Eliot, in the very passage in which he attacks the "Ode" has indicated the general line which we are to take in its defense. In that passage, Eliot goes on to contrast the closing lines of the "Ode" with a line from *King Lear,* "Ripeness is all." Keats's lines strike him as false; Shakespeare's, on the other hand, as not clearly false, and as possibly quite true. Shakespeare's generalization, in other words, avoids raising the question of truth. But is it really a question of truth and falsity? One is tempted to account for the difference of effect which Eliot feels in this way: "Ripeness is all" is a statement put in the mouth of a dramatic character and a statement which is governed and qualified by the whole context of the play. It does not directly challenge an examination into its truth because its relevance is pointed up and modified by the dramatic context.

Now, suppose that one could show that Keats's lines, *in quite the same way,* constitute a speech, a consciously riddling paradox, put in the mouth of a particular character, and modified by the total context of the poem. If we could demonstrate that the speech was "in character," was dramatically appropriate, was properly prepared for—then would not the lines have all the justification of "Ripeness is all"? In such case, should we not have waived the question of the scientific or philosophic truth of the lines in favor of the application of a principle curiously like that of dramatic propriety? I suggest that some such principle is the only one legitimately to be invoked in any case. Be this as it may, the "Ode on a Grecian Urn" provides us with as neat an instance as one could wish in order to test the implications of such a maneuver.

It has seemed best to be perfectly frank about procedure: the poem is to be read in order to see whether the last lines of the poem are not, after all, dramatically prepared for. Yet there are some claims to be made upon the reader too, claims which he, for his part, will have to be prepared to honor. He must not be allowed to dismiss the early characterizations of the urn as merely so much vaguely beautiful description. He must not be too much surprised if "mere decoration" turns out to be meaningful symbolism—or if ironies develop where he has been taught to expect only sensuous pictures. Most of all, if the teasing riddle spoken finally by the urn is not to strike him as a bewildering break in tone, he must not be too much disturbed to have the element of paradox latent in the poem emphasized, even in those parts of the poem which have none of the energetic crackle of wit with which he usually associates paradox. This is surely not too much to ask of the reader—namely, to assume that Keats meant what he said and that he chose his words with care. After all, the poem begins on a note of paradox, though a mild one: for we ordinarily do not expect an urn to speak at all; and yet, Keats does more than this: he begins his poem by emphasizing the apparent contradiction.

The silence of the urn is stressed—it is a "bride of quietness"; it is a "foster-child of silence," but the urn is a "historian" too. Historians tell the truth, or are at least expected to tell the truth. What is a "Sylvan historian?" A historian who is like the forest rustic, a woodlander? Or, a historian who writes histories of the forest? Presumably, the urn is sylvan in both senses. True, the latter meaning is uppermost: the urn can "express/A flowery tale more sweetly than our rhyme," and what the urn goes on to express is a "leaf-fring'd legend" of "Tempe or the dales of Arcady." But the urn, like the "leaf-fring'd legend" which it tells, is covered with emblems of the fields and forests: "Overwrought,/ With forest branches and the trodden weed." When we consider the way in which the urn utters its history, the fact that it must be sylvan in both senses is seen as inevitable. Perhaps too the fact that it is a rural historian, a rustic, a peasant historian, qualifies in our minds the dignity and the "truth" of the histories which it recites. Its histories, Keats has already conceded, may be characterized as "tales"—not formal history at all.

The sylvan historian certainly supplies no names and dates—"What men or gods are these?" the poet asks. What it does give is action—of men *or* gods, of godlike men or of superhuman (though not daemonic) gods—action, which is not the less intense for all that the urn is cool marble. The words "mad" and "ecstasy" occur, but it is the quiet, rigid urn which gives the dynamic picture. And the paradox goes further: the scene is one of violent love-making, a Bacchanalian scene, but the urn itself is like a "still unravish'd bride," or like a child, a child "of silence and slow time." It is not merely like a child, but like a "foster-child." The exactness of the term can be defended. "Silence and slow time," it is suggested, are not the true parents, but foster-parents. They are too old, one feels, to have borne the child themselves. Moreover, they dote upon the "child" as grandparents do. The urn is fresh and unblemished; it is still young, for all its antiquity, and time which destroys so much has "fostered" it.

With Stanza II we move into the world presented by the urn, into an examination, not of the urn as a whole—as an entity with its own form—but of the details which overlay it. But as we enter that world, the paradox of silent speech is carried on, this time in terms of the objects portrayed on the vase.

The first lines of the stanza state a rather bold paradox—even the dulling effect of many readings has hardly blunted it. At least we can easily revive its sharpness. Attended to with

care, it is a statement which is preposterous, and yet true—
true on the same level on which the original metaphor of the
speaking urn is true. The unheard music is sweeter than any
audible music. The poet has rather cunningly enforced his
conceit by using the phrase, "ye soft pipes." Actually, we
might accept the poet's metaphor without being forced to
accept the adjective "soft." The pipes might, although "unheard," be shrill, just as the action which is frozen in the
figures on the urn can be violent and ecstatic as in Stanza I
and slow and dignified as in Stanza IV (the procession to the
sacrifice). Yet, by characterizing the pipes as "soft," the poet
has provided a sort of realistic basis for his metaphor: the
pipes, it is suggested, are playing very softly; if we listen
carefully, we can hear them; their music is just below the
threshold of normal sound.

This general paradox runs through the stanza: action goes
on though the actors are motionless; the song will not cease;
the lover cannot leave his song; the maiden, always to be
kissed, never actually kissed, will remain changelessly beautiful. The maiden is, indeed, like the urn itself, a "still unravished bride of quietness"—not even ravished by a kiss;
and it is implied, perhaps, that her changeless beauty, like
that of the urn, springs from this fact.

The poet is obviously stressing the fresh, unwearied charm
of the scene itself which can defy time and is deathless. But,
at the same time, the poet is being perfectly fair to the terms
of his metaphor. The beauty portrayed is deathless because
it is lifeless. And it would be possible to shift the tone easily
and ever so slightly by insisting more heavily on some of the
phrasings so as to give them a darker implication. Thus, in
the case of "thou canst not leave/Thy song," one could
interpret: the musician cannot leave the song even if he
would: he is fettered to it, a prisoner. In the same way, one
could enlarge on the hint that the lover is not wholly satisfied
and content: "never canst thou kiss,/ . . . yet, *do not
grieve.*" These items are mentioned here, not because one
wishes to maintain that the poet is bitterly ironical, but because it is important for us to see that even here the

paradox is being used fairly, particularly in view of the shift in tone which comes in the next stanza.

This third stanza represents, as various critics have pointed out, a recapitulation of earlier motifs. The boughs which cannot shed their leaves, the unwearied melodist, and the ever-ardent lover reappear. Indeed, I am not sure that this stanza can altogether be defended against the charge that it represents a falling-off from the delicate but firm precision of the earlier stanzas. There is a tendency to linger over the scene sentimentally: the repetition of the word "happy" is perhaps symptomatic of what is occurring. Here, if anywhere, in my opinion, is to be found the blemish on the ode—not in the last two lines. Yet, if we are to attempt a defense of the third stanza, we shall come nearest success by emphasizing the paradoxical implications of the repeated items; for whatever development there is in the stanza inheres in the increased stress on the paradoxical element. For example, the boughs cannot "bid the Spring adieu," a phrase which repeats "nor ever can those trees be bare," but the new line strengthens the implications of speaking: the falling leaves are a gesture, a word of farewell to the joy of spring. The melodist of Stanza II played sweeter music because unheard, but here, in the third stanza, it is implied that he does not tire of his song for the same reason that the lover does not tire of his love—neither song nor love is consummated. The songs are "for ever new" because they cannot be completed.

The paradox is carried further in the case of the lover whose love is "For ever warm and still to be enjoy'd." We are really dealing with an ambiguity here, for we can take "still to be enjoy'd" as an adjectival phrase on the same level as "warm"—that is, "still virginal and warm." But the tenor of the whole poem suggests that the warmth of the love depends upon the fact that it has not been enjoyed—that is, "warm and still to be enjoy'd" may mean also "warm *because* still to be enjoy'd."

But though the poet has developed and extended his metaphors furthest here in this third stanza, the ironic counterpoise is developed furthest too. The love which a line earlier was "warm" and "panting" becomes suddenly in the next line, "All breathing human passion far above." But if it is *above* all breathing passion, it is, after all, outside the realm of breathing passion, and therefore, not human passion at all.

(If one argues that we are to take "All breathing human passion" as qualified by "That leaves a heart high-sorrowful and cloy'd"—that is, if one argues that Keats is saying that the love depicted on the urn is above only that human passion which leaves one cloyed and not above human passion in general, he misses the point. For Keats in the "Ode" is stressing the ironic fact that all human passion *does* leave one cloyed; hence the superiority of art.)

The purpose in emphasizing the ironic undercurrent in the foregoing lines is not at all to disparage Keats—to point up implications of his poem of which he was himself unaware. Far from it: the poet knows precisely what he is doing. The point is to be made simply in order to make sure that we are completely aware of what he *is* doing. Garrod, sensing this ironic undercurrent, seems to interpret it as an element over which Keats was not able to exercise full control. He says: "Truth to his main theme [the fixity given by art to forms which in life are impermanent] has taken Keats farther than he meant to go. The pure and ideal art of this 'cold Pastoral,' this 'silent form,' *has* a cold silentness which in some degree saddens him. In the last lines of the fourth stanza, especially the last three lines . . . every reader is conscious, I should suppose, of an undertone of sadness, of disappointment." The undertone is there, but Keats has not been taken "farther than he meant to go." Keats's attitude, even in the early stanzas, is more complex than Garrod would allow: it is more complex and more ironic, and a recognition of this is important if we are to be able to relate the last stanza to the rest of the "Ode." Keats is perfectly aware that the frozen moment of loveliness is more dynamic than is the fluid world of reality *only* because it is frozen. The love depicted on the urn remains warm and young because it is not human flesh at all but cold, ancient marble.

With Stanza IV, we are still within the world depicted by

the urn, but the scene presented in this stanza forms a contrast to the earlier scenes. It emphasizes, not individual aspiration and desire, but communal life. It constitutes another chapter in the history that the "Sylvan historian" has to tell. And again, names and dates have been omitted. We are not told to what god's altar the procession moves, nor the occasion of the sacrifice.

Moreover, the little town from which the celebrants come is unknown; and the poet rather goes out of his way to leave us the widest possible option in locating it. It may be a mountain town, or a river town, or a tiny seaport. Yet, of course, there is a sense in which the nature of the town—the essential character of the town—is actually suggested by the figured urn. But it is not given explicitly. The poet is willing to leave much to our imaginations; and yet the stanza in its organization of imagery and rhythm does describe the town clearly enough; it is small, it is quiet, its people are knit together as an organic whole, and on a "pious morn" such as this, its whole population has turned out to take part in the ritual.

The stanza has been justly admired. Its magic of effect defies reduction to any formula. Yet, without pretending to "account" for the effect in any mechanical fashion, one can point to some of the elements active in securing the effect: there is the suggestiveness of the word "green" in "green altar"— something natural, spontaneous, living; there is the suggestion that the little town is caught in a curve of the seashore, or nestled in a fold of the mountains—at any rate, is something secluded and something naturally related to its terrain; there is the effect of the phrase "peaceful citadel," a phrase which involves a clash between the ideas of war and peace and resolves it in the sense of stability and independence without imperialistic ambition—the sense of stable repose.

But to return to the larger pattern of the poem: Keats does something in this fourth stanza which is highly interesting in itself and thoroughly relevant to the sense in which the urn is a historian. One of the most moving passages in the poem is that in which the poet speculates on the strange emptiness of the little town which, of course, has not been pictured on the urn at all.

The little town which has been merely implied by the procession portrayed on the urn is endowed with a poignance beyond anything else in the poem. Its streets "for evermore/ Will silent me," its desolation forever shrouded in a mystery. No one in the figured procession will ever be able to go back to the town to break the silence there, not even one to tell the stranger there why the town remains desolate.

If one attends closely to what Keats is doing here, he may easily come to feel that the poet is indulging himself in an ingenious fancy, an indulgence, however, which is gratuitous and finally silly; that is, the poet has created in his own imagination the town implied by the procession of worshipers, has given it a special character of desolation and loneliness, and then has gone on to treat it as if it were a real town to which a stranger might actually come and be puzzled by its emptiness. (I can see no other interpretation of the lines, "and not a soul to tell/Why thou art desolate can e'er return.") But, actually, of course, no one will ever discover the town except by the very same process by which Keats has discovered it: namely, through the figured urn, and then, of course, he will not need to ask why it is empty. One can well imagine what a typical eighteenth-century critic would have made of this flaw in logic.

It will not be too difficult, however, to show that Keats's extension of the fancy is not irrelevant to the poem as a whole. The "reality" of the little town has a very close relation to the urn's character as a historian. If the earlier stanzas have been concerned with such paradoxes as the ability of static carving to convey dynamic action, of the soundless pipes to play music sweeter than that of the heard melody, of the figured lover to have a love more warm and panting than that of breathing flesh and blood, so in the same way the town implied by the urn comes to have a richer and more important history than that of actual cities. Indeed, the imagined town is to the figured procession as the unheard melody is to the carved pipes of the unwearied melodist. And the poet, by pretending to take the town as real—so real that he can imagine the effect of its silent streets upon the stranger who chances to come into it—has suggested in the most powerful way possible its essential reality for him—and for us. It is a case of the doctor's taking his own medicine: the poet is prepared to stand by the illusion of his own making.

With Stanza V we move back out of the enchanted world portrayed by the urn to consider the urn itself once more as a whole, as an object. The shift in point of view is marked with the first line of the stanza by the apostrophe, "O Attic shape . . ." It is the urn itself as a formed thing, as an autonomous world, to which the poet addresses these last words. And the rich, almost breathing world which the poet has conjured up for us contracts and hardens into the decorated motifs on the urn itself: "with brede/ Of marble men and maidens overwrought." The beings who have a life above life—"All breathing human passion far above"—are marble, after all.

This last is a matter which, of course, the poet has never denied. The recognition that the men and maidens are frozen, fixed, arrested, has, as we have already seen, run through the second, third, and fourth stanzas as an ironic undercurrent. The central paradox of the poem, thus, comes to conclusion in the phrase, "Cold Pastoral." The word "pastoral" suggests warmth, spontaneity, the natural and the informal as well as the idyllic, the simple, and the informally charming. What the urn tells is a "flowery tale," a "leaf-fring'd legend," but the "sylvan historian" works in terms of marble. The urn itself is cold, and the life beyond life which it expresses is life which has been formed, arranged. The urn itself is a "silent form," and it speaks, not by means of statement, but by "teasing us out of thought." It is as enigmatic as eternity is, for, like eternity, its history is beyond time, outside time, and for this very reason bewilders our time-ridden minds: it teases us.

The marble men and maidens of the urn will not age as flesh-and-blood men and women will: "When old age shall this generation waste." (The word "generation," by the way, is very rich. It means on one level "that which is generated" —that which springs from human loins—Adam's breed; and yet, so intimately is death wedded to men, the word "generation" itself has become, as here, a measure of time.) The marble men and women lie outside time. The urn which they adorn will remain. The "Sylvan historian" will recite its history to other generations.

What will it say to them? Presumably, what it says to the poet now: that "formed experience," imaginative insight, embodies the basic and fundamental perception of man and nature. The urn is beautiful, and yet its beauty is based— what else is the poem concerned with?—on an imaginative perception of essentials. Such a vision is beautiful but it is also true. The sylvan historian presents us with beautiful histories, but they are true histories, and it is a good historian.

Moreover, the "truth" which the sylvan historian gives is the only kind of truth which we are likely to get on this earth, and, furthermore, it is the only kind that we *have* to have. The names, dates, and special circumstances, the wealth of data—these the sylvan historian quietly ignores. But we shall never get all the facts anyway—there is no end to the accumulation of facts. Moreover, mere accumulations of facts—a point our own generation is only beginning to realize—are meaningless. The sylvan historian does better than that: it takes a few details and so orders them that we have not only beauty but insight into essential truth. Its "history," in short, is a history without footnotes. It has the validity of myth—not myth as a pretty but irrelevant make-believe, an idle fancy, but myth as a valid perception into reality.

So much for the "meaning" of the last lines of the "Ode." It is an interpretation which differs little from past interpretations. It is put forward here with no pretension to novelty. What is important is the fact that it can be derived from the context of the "Ode" itself.

And now, what of the objection that the final lines break the tone of the poem with a display of misplaced sententiousness? One can summarize the answer already implied thus: throughout the poem the poet has stressed the paradox of the speaking urn. First, the urn itself can tell a story, can give a history. Then, the various figures depicted upon the urn play music or speak or sing. If we have been alive to these items, we shall not, perhaps, be too much surprised to have the urn speak once more, not in the sense in which it tells a story—a metaphor which is rather easy to accept—but, to have it speak on a higher level, to have it make a commentary on its own nature. If the urn has been properly dramatized, if we have followed the development of the metaphors, if we have been alive to the paradoxes which work throughout the poem, perhaps then, we shall be prepared for the enigmatic, final paradox which the "silent form" utters. But in that case, we shall not feel that the generalization, unqualified and to be taken literally, is meant to march out of its context to compete with the scientific and philosophical generalizations which dominate our world.

"Beauty is truth, truth beauty" has precisely the same status, and the same justification as Shakespeare's "Ripeness is all." It is a speech "in character" and supported by a dramatic context.

To conclude thus may seem to weight the principle of dramatic propriety with more than it can bear. This would not be fair to the complexity of the problem of truth in art nor fair to Keats's little parable. Granted; and yet the principle of dramatic propriety may take us further than would first appear. Respect for it may at least ensure our dealing with the problem of truth at the level on which it is really relevant to literature. If we can see that the assertions made in a poem are to be taken as part of an organic context, if we can resist the temptation to deal with them in isolation, then we may be willing to go on to deal with the world-view, or "philosophy," or "truth" of the *poem as a whole* in terms of its dramatic wholeness: that is, we shall not neglect the maturity of attitude, the dramatic tension, the emotional *and* intellectual coherence in favor of some statement of theme abstracted from it by paraphrase. Perhaps, best of all, we might learn to distrust our ability to represent any poem adequately by paraphrase. Such a distrust is healthy. Keats's sylvan historian, who is not above "teasing" us, exhibits such a distrust, and perhaps the point of what the sylvan historian "says" is to confirm us in our distrust.

THE ARCHETYPAL
APPROACH:

LITERATURE
IN THE LIGHT OF MYTH

Introduction

A CRITICAL APPROACH that has been gaining considerable attention recently is the archetypal, sometimes called the totemic, mythological, or ritualistic. It occupies a curious position among other methods: it requires close textual readings, like the formalistic, and yet it is concerned humanistically with more than the intrinsic value of aesthetic satisfaction; it seems psychological insofar as it analyzes the work of art's appeal to the audience (in a way, extending Richards' investigations of the poem-reader relationship) and yet sociological in its attendance upon basic cultural patterns as central to that appeal; it is historical in its investigation of a cultural or social past, but nonhistorical in its demonstration of literature's timeless value, independent of particular periods.

To avoid further circumscribing, one can delineate the method as a demonstration of some basic cultural pattern of great meaning and appeal to humanity in a work of art. Such an approach reflects the strong contemporary interest in myth, and the influence of two figures whose work has been of great importance to us: Frazer and Jung.

The major work of Sir James George Frazer, the Scottish anthropologist, was, of course, *The Golden Bough,* which appeared in twelve volumes from 1890 to 1915. They constitute a monumental study of magic and religion, tracing numerous myths back to prehistoric beginnings. In the twenties, a number of scholars, mostly Cantabrigian, turned their knowledge of the work of Frazer and of Sir Edward Tylor[1] to a new kind of study of the classics. The group, composed of Jane Harrison, F. M. Cornford, Gilbert Murray, Andrew Lang and others, dealt with the ritual conflicts underlying the work of the Greek tragedians and Homer. Cornford, for ex-

[1] Tylor had been as active as Frazer in the study of myth. His chief work was *Primitive Culture,* 1871.

ample, examined the ritualistic basis of Greek comedy in one study, and the ritual figure of the Greek god-king in another; Miss Harrison explored the social origins of Greek religion. Their general view has been summarized in Miss Harrison's *Ancient Art and Ritual*, 1913; and their applications are both interesting in themselves, and valuable in establishing an approach that later critics were to pursue. One value of academic scholarship is nowhere better illustrated than here, since the work of these writers and of some who came after them was a direct influence upon the creative use of myth by Joyce and others.

Carl Gustav Jung, originally associated with Freud, departed from the work of his master with several concepts. So far as archetypal criticism is concerned, his chief contribution is the theory of the collective unconsciousness: that civilized man preserves, though unconsciously, those prehistorical areas of knowledge which he articulated obliquely in myth. If valid, the speculation explains the somewhat mysterious appeal of mythical stories long after the supernatural elements in them have ceased to command belief.

The two forces represented by Frazer and Jung—asserting the validity of myth, and its retention in the social memory —strongly appealed to the creative imagination. D. H. Lawrence's motif of "blood consciousness" is obviously close to the theory that sophisticated man should respond affirmatively to the elemental forces which alone can instruct him in the proper, "natural" modes of living. In his notes to *The Wasteland*, T. S. Eliot acknowledges his debt to Jesse Weston's *From Ritual to Romance*, as well as to an earlier work in anthropology, "one which has influenced our generation profoundly; I mean *The Golden Bough*." For Eliot, one of the main uses of these studies was their establishment of universal patterns of man, whatever his time and place, which enabled the poet to make simultaneous parallels to and contrasts with figures and situations in the contemporary wasteland. Precisely this advantage has led other writers to myth: Robert Graves, James Joyce, and Yeats; and most recently C. S. Lewis has illustrated the appeal by retelling the story of Psyche and Cupid in such a way as to make it a prefiguration of man's struggle toward eternal love.

Inevitably, literary critics were challenged to examine literature with the hope of discovering the existence of underlying mythological patterns. The resulting analysis comes from the critic's sense that "the deepest meanings, meanings which extend beyond the single work to a whole body of books, are to be sought in the archetypal symbols to which . . . writers compulsively turn." [2] Freud had established that rituals and taboos were dealt with consciously by primitive man, but unconsciously by civilized man. Freudians tended to look upon the atavistic retention of such taboos as forms of illness. The Jungians, however, regarded myth not as the dream of the inhibited individual person, but as protoplastic pattern of the race which, so far as the individual repeats it, bespeaks not illness but his natural participation in the collective unconsciousness. Myth is, in the terms of Erich Fromm, "a message from ourselves to ourselves, a secret language which enables us to treat inner as if outer event." [3] The artist, thus, is not a neurotic but a "shaman, a mythmaker, speaking out of his unconscious a primordial truth." [4] Archetypal criticism, then, aims to discover and decode the secret language in literary works so that it may have for us a more rational meaning.

D. H. Lawrence's *Studies in Classic American Literature,* 1923, as one might expect from his creative interest in the nonrational forces of life, exhibits an inclination to consider various fictitious characters (Natty Bumppo, Hester Prynne) as archetypes, and various plots as fulfilling fundamental patterns. Maud Bodkin's *Archetypal Patterns in Poetry,* 1934, is a classic of its kind. Kenneth Burke often relies—for ex-

[2] Leslie Fiedler in Lewis Leary, ed., *Contemporary Literary Scholarship,* p. 170.

[3] As summarized by W. Y. Tindall in *Forces in Modern British Literature,* p. 311.

[4] C. Hugh Holman, "The Defense of Art: Criticism since 1930," in Floyd Stovall, ed., *The Development of American Criticism,* p. 218.

ample, in his concept of "symbolic action"—on social anthropology. For him, the artist is often a "medicine man" and the work of art, his "medicine." [5] In pursuit of the implied relationship between poet, poem, and audience, Burke often discusses taboos, fetishes, ritual paradigms. In one of his best essays, for example, "Antony in Behalf of the Play," he works out the strategy of Shakespeare's drama as rendered necessary by the traditional feelings of the audience toward authority, revolution, and scapegoat. Ritual patterns in Shakespeare have also been studied by others: Colin Still, in *The Timeless Theme,* 1936, and G. Wilson Knight in several of his works.

Archetypal criticism does not necessarily go back to specific myths; it may discover basic cultural patterns which assume a mythic quality in their permanence within a particular culture. I am thinking of such studies as those made by Leslie Fiedler. What he has uncovered (some hostile critics would say "invented") is an American cultural pattern involving a relationship between men, reflected sometimes in the rituals of boyhood gangs, sometimes in unconsciously symbolic ceremonies of adults. He finds this scheme employed in American novels—*The Adventures of Huckleberry Finn,* and *Moby-Dick* especially—and in the social mores of cowboys in Montana. His analyses are disturbing to many because, I believe, of the discomforts many feel about the homosexual quality of the pattern he investigates.

This uneasiness illustrates the dichotomous attitude of many readers toward this approach. On the one hand, more critics are turning to the anthropological study of literature; on the other, animadversions are made and results often ridiculed. One basic objection is that archetypal criticism does not lead to evaluation of literature so much as to an explanation of the fundamental appeal of certain writing. Another is the charge that the practitioners are notable more for their ingenuity than for the validity of what they have to say. And, of course, uncontrolled totemic criticism has come in for the

[5] Ransom's terms.

sort of fleering that Malcolm Cowley has showered on Richard Chase's *Herman Melville* for stewing together "a mess of Freudian and Christian symbols." In appraising the school in general, Cowley says "far too many of the readings are more like spiritualistic seances or demonstrations of popular magic. When the critic utters an incantation, waving his sorcerer's wand—presto!—everything is transformed into something else." [6]

But whether done well or ill, the totemic approach obviously reflects the contemporary dissatisfaction with the scientific concept of man as, at his highest, rational. Anthropological literature seeks to restore to us our entire humanity, a humanity which values the primitive elements in human nature. In contrast to the splitting of the human mind by emphasizing the warfare between the conscious and the subconscious processes, anthropological literature reestablishes us as members of the ancient race of man. And archetypal criticism seeks to discover in literature the dramatizations of this membership.

[6] *The Literary Situation* (Compass Books edition), p. 16.

Bibliographical Note

The three studies at the base of archetypal criticism are Sir Edward Tylor, *Primitive Culture,* 1871; Sir James Frazer, *The Golden Bough,* 1890-1915, and the writings of Carl Jung, who most fully expresses his concept of archetypes in "On the Relation of Analytic Psychology to Poetic Art" in *Contributions to Analytic Psychology,* 1928, "Psychology and Literature" in *Modern Man in Search of a Soul,* 1933, and *The Integration of the Personality* (translated by Stanley Dell), 1940.

British scholars were among the first to work in the field. *Anthropology and the Classics,* edited by R. R. Marret, contains pieces by Gilbert Murray and Andrew Lang. Other works are Jane Harrison, *Themis,* 1912, and *Ancient Art and Ritual,* 1913; Gilbert Murray, *Euripides and his Age,* 1913; and F. M. Cornford, *The Origin of Attic Comedy,* 1914.

Two later English studies of significance are Jesse Weston, *From Ritual to Romance,* 1920, one of T. S. Eliot's important sources, and Lord Ragland, *The Hero: A Study in Tradition, Myth, and Drama,* 1937, which analyzes the heroic figures of various cultures as versions of one archetype.

Examples of the method in practice would have to include Maud Bodkin, *Archetypal Patterns in Poetry,* 1934, which studies the influence of the "stored achievement" of the community upon authors. Among other leading examples are Northrup Frye, *Fearful Symmetry: A Study of Blake,* 1947, and *Anatomy of Criticism,* 1957; Richard Chase, *Quest for Myth,* 1949, and *Herman Melville: A Critical Study,* 1949; Francis Furgusson, *The Idea of a Theater,* 1949, and *The Human Image in Dramatic Literature,* 1957; and Leslie Fiedler, *An End to Innocence,* 1955, *No! in Thunder,* 1960, and *Love and Death in the American Novel,* 1960. *Chimera,* in the Spring of 1946, contains a symposium on the method, with pieces by Louise Bogan, William Troy, Jacques Barzun, and others. A number of pieces by Troy appearing in *Partisan Review* and *Kenyon Review* are excellent examples.

The most recent attack upon the approach is by Malcolm Cowley in *The Literary Situation,* 1954. An unfriendly article is by W. W. Douglas, "The Meaning of 'Myth' in Modern Criticism," *Modern Philology,* L, (1953).

Hamlet and Orestes

By Gilbert Murray

In the first of these studies we considered the conscious study and imitation of classical literature revealed in Milton's poetry. In the second we considered the origin of that classical literature itself—not indeed the models which it consciously imitated, but the quarry out of which its marbles were hewn, or the spring whose waters ran in its great rivers. In the last chapter we saw how this original raw material of poetry, the primitive religious Molpê, for the most part was not wrought to its highest forms except by passing through fire and torment, and that for this reason poetry still, in a sense, finds its models in the Heroic Age. But the unconscious tradition in poetry is not only greater in extent, it also reaches much further back into the past, than any deliberate human imitation.

I propose now to consider the influence of this unconscious tradition in a region where its presence has not been suspected.

My subject is the study of two great tragic characters, Hamlet and Orestes, regarded as traditional types. I do not compare play with play, but simply character with character, though in the course of the comparison I shall naturally consider the situations in which my heroes are placed and the other persons with whom they are associated.

Orestes in Greek is very clearly a traditional character. He occurs in poem after poem, in tragedy after tragedy, varying slightly in each one but always true to type. He is, I think, the most central and typical tragic hero on the Greek stage; and he occurs in no less than seven of our extant tragedies—eight if we count the *Iphigenia in Aulis,* where he is an infant—whereas Oedipus, for instance, only comes in three and Agamemnon in four. I shall use all these seven plays as material: namely, Aeschylus, *Choephoroe* and *Eumenides;* Sophocles, *Electra;* and Euripides, *Electra, Orestes, Iphigenia in Tauris* and *Andromache*. And we must realize that before any of these plays was written Orestes was a well established character both in religious worship and in epic and lyric tradition.

As for *Hamlet*, I note, in passing, the well known fragments of evidence which indicate the existence of a Hamlet tragedy before the publication of Shakespeare's Second Quarto in 1604. These are:

1602. A phrase in Dekker's *Satiromastix*, "My name's Hamlet: Revenge!"

1598. Gabriel Harvey's remarks about Shakespeare's *Hamlet*. The true date of this entry is disputed.

1596. Lodge, *Wit's Miserie and the World's Madness*: "He looks as pale as the ghost which cried so miserably at the theater like an oysterwife, Hamlet, revenge."

1594. Henslowe's Diary records a play called *Hamlet* as acted at Newington Butts Theatre on June 9.

The earliest reference seems to be in Nash's *Epistle* prefixed to Greene's *Menaphon*: it is dated 1589, but was perhaps printed in 1587. "Yet English Seneca read by candle light yeeldes many good sentences, as Bloud is a beggar, and so foorth: and if you intreate him faire in a frosty morning, he will affoord you whole Hamlets, I should say handfulls of tragicall speeches."

The play of *Hamlet* is extant in three main forms:

The First Quarto, dated 1603, but perhaps printed in 1602. It is entitled "The Tragicall Historie of Hamlet *Prince of Denmark* by William Shake-speare, As it hath been at divers times acted by his Highnesse servants in the Cittie of London: as also in the two Vniversities of Cambridge and Oxford and else-where." It is much shorter than the *Hamlet* which we commonly read, having only 2,143 lines, many of them incomplete, as against the 3,891 of the Globe edition. It differs from our version also in the order of the scenes and to some extent in plot. For instance, the Queen's innocence of her husband's murder is made quite explicit: when she hears how it was wrought she exclaims:

> *But, as I have a soule, I sweare by Heaven*
> *I never knew of this most horride murder;*

and thereafter she acts confidentially with Hamlet and Horatio. Also some of the names are different: for Polonius we have Corambis, and for Reynaldo, Montano.

The Second Quarto, dated 1604, describes itself as "enlarged to almoste as much againe as it was, according to the true and perfecte coppie."

Thirdly, there is the Folio of 1623. This omits a good deal that was in the Second Quarto, and contains some passages which are not in that edition but have their parallels in the First Quarto.

Thus *Hamlet*, like most of the great Elizabethan plays, presents itself to us as a whole that has been gradually built up, not as a single definitive creation made by one man in one effort. There was an old play called *Hamlet* extant about 1587, perhaps written by Kyd. It was worked over and improved by Shakespeare; improved doubtless again and again in the course of its different productions. We can trace additions; we can even trace changes of mind or repentances, as when the Folio of 1623 goes back to a discarded passage in the First Quarto. It is a live and growing play, apt no doubt to be slightly different at each performance, and growing steadily more profound, more rich, and more varied in its appeal.

And before it was an English play, it was a Scandinavian story: a very ancient Northern tale, not invented by any person, but just living, and doubtless from time to time growing and decaying, in oral tradition. It is recorded at length, of course with some remodeling, both conscious and unconscious, by Saxo Grammaticus in his great *History of the Danes* (*Gesta Danorum*), Books III and IV. Saxo wrote about the year 1185; he calls his hero Amlehtus, or Amloði, Prince of Jutland, and has worked in material that seems to come from the classical story of Brutus—Brutus the Fool, who cast out the Tarquins—and the deeds of Anlaf Curan, King of Ireland. But the story of Hamlet existed long before Saxo; for the prose *Edda* happens to quote a song by the

poet Snaebjørn, composed about 980, with a passing reference to "Amloði." And it must mean our Amloði; for our
Amloði in his pretended madness was a great riddle-maker,
and the song refers to one of his best riddles. He speaks in
Saxo of the sand as meal ground by the sea; and Snaebjørn's
song calls the sea "Amloði's meal-bin."

Besides Saxo we have a later form of the same legend in
the Icelandic *Ambales Saga.* The earliest extant manuscripts
of this belong to the seventeenth century.

Thus our sources for *Hamlet* will be (1) the various versions of the play known to us, (2) the story in Saxo Grammaticus and the *Ambales Saga,* and (3) some occasional
variants of these sagas.[1]

II

Now to our comparison.

1. The general situation. In all the versions, both Northern and Greek, the hero is the son of a king who has been
murdered and succeeded on the throne by a younger kinsman—a cousin, Aegisthus, in the Greek; a younger brother,
Feng or Claudius, in the Northern. The dead king's wife has
married his murderer. The hero, driven by supernatural commands, undertakes and carries through the duty of vengeance.

In Shakespeare the hero dies as his vengeance is accom-
plished; but this seems to be an innovation. In Saxo, *Ambales,*
and the Greek he duly succeeds to the kingdom. In Saxo there
is no mention of a ghost; the duty of vengeance is perhaps
accepted as natural. In *Ambales,* however, there are angels;
in the English, a ghost; in the Greek, dreams and visions of
the dead father, and an oracle.

2. In all versions of the story there is some shyness about
the mother-murder. In Saxo the mother is not slain; in
Shakespeare she is slain by accident, not deliberately murdered; in *Ambales* she is warned and leaves the burning hall

[1] There are, of course, numerous variants and offshoots of the
Hamlet story. See *Corpus Hamleticum* by Professor Josef Schick
of Munich.

just in time. In one of the variants the mother refuses to leave the hall and is burnt with her husband.[2] In the Greek versions she is deliberately slain, but the horror of the deed unseats the hero's reason. We shall consider this mother more at length later on.

3. In all the versions the hero is in some way under the shadow of madness. This is immensely important, indeed essential, in his whole dramatic character. It is present in all the versions, but is somewhat different in each.

In *Hamlet* the madness is assumed, but I trust I am safe in saying that there is something in the hero's character which at least makes one wonder if it is entirely assumed. I think the same may be said of Amloði and Ambales.

In the Greek the complete madness comes only as a result of the mother-murder; yet here too there is that in the hero's character which makes it easy for him to go mad. In the *Choephoroe*, where we see him before the deed, he is not normal. His language is strange and broken amid its amazing eloquence; he is a haunted man. In other plays, after the deed, he is seldom actually raving. But, like Hamlet in his mother's chamber, he sees visions which others cannot:

> *You cannot see them: only I can see.*[3]

He indulges freely in soliloquies;[4] especially, like Hamlet, he is subject to paralyzing doubts and hesitations, alternating with hot fits. For instance, once in the *Iphigenia* he suddenly wishes to fly and give up his whole enterprise, and has to be checked by Pylades:

> *O God, where hast thou brought me? what new snare*
> *Is this?—I slew my mother, I avenged*

[2] Halfdan is killed by his brother Frodi, who also takes his wife. Halfdan's sons, Helgi and Hroar, eventually burn Frodi at a feast. See Professor Elton's appendix to his translation of Saxo, edited by York Powell.
[3] *Choephoroe*, 1061; cf. *Orestes*, 255–279.
[4] *Iphigenia in Tauris*, 77–94, *Electra*, 367–390; cf. *Iphigenia in Tauris*, 940–978; *Choephoroe*, 268–305, and last scene.

My father at thy bidding. I have ranged
A homeless world, hunted by shapes of pain. . . .
. . . We still have time to fly for home,
Back to the galley quick, ere worse things come.

PYLADES

To fly we dare not, brother: 't is a thing
Not of our custom.[5]

Again, in the *Electra* he suspects that the god who commands
him to take vengeance may be an evil spirit in disguise:

How if some fiend of Hell
Hid in God's likeness spake that oracle?

One is reminded of Hamlet's words:

The spirit that I have seen
May be the devil.[6]

At the moment before the actual crisis he is seized with
horror and tries to hold back. In the *Choephoroe* this is given
in a line or two:

Pylades,
What can I? Dare I let my mother live?[7]

or with a different punctuation: "Let me spare my mother!"
In the *Electra* it is a whole scene, where he actually for the
moment forgets what it is that he has to do; he only remembers that it has something to do with his mother. Again he
vows, too late, after the mother-murder, that, if his dead
father had known all, he would never have urged him to such
a deed; he would rather

have knelt down
And hung his wreath of prayers about my beard,
To leave him unavenged.[8]

[5] *Iphigenia in Tauris,* 93–103.
[6] *Electra,* 979; *Hamlet,* II, 2.
[7] *Choephoroe,* 899.
[8] *Orestes,* 288–293.

In Shakespeare this belief is made a fact: the Ghost specially charges Hamlet not to kill Gertrude:

> *Taint not thy mind, nor let thy soul contrive*
> *Against thy Mother aught.*[9]

Is it too much to say that, in all these strangely characteristic speeches of Orestes, every line might have been spoken by Hamlet, and hardly a line by any other tragic character except those directly influenced by Orestes or Hamlet?

Now what do we find in the sagas? Both in Saxo and in *Ambales* the madness is assumed, entirely or mainly, but in its quality also it is utterly different from that of Shakespeare's hero. The saga Hamlet is not a highly wrought and sensitive man with his mind shaken by a terrible experience, he is a Fool, a gross Jester, covered with dirt and ashes, grinning and mowing and eating like a hog, spared by the murderer simply because he is considered too witless to be dangerous. The name "Amloði" itself means a fool. This side is emphasized most in *Ambales,* but it is clear enough in Saxo also and explains why he has combined his hero with the Fool, Brutus. Hamlet is a Fool, though his folly is partly assumed and hides unsuspected cunning.

4. The Fool.—It is very remarkable that Shakespeare, who did such wonders in his idealized and half-mystic treatment of the real Fool, should also have made his greatest tragic hero out of a Fool transfigured. Let us spend a few moments on noticing the remnants of the old Fool that subsist in the transfigured hero of the tragedies. For one thing, as has often been remarked, Hamlet's actual language is at times exactly that of the regular Shakespearean Fool: for example, with Polonius in Act II, scene 2; just before the play in Act III, scene 2, and after. But apart from that, there are other significant elements.

(*a*) The Fool's disguise.—Amloði and Brutus and Shakespeare's Hamlet feign madness; Orestes does not. Yet the element of disguise is very strong in Orestes. He is always

[9] *Hamlet,* I, 5; cf. also the tone in III, 4.

disguising his feelings: he does so in the *Choephoroe*, Sophocles' *Electra*, Euripides' *Electra* and *Iphigenia in Tauris*. In two passages further, he narrates how, in other circumstances, he had to disguise them:

I suffered in silence and made pretence not to see.[10]
I suffered, Oh, I suffered; but as things drove me I endured.[11]

This is like Shakespeare's Hamlet. It is also very like the saga Hamlet, who deliberately laughs in pretended idiocy to see his brother hanged.

Again, it is a marked feature of Orestes to be present in disguise, especially when he is supposed to be dead, and then at some crisis to reveal himself with startling effect. He is apt to be greeted by such words as "Undreamed-of phantom!" or "Who is this risen from the dead?" [12] He is present disguised and unknown in the *Choephoroe*, Sophocles' *Electra*, Euripides' *Electra* and *Iphigenia in Tauris;* he is in nearly every case supposed to be dead. In the *Choephoroe* and Sophocles' *Electra* he brings the funeral urn that is supposed to contain his own ashes; in the *Iphigenia* he interrupts his own funeral rites.

No other character in Greek tragedy behaves in this extraordinary way. But Saxo's Amloði does. When Amloði goes to England, he is suposed to be dead, and his funeral feast is in progress, when he walks in, "striking all men utterly aghast." [13]

In *Hamlet* there is surely a remnant of this motive, considerably softened. In Act V, 2, the Gravedigger scene, Hamlet has been present in disguise while the Gravedigger and the public thought he was in England, and the King and his confidants must have believed him dead, as they do in Saxo. Then comes the funeral—not his own, but Ophelia's; he stays hidden for a time, and then springs out, revealing himself: "This is I, Hamlet the Dane!" The words seem like

[10] *Iphigenia in Tauris,* 956.
[11] *Andromache,* 980.
[12] *Orestes,* 385, 879, 478 f.; *Iphigenia,* 1361 (cf. 1321).
[13] *Gesta Danorum,* IV, 95.

an echo of that cry that is so typical in the Greek tragedies:
" 'Tis I, Orestes, Agamemnon's son!" [14] One is reminded, too,
of the quotation from the pre-Shakespearean *Hamlet* in
Dekker's *Satiromastix* of 1602: "My name's Hamlet! Revenge!" It may well be that these melodramatic appearances
were more prominent in the tradition before Shakespeare.

(*b*) The disorder of the Fool.—This disguise motive has
led us away from the Fool, though it is closely connected
with him. Another curious element of the Fool that lingers
on is his dirtiness and disorder in dress. Saxo says that Amloði "remained always in his mother's house, utterly listless
and unclean, flinging himself on the ground and bespattering
his person with foul dirt." [15] Ambales was worse; enough to
say that he slept in his mother's room and "ashes and filth
reeked off him." [16] We remember Ophelia's description of
Hamlet's coming to her chamber:

> *his doublet all unbraced;*
> *No hat upon his head; his stockings fouled,*
> *Ungartered and down-gyvèd to the ankle,*
> *Pale as his shirt . . .* [17]

Similarly, Orestes, at the beginning of the play that bears his
name, is found with his sister, ghastly pale, with foam on
his mouth, gouts of rheum in his eyes, his long hair matted
with dirt and "made wild with long unwashenness." "Poor
curls, poor filthy face," his sister says to him. [18] In the *Electra*,
too, he is taken for a brigand,[19] which suggests some lack of
neatness in dress; in the *Iphigenia* we hear of his foaming at
the mouth and rolling on the ground.[20] In both plays, it is
true, Orestes carries with him an air of princely birth, but

[14] *Andromache*, 884; *Iphigenia*, 1361; cf. his sudden apparitions
in *Choephoroe*, 212 ff., *Electra*, 220, also the recognition scenes.
[15] Saxo, 88.
[16] *Ambales*, pp. 73–75, 77.
[17] *Hamlet*, II, i.
[18] *Electra*, 219.
[19] *Orestes*, 219–226; cf. 880 ff.
[20] *Iphigenia in Tauris*, 307 f.

so, no doubt, did Hamlet, whatever state his stockings were in.

(c) *The Fool's rudeness of speech.*—Besides being dirty and talking in riddles, the Fool was abusive and gross in his language. This is the case to some degree in Saxo, though no doubt the monk has softened Amloði's words. It is much emphasized in Ambales. That hero's language is habitually outrageous, especially to women. This outrageousness of speech has clearly descended to Hamlet, in whom it seems to be definitely intended as a morbid trait. He is obsessed by revolting images. He does

> *like a whore unpack his heart in words*
> *And fall a-cursing like a very drab,*

and he rages at himself because of it.

(d) *The Fool on women.*—Now the general style of Greek tragedy will not admit any gross language. So Orestes has lost this trait. But a trace of it perhaps remains. Both Orestes and Hamlet are given to expressing violently cynical opinions about women.[21] The *Orestes* bristles with parallels to the ravings of Hamlet's "Get-thee-to-a-nunnery" scene.[22] The hero is haunted by his "most pernicious woman." All women want to murder their husbands; it is only a question of time. Then they will fly in tears to their children, show their breasts, and cry for sympathy. We may, perhaps, couple with these passages the famous speech where he denies any blood relationship with his mother,[23] and the horrible mad line where he says he could never weary of killing evil women.[24]

Both heroes also tend—if I may use such an expression—to bully any woman they are left alone with. Amloði in Saxo mishandles his foster sister—though the passage is obscure—and utters violent reproaches to the Queen. (The scene is

[21] *Orestes,* 246–251, 566–572, 935–942.
[22] *Hamlet,* III, 1.
[23] *Orestes,* 552 ff., based on the quibble in Aeschylus' *Eumenides,* 657–661.
[24] *Orestes,* 1590.

taken over by Shakespeare.) Ambales is habitually misbehaving in this way. Hamlet bullies Ophelia cruelly and "speaks daggers" to the Queen. He never meets any other woman. Orestes is very surly to Iphigenia;[25] draws his sword on Electra in one play, and takes her for a devil in another;[26] holds his dagger at the throat of Hermione till she faints;[27] denounces, threatens, and kills Clytemnestra, and tries to kill Helen. There are not many tragic heroes with such an extreme antifeminist record.

The above, I think, are, all of them, elements that go deep into the character of the hero as a stage figure. I will now add some slighter and more external points of resemblance.

1. In both traditions the hero has been away from home when the main drama begins, Orestes in Phocis, Hamlet in Wittenberg. This point, as we shall see later, has some significance.

2. The hero in both traditions—and in both rather strangely —goes on a ship, is captured by enemies who want to kill him, but escapes. And as Hamlet has a sort of double escape, first from the King's treacherous letter, and next from the pirates, so Orestes, in the *Iphigenia,* escapes once from the Taurians who catch him on the shore, and again from the pursuers in the ship. Ambales has similar adventures at sea; and the original Amloði seems to have had nautical connections, since the sea was his meal-bin, and the ship's rudder his knife.[28]

3. Much more curious, and indeed extraordinary, is the following point, which occurs in Saxo, *Ambales,* and the Greek, but not in Shakespeare. We have seen that the hero is always a good deal connected with the dead, with graves and ghosts and funerals. In the sagas on one occasion he wins a great battle after a preliminary defeat, by a somewhat ghastly strategem. He picks up his dead—or his dead and wounded

[25] *Iphigenia,* 482 ff.
[26] *Electra,* 220 ff.; *Orestes,* 264.
[27] *Orestes,* 1575 ff.
[28] See also a pamphlet, *Grotta Söngr and the Orkney and Shetland Quern,* by A. W. Johnston, 1912.

—and ties them upright to stakes and rocks, so that, when his pursuers renew their attack, they find themselves affronted by an army of dead men standing upright, and fly in dismay. Now in the *Electra*, Orestes prays to his father:

> Girt with thine own dead armies wake, Oh wake,[29]

or, quite literally, "Come bringing every dead man as a fellow fighter." One would almost think here that there was some direct influence—of course with a misunderstanding. But the parallel may be a mere chance.

4. I would not lay much stress on the coincidence about the serpent. Clytemnestra dreams that she gives birth to a serpent, which bites her breast. Orestes, hearing of it, accepts the omen: he will be the serpent. And at the last moment, Clytemnestra so recognizes him:

> Oh, God;
> This is the serpent that I bore and suckled.

We are reminded of the Ghost's words:

> The serpent that did sting thy father's life
> Now wears his crown.[30]

However, Shakespeare abounds in serpents, and I have found no trace of this serpent motive in the sagas.

5. Nor yet would I make anything of the point that both Hamlet and Orestes on one occasion have the enemy in their power and put off killing him in order to provide a worse death afterwards. This is important in *Hamlet*—

> Now might I do it pat, now he is praying;[31]

but only occurs as a slight incident in Sophocles' *Electra*,[32]

[29] *Electra,* 680.
[30] *Choephoroe,* 527–550, 928; *Orestes,* 479; *Hamlet,* I, 5.
[31] *Hamlet,* III, 3.
[32] Sophocles, *Electra,* 1491 ff.

and may be due merely to the Greek rule of having no violent deaths on the stage. Nor is there much significance in the fact that in both traditions the hero has a scene in which he hears the details of his father's death and bursts into uncontrollable grief.[33] Such a scene is in both cases almost unavoidable.

Let us now follow this father for a little while. He was, perhaps naturally, a great warrior. He "slew Troy's thousands"; he "smote the sledded Polacks on the ice." It is a particular reproach that the son of such a man should be so slow-tempered, "peaking like John-a-dreams," and so chary of shedding blood.[34] The father was also generally idealized and made magnificent. He had some manly faults, yet ."He was a man, taking him all in all." He was "a king of kings." [35] A special contrast is drawn between him and his successor:

> It was so easy to be true. A King
> Was thine, not feebler, not in any thing
> Below Aegisthus; one whom Hellas chose
> Above all kings.[36]

One might continue: "Look on this picture and on this."

We may also notice that the successor, besides the vices which are necessary, or at least desirable, in his position, is in both cases accused of drunkenness,[37] which seems irrelevant and unusual.

Lastly, and more important, one of the greatest horrors about the father's death in both traditions is that he died without the due religious observances. In the Greek tragedies, this lack of religious burial is almost the central horror of the whole story. Wherever it is mentioned it comes as something intolerable, maddening; it breaks Orestes down. A good

[33] *Choephoroe*, 430 ff.; Euripides, *Electra*, 290; *Hamlet*, I, 5, "Oh, all you host of heaven," etc.
[34] *Electra*, 275 ff., 336 ff.; cf. 130, 245.
[35] *Ibid.*, 1066 ff.
[36] *Ibid.*, 320 ff., 917, 1080.
[37] *Hamlet*, I, 4; *Electra*, 326.

instance is the scene in the *Choephoroe*, where Orestes and Electra are kneeling at their father's grave, awakening the dead and working their own passion to the murder point.

ELECTRA

Ah, pitiless one, my mother, mine enemy! With an enemy's burial didst thou bury him: thy King without his people, without dying rites; thine husband without a tear!

ORESTES

All, all, in dishonour thou tellest it, woe is me! And for that dishonouring she shall pay her punishment: by the will of the Gods, by the will of my hands: Oh, let me but slay, and then perish!

He is now ripe for the hearing of the last horror:

LEADER OF THE CHORUS

His body was mangled to lay his ghost! There, learn it all . . .

and the scene becomes hysterical.[38]

The atmosphere is quite different in the English. But the lack of dying rites remains, and retains a strange dreadfulness:

> *Cut off even in the blossom of my sin,*
> *Unhousel'd, disappointed, unanel'd.*

To turn to the other characters: in both the dramatic traditions the hero has a faithful friend and confidant, who also arrives from Phocis-Wittenberg, and advises him about his revenge. This friend, when the hero is threatened with death, wishes to die too, but is prevented by the hero and told to "absent him from felicity awhile." [39] This motive is worked out more at length in the Greek than in the English.

[38] *Choephoroe*, 435 ff.; cf. Sophocles, *Electra*, 443 ff; Euripides, *Electra*, 289, 323 ff.
[39] *Orestes*, 1069 ff.; *Iphigenia*, 675 ff.; *Hamlet*, V, 2.

Also the friendship between Orestes and Pylades is more intense than—between Hamlet and Horatio; naturally, since devoted friendship always plays a greater part in antiquity. But Hamlet's words are strong:

> Give me that man
> That is not passion's slave, and I will wear him
> In my heart's core, ay, in my heart of heart,
> As I do thee.[40]

I find no Pylades-Horatio in the sagas; though there is a brother to Hamlet, sometimes older and sometimes a twin. In some of the variants also, such as the stories of Helgi and Hroar, there are pairs of avengers, one of whom is mad, or behaves like a madman.

Next comes a curious point. At first sight it seems as if all the Electra motive were lacking in the modern play, all the Ophelia-Polonius motive in the ancient. Yet I am not sure.

In all the ancient plays Orestes is closely connected with a strange couple—a young woman and a very old man. They are his sister Electra and her only true friend, an old and trusted servant of the dead King, who saved Orestes' life in childhood. In Euripides this old man habitually addresses Electra as "my daughter"—not merely as "child" ($\pi a\hat{i}s$), but really "daughter" ($\theta\nu\gamma\acute{a}\tau\eta\rho$),[41] while she in return carefully avoids calling him "Father," because that is to her a sacred name and she will never use it lightly. But in Sophocles she says emphatically:

> "Hail, Father. For it is as if in thee
> I saw my father!"[42]

In the Elizabethan play this couple—if we may so beg the question—has been transformed. The sister is now the mistress, Ophelia; the old servant of the King—for so we must surely describe Polonius or Corambis—remains, but has be-

[40] *Hamlet,* III, 2.
[41] Euripides, *Electra,* 493, 563.
[42] Sophocles, *Electra,* 1361.

come Ophelia's real father. And the relations of both to the hero are quite different.

The change is made more intelligible when we look at the sagas. There the young woman is not a sister but a foster sister; like Electra she helps Amloði, like Ophelia she is his beloved. The old servant of the King is not her father—so far like the Greek; but there the likeness stops. He spies on Amloði in his mother's chamber and is killed for his pains, as in the English.

We may notice, further, that in all the Electra plays alike a peculiar effect is got from Orestes' first sight of his sister, either walking in a funeral procession or alone in mourning garb.[43] He takes her for a slave, and cries, "Can that be the unhappy Electra?" A similar but stronger effect is reached in *Hamlet*,[44] when Hamlet, seeing an unknown funeral procession approach, gradually discovers whose it is and cries in horror: "What, the fair Ophelia?"

Lastly, there is something peculiar, at any rate in the Northern tradition—I will take the Greek later—about the hero's mother. Essentially it is this: she has married the murderer of her first husband and is in part implicated in the murder, and yet the tradition instinctively keeps her sympathetic. In our *Hamlet* she is startled to hear that her first husband was murdered, yet one does not feel clear that she is perfectly honest with herself. She did not know Claudius had poisoned him, but probably that was because she obstinately refused to put together things which she did know and which pointed towards that conclusion. At any rate, though she does not betray Hamlet, she sticks to Claudius and shares his doom. In the First Quarto she is more definitely innocent of the murder; when she learns of it she changes sides, protects Hamlet, and acts in confidence with Horatio. In Saxo her attitude is as ambiguous as in the later *Hamlet;* she is friendly to Amloði and does not betray him, yet does not turn against Feng either.

[43] *Choephoroe,* 16; Sophocles, *Electra,* 80; Euripides, *Electra,* 107 ff.
[44] Act V, scene 1.

A wife who loves her husband and bears him children, and then is wedded to his slayer and equally loves him, and does it all in a natural and unemotional manner: it seems somewhat unusual.

And one's surprise is a little increased to find that in Saxo Amlóði's wife, Hermutrude, behaves in the same way as his mother has done. On Amlóði's death she marries his slayer, Wiglek. Again, there is an Irish king, historical to a great degree, who has got deeply entangled with the Hamlet story. His name is Anlaf Curan. Now his wife, Gormflaith, carried this practice so far that the chronicler comments on it. After Anlaf's defeat at Tara she married his conqueror Malachy, and on Malachy's defeat she married Malachy's conqueror Brian. We will consider later the Greek parallels to this enigmatic lady. For the present we must admit that she is very unlike the Clytemnestra of Greek tragedy, whose motives are studied in every detail, who boldly hates her husband and murders him. But there are traces in Homer of a far less passionate Clytemnestra.

III

Now I hope I have not tried artificially to make a case or to press my facts too hard. I think it will be conceded that the points of similarity, some fundamental and some perhaps superficial, between these two tragic heroes are rather extraordinary, and are made the more striking by the fact that Hamlet and Orestes are respectively the very greatest or most famous heroes of the world's two great ages of tragedy.

The points of similarity, we must notice, fall into two parts. There are, first, the broad similarities of situation between what we may call the original sagas on both sides; that is, the general story of Orestes and of Hamlet respectively. But, secondly, there is something much more remarkable: when these sagas were worked up into tragedies, quite independently and on very different lines, by the great dramatists of Greece and England, not only do most of the old similarities remain, but a number of new similarities are developed. That is, Aeschylus, Euripides, and Shakespeare are strikingly similar in certain points which do not occur at all in Saxo or *Ambales* or the Greek epic. For instance, the hero's madness is the same in Shakespeare and Euripides, but is totally different from the madness in Saxo or *Ambales*.

What is the connection? All critics seem to be agreed that Shakespeare did not study these Greek tragedians directly. And, if any one should suggest that he did, there are many considerations which would, I think, make that hypothesis unserviceable. Of course, it is likely enough that some of Shakespeare's university friends, who knew Greek, may have told him in conversation of various stories or scenes or effects in Greek plays. Miss Spens suggests the name of Marston. She shows that he consciously imitated the Greek—for instance, in getting a special effect out of the absence of funeral rites— and probably had considerable influence on Shakespeare. This is a highly important line of inquiry, but such an explanation would not carry us very far with Shakespeare, and would be no help with Saxo.

Neither can it be indirect imitation through Seneca. Orestes only appears once in the whole of Seneca, and then he is a baby unable to speak.[45] And in any case Saxo does not seem to have studied Seneca.

Will Scandinavian mercenaries at the Court of Byzantium help us? Or, simpler perhaps, will the Roman conquest of Britain? Both these channels were doubtless important in opening up a connection between the North and the Mediterranean, and revealing to the Northmen the rich world of classical story. But neither explanation is at all adequate. It might possibly provide a bridge between the traditional Orestes and Saxo's Amloði; but they are not in any pressing need of a bridge. It does not provide any bridge where it is chiefly wanted, between the Orestes of tragedy and Shakespeare's Hamlet.

There seems to have been, so far as our recorded history goes, no chance of imitation, either direct or indirect. Are

[45] Seneca, *Agamemnon,* 910–943.

we thrown back, then, on a much broader and simpler though rather terrifying hypothesis, that the field of tragedy is by nature so limited that these similarities are inevitable? Certain situations and stories and characters—certain subjects, we may say, for shortness—are naturally tragic; these subjects are quite few in number, and, consequently, two poets or sets of poets trying to find or invent tragic subjects are pretty sure to fall into the same paths. I think there is some truth in this suggestion; and I shall make use of something like it later. But I do not think that in itself it is enough, or nearly enough, to explain such close similarities, both detailed and fundamental, as those we are considering. I feel as I look at these two traditions that there must be a connection somewhere.

There is none within the limits of our historical record; but can there be any outside? There is none between the dramas, nor even directly between the sagas; but can there be some original connection between the myths, or the primitive religious rituals, on which the dramas are ultimately based? And can it be that in the last analysis the similarities between Euripides and Shakespeare are simply due to the natural working out, by playwrights of special genius, of the dramatic possibilities latent in that original seed? If this is so, it will lead us to some interesting conclusions.

To begin with, then, can we discover the original myth out of which the Greek Orestes-saga has grown? (I do not deny the possible presence of an historical element also; but if history is there, there is certainly myth mixed up with it.) The saga contains two parts:

(1) Agamemnon, "king of men," is dethroned and slain by a younger kinsman, the banished Aegisthus, who is helped by the Queen. (2) His successor, in turn, dreads and tries to destroy the next heir to the throne, Orestes, who, however, comes home secretly and, helped by a young Queen, Electra, slays him and the Queen with him.

The story falls into its place in a clearly marked group of Greek or pre-Greek legends. Let us recall the primeval kings of the world in Hesiod.

First there was Ouranos and his wife Gaia. Ouranos lived in dread of his children, and "hid them away" till his son Kronos rose and cast him out, helped by the Queen-Mother Gaia.

Then came King Kronos with his wife Rhea. He, too, feared his children and "swallowed them," till his son Zeus rose and cast him out, helped by the Queen-Mother Rhea.

Then, thirdly—but the story cannot continue. For Zeus is still ruling and cannot have been cast out. But he was saved by a narrow margin. He was about to marry the sea-maiden Thetis, when Prometheus warned him that, if he did so, the son of Thetis would be greater than he and cast him out from heaven. And, great as is my love for Thetis, I have little doubt that she would have been found helping her son in his criminal behavior.

In the above cases the new usurper is represented as the son of the old King and Queen. Consequently the Queen-Mother, though she helps him, does not marry him, as she does when he is merely a younger kinsman. But there is one great saga in which the marriage of mother and son has remained, quite unsoftened and unexpurgated. In Thebes King Laïus and his wife Jocasta knew that their son would slay and dethrone his father. Laïus orders the son's death, but he is saved by the Queen-Mother, and, after slaying and dethroning his father, marries her. She is afterwards slain or dethroned with him, as Clytemnestra is with Aegisthus, and Gertrude with Claudius.

There is clearly a common element in all these stories, and the reader will doubtless have recognized it. It is the world-wide ritual story of what we may call the Golden-Bough Kings. That ritual story is, as I have tried to show elsewhere, the fundamental conception that forms the basis of Greek tragedy, and not Greek tragedy only. It forms the basis of the traditional Mummers' Play, which, though deeply degraded and vulgarized, is not quite dead yet in the countries of Northern Europe and lies at the root of so large a part of all the religions of mankind.

It is unnecessary, I hope, to make any long explanation of

the Vegetation-kings or Year-daemons. But there are perhaps two points that we should remember, to save us from confusion later on. First, there are two early modes of reckoning: you can reckon by seasons or half-years, by summers and winters; or you can reckon with the whole year as your unit. On the first system a Summer-king or Vegetation-spirit is slain by Winter and rises from the dead in the spring. On the second each Year-king comes first as a wintry slayer, weds the queen, grows proud and royal, and then is slain by the Avenger of his predecessor. These two conceptions cause some confusion in the myths, as they do in most forms of the Mummers' Play.

The second point to remember is that this death and vengeance was really enacted among our remote ancestors in terms of human bloodshed. The sacred king really had "slain the slayer" and was doomed himself to be slain. The queen might either be taken on by her husband's slayer, or else slain with her husband. It is no pale myth or allegory that has so deeply dyed the first pages of human history. It is man's passionate desire for the food that will save him from starvation, his passionate memory of the streams of blood, willing and unwilling, that have been shed to keep him alive. But for all this subject I must refer the reader to the classic expositions of the *Golden Bough,* and their brilliant development in Dr. Jane Harrison's *Themis.*

Thus Orestes, the madman and king-slayer, takes his place beside Brutus the Fool, who expelled the Tarquins, and Amloði the Fool, who burnt King Feng at his winter feast. The great Greek scholar, Hermann Usener, some years since, on quite other grounds, identified Orestes as a Winter-god, a slayer of the Summer.[46] He is the man of the cold mountains who slays annually the Red Neoptolemus at Delphi; he is the ally of death and the dead; he comes suddenly in the dark; he is mad and raging, like the Winter-god Maimaktes and the November storms. In Athenian ritual, it seems, a cloak was actually woven for him in late autumn, lest he

[46] *Heilige Handlung,* in the *Archiv für Religionswissenschaft,* 1904.

should be too cold.[47] Thus he is quite unlike the various bright heroes who slay dragons of darkness; he finds his comrade in the Bitter Fool—may we say the bitter Amloði?—of many Mummers' Plays, who is the Slayer of the Joyous King.

This is all very well for Orestes; but can we talk thus of Hamlet-Amloði? Is it possible to bring him into the region of myth, and myth of the same kind that we find in Greece? Here I am quite off my accustomed beat, and must speak with diffidence and under correction from my betters. But it seems beyond doubt, even to my most imperfect scrutiny of the material, that the same forms of myth and the same range of primitive religious conceptions are to be found in Scandinavia as in other Aryan countries.

There are several wives in the Ynglinga saga who seem to belong to the Gaia–Rhea–Clytemnestra–Jocasta type. For instance, King Vanlandi was married to Drifa of Finland, and was killed by her in conjunction with their son Visburr, who succeeded to the kingdom. (The slaying was done by witchcraft; but no jury could, I think, exculpate Visburr.)

Visburr in turn married the daughter of Aude the Wealthy. Like Agamemnon, he was unfaithful to his wife, so she left him and sent her two sons to talk to him, and duly, in the proper ritual manner, to burn him in his house—just as the Hamlet of saga burned King Feng, just as the actual Northern villagers at their festival burned the Old Year.

Again, there are clear traces of kings who are sacrificed and are succeeded by their slayers. Most of the Yngling kings die in sacrificial ways. One is confessedly sacrificed to avert famine, one killed by a sacrificial bull, one falls off his horse in a temple and dies, one burns himself on a pyre at a festival. Another—like Ouranos and Kronos and the other child-swallowers—sacrifices one of his sons periodically in order to prolong his own life. I cite these cases merely to show that such ideas were apparently current in primitive Norse society as well as elsewhere. But the matter is really clinched by

[47] Aristophanes, *Birds*, 712.

Saxo himself. He not only gives us the tale of Ole, King of the Beggars, who came in disguise, with one servant dressed as a woman, to King Thore's house, got himself hailed as king in mockery, and then slew Thore and took the crown. He definitely tells us, in a story about the Sclavs, that "by public law of the ancients the succession to the throne belonged to him who should slay the king." [48]

So that when we find that the Hamlet of saga resembles Orestes so closely; when we find that he is the Bitter Fool and king-slayer; when especially we find that this strange part of wedding—if not helping—their husband's slayer and successor is played alike by Hamlet's mother, whatever her name, Gerutha, Gertrude, or Amba; and by Amloði's mother and by Ambales' mother, and by the mother of divers variants of Hamlet, like Helgi and Hroar; and by Hamlet's wife, and by the wife of Anlaf Curan, who is partly identified with Hamlet, we can hardly hesitate to draw the same sort of conclusion as would naturally follow in a Greek story. Hamlet is more deeply involved in this Clytemnestra-like atmosphere than any person I know of outside Hesiod. And one cannot fail to be reminded of Oedipus and Jocasta by the fact, which is itself of no value in the story but is preserved both in Saxo and the *Ambales Saga*, that Amloði slept in his mother's chamber.[49]

There is something strangely characteristic in the saga treatment of this ancient Queen-Mother, a woman under the shadow of adultery, the shadow of incest, the shadow of murder, who is yet left in most of the stories a motherly and sympathetic character. Clytemnestra is an exception, and perhaps Gormflaith. But Gaia, Rhea, and even Jocasta, are all motherly and sympathetic. So is Gerutha, the wife of Ørvandil and the mother of Amleth, and Amba the mother of Ambales.[50] So is Groa, the usual wife of Ørvandil, who is probably the same person as Gerutha. "Groa," says Professor

[48] *Gesta Danorum*, 254, 277.
[49] Saxo, 88; *Ambales*, p. 119, *et ante*, ed. Gollancz.
[50] In the extant form of the *Ambales Saga* Amba's personal chastity is preserved by a miracle; such an exception approves the rule.

Rydberg, "was a tender person devoted to the members of her family." The trait remains even in Shakespeare. "Gertrude," says Professor Bradley, "had a soft animal nature. . . . She loved to be happy like a sheep in the sun, and to do her justice she loved to see others happy, like more sheep in the sun." Just the right character for our Mother Earth! For, of course, that is who she is. The Greek stories speak her name openly: Gaia and Rhea are confessed Earth-Mothers, Jocasta only a few stages less so. One cannot apply moral disapproval to the annual remarriages of Mother Earth with the new Spring-god; nor yet possibly to the impersonal and compulsory marriages of the human queen in certain very primitive stages of society. But later on, when life has become more self-conscious and sensitive, if once a poet or dramatist gets to thinking of the story, and tries to realize the position and feelings of this eternally traitorous wife, this eternally fostering and protecting mother, he cannot but feel in her that element of inward conflict which is the seed of great drama. She is torn between husband, lover, and son; and the avenging son, the mother-murderer, how is he torn?

English tragedy has followed the son. Yet Gerutha, Amba, Gertrude, Hermutrude, Gormflaith, Gaia, Rhea, Jocasta—there is tragedy in all of them, and it is in the main the same tragedy. Why does the most tragic of all of them, Clytemnestra, stand out of the picture?

We can only surmise. For one thing, Clytemnestra, like Gertrude in some stories, has both the normal experiences of the primitive king's wife. She both marries her husband's slayer and is slain by his avenger; and both parts of her story are equally emphasized, which is not the case with the other heroines. Their deaths are generally softened or ignored. But, apart from this, I am inclined to lay most stress on the deliberate tragic art of Aeschylus. He received perhaps from the tradition a Clytemnestra not much more articulate than Gerutha; but it needed only a turn of the wrist to change her from a silent and passive figure to a woman seething with tragic passions. If Saxo had been a man like Aeschylus, or if Shakespeare had made Gertrude his central figure instead of Hamlet, Clytemnestra would perhaps not have stood so much alone.

And what of Hamlet himself as a mythical character? I find, almost to my surprise, exactly the evidence I should have liked to find. Hamlet in Saxo is the son of Horvendillus or Ørvandil, an ancient Teutonic god connected with dawn and the spring. His great toe, for instance, is now the morning star. (It was frozen off; that is why it shines like ice.) His wife was Groa, who is said to be the Green Earth; he slew his enemy Collerus—Kollr the Hooded, or perhaps the Cold—in what Saxo calls "a sweet and spring-green spot" in a budding wood. He was slain by his brother and avenged by his son. The sort of conclusion toward which I, on my different lines, was groping had already been drawn by several of the recognized Scandinavian authorities: notably by Professor Gollancz (who especially calls attention to the part played by the hero's mother), by Adolf Zinzow, and by Victor Rydberg. Professor Elton is more guarded, but his conclusions point, on the whole, in the same direction. And the whole of the evidence has been greatly strengthened since these words were first published, by the appearance of Miss Phillpotts's remarkable book, *The Elder Edda*.[51]

Thus, if these arguments are trustworthy, we finally run the Hamlet-saga to earth in the same ground as the Orestes-saga: in that prehistoric and world-wide ritual battle of Summer and Winter, of Life and Death, which has played so vast a part in the mental development of the human race and especially, as Mr. E. K. Chambers has shown us, in the history of medieval drama. Both heroes have the notes of the winter

[51] Gollancz, *Hamlet in Iceland*, Introduction; Zinzow, *Die Hamlet saga an und mit verwandten Sagen erläutert*, 1877; Rydberg, *Teutonic Mythology*, English tr. by Anderson, 1889; Elton, Appendix II to his translation of Saxo, edited by York Powell; Bertha S. Phillpotts, *The Elder Edda* (Cambridge, 1920). Rydberg goes so far as to identify Hamlet with Orvandil's famous son Swipdag. "Two Dissertations on the Hamlet of Saxo and of Shakespeare" by R. G. Latham contain linguistic and mythological suggestions. I have not come across the works of Gubernatis mentioned in Ward, *English Dramatic Literature*, ii, 165.

about them rather than summer, though both are on the side
of right against wrong. Hamlet is no joyous and triumphant
slayer. He is clad in black, he rages alone, he is the Bitter
Fool who must slay the King.[52]

IV

It seems a strange thing, this gradual shaping and reshaping
of a primitive folktale, in itself rather empty and devoid of
character, until it issues in a great tragedy which shakes the
world. Yet in Greek literature, I am sure, the process is a
common, almost a normal, one. Myth is defined by a Greek
writer as τὰ λεγόμενα ἐπὶ τοῖς δρωμένοις, "the things said over
a ritual act." For a certain agricultural rite, let us suppose,
you tore a corn sheaf in pieces and scattered the grain; and
to explain why you did so, you told a myth. "There was once
a young and beautiful prince who was torn in pieces. . . ."
Was he torn by hounds or wild beasts in requital for some
strange sin? Or was he utterly innocent, torn by mad Thracian
women or devilish Titans, or the working of an unjust curse?
As the group in the village talks together, and begins to muse
and wonder and make unconscious poetry, the story gets
better and stronger and ends by being the tragedy of Pen-
theus or Hippolytus or Actaeon or Dionysus himself. Of
course, an element of history must be present also. Life was
not eventless in primitive times any more than it is now.
Things happened, and people were moved by them at the
time and talked about them afterwards. But to observe
exactly, and to remember and report exactly, is one of the
very latest and rarest of human accomplishments. By the
help of much written record and much mental training we
can now manage it pretty well. But early man was at the time
too excited to observe, and afterwards too indifferent to
record, and always too much beset by fixed forms of thought
ever to take in concrete facts exactly. (As a matter of fact,
he did not even wish to do so; he was aiming at something

[52] I believe this figure of the Fool to be capable of further analysis, but will not pursue the question here.

quite different.) In any case, the facts, as they happened, were thrown swiftly into the same crucible as the myths. Men did not research. They did not keep names and dates distinct. They talked together and wondered and followed their musings, till a historical king of Ireland grew very like the old mythical Amloði, a historical king of Mycenae took on part of the story of a primitive Ouranos or Sky-King wedded to an Earth-Mother. And in later times it was the myth that lived and grew great rather than the history. The things that thrill and amaze us in *Hamlet* or the *Agamemnon* are not any historical particulars about medieval Elsinore or prehistoric Mycenae, but things belonging to the old stories and the old magic rites, which stirred and thrilled our forefathers five and six thousand years ago; set them dancing all night on the hills, tearing beasts and men in pieces, and giving up their own bodies to a ghastly death, in hope thereby to keep the green world from dying and to be the saviors of their own people.

I am not trying to utter a paradox, or even to formulate a theory. I am not for a moment questioning or belittling the existence, or the overwhelming artistic value, of individual genius. I trust no one will suspect me of so doing. I am simply trying to understand a phenomenon which seems, before the days of the printed book and the widespread reading public, to have occurred quite normally and constantly in works of imaginative literature, and doubtless in some degree is occurring still.

What does our hypothesis imply? It seems to imply, first, a great unconscious solidarity and continuity, lasting from age to age, among all the children of the poets, both the makers and the callers-forth, both the artists and the audiences. In artistic creation, as in all the rest of life, the traditional element is far larger, the purely inventive element far smaller, than the unsophisticated man supposes.

Further, it implies that in the process of *traditio*—that is, of being handed on from generation to generation, constantly modified and expurgated, refelt and rethought—a subject sometimes shows a curious power of almost eternal durability. It can be vastly altered; it may seem utterly transformed. Yet some inherent quality still remains, and significant details are repeated quite unconsciously by generation after generation of poets. Nay, more. It seems to show that often there is latent in some primitive myth a wealth of detailed drama, waiting only for the dramatist of genius to discover it and draw it forth. Of course, we must not exaggerate this point. We must not say that *Hamlet* or the *Electra* is latent in the original ritual as a flower is latent in the seed. The seed, if it just gets its food, is bound to develop along a certain fixed line; the myth or ritual is not. It depends for its development on too many live people and too many changing and complex conditions. We can only say that some natural line of growth is there, and in the case before us it seems to have asserted itself both in large features and in fine details, in a rather extraordinary way. The two societies in which the Hamlet and Orestes tragedies arose were very dissimilar; the poets were quite different in character, and quite independent; even the particular plays themselves differed greatly in plot and setting and technique and most other qualities; the only point of contact lies at their common origin many thousand years ago, and yet the fundamental identity still shows itself, almost unmistakable.

This conception may seem strange; but after all, in the history of religion it is already a proved and accepted fact, this "almost eternal durability" of primitive conceptions and even primitive rites. Our hypothesis will imply that what is already known to happen in religion may also occur in imaginative drama.

If this is so, it seems only natural that those subjects, or some of those subjects, which particularly stirred the interest of primitive men, should still have an appeal to certain very deep-rooted human instincts. I do not say that they will always move us now; but, when they do, they will tend to do so in ways which we recognize as particularly profound and poetical. This comes in part from their original quality; in part, I suspect, it depends on mere repetition. We all know the emotional charm possessed by famous and familiar words and names, even to hearers who do not understand the words and know little of the bearers of the names. I suspect that a charm of that sort lies in these stories and situations, which are—I cannot quite keep clear of metaphor—deeply implanted in the memory of the race, stamped, as it were, upon our physical organism. We have forgotten their faces and their voices; we say that they are strange to us. Yet there is that within us which leaps at the sight of them, a cry of the blood which tells us we have known them always.

Of course, it is an essential part of the whole process of Tradition that the mythical material is constantly castigated and rekindled by comparison with real life. That is where realism comes in, and literary skill and imagination. An element drawn from real life was there, no doubt, even at the beginning. The earliest myth-maker never invented in a vacuum. He really tried—in Aristotle's famous phrase—to tell "the sort of thing that would happen"; only his conception of "what would happen" was, by our standards, a little wild. Then, as man's experience of life grew larger and calmer and more objective, his conception of "the sort of thing that would happen" grew more competent. It grew ever nearer to the truth of Nature, to its variety, to its reasonableness, to its infinite subtlety. And in the greatest ages of literature there seems to be, among other things, a power of preserving due proportion between these opposite elements—the expression of boundless primitive emotion and the subtle and delicate representation of life. In plays like *Hamlet* or the *Agamemnon* or the *Electra* we have certainly fine and flexible character study, a varied and well wrought story, a full command of the technical instruments of the poet and the dramatist; but we have also, I suspect, strange, unanalyzed vibration below the surface, an undercurrent of desires and fears and passions, long slumbering yet eternally familiar, which have for thousands of years lain near the root of our most intimate emotions and been wrought into the fabric of our most magical dreams. How far into past ages this stream may reach back, I dare not even surmise; but it seems as if the power of stirring it or moving with it were one of the last secrets of genius.

The Turn of the Screw as Poem

By Robert Heilman

THERE IS probably no other short work of fiction which has been the center, during the first fifty years of its life, of such regular attention and speculation as have been called forth by Henry James's *The Turn of the Screw*. The more obvious reasons for this phenomenon—those summarized, for instance, in Heywood Broun's rather uncomplex description of *The Turn* as "the thriller of thrillers, the last word in creeping horror stories"—actually explain almost nothing. For thrillers that exert a "hideous thralldom" are incontinently begotten and die, like movies, each year; and the continuing devotion to *The Turn* has hardly been that of the multitudes in search of hashish. That devotion is significant, indeed, because it has been critical; *The Turn* has elicited special comment from such writers as Edmund Wilson, Philip Rahv, F. O. Matthiessen, Katherine Anne Porter, Mark Van Doren, Allen Tate. Since the book first appeared, there has been a series of interpretations; as these come forth periodically, and as the alterations in them show the different decades endeavoring to adjust James's materials to new interpretative methods, what is unmistakable is that James has hit upon some fundamental truth of experience that no generation can ignore and that each generation wishes to restate in its own terms. For half a century sensitive readers have felt the story exert a pull that far transcends any effects springing from the cool manipulations of mystery-mongers. Mr. Matthiessen's remark that the story exhibits James's "extraordinary command of . . . the darkness of moral evil" suggests the nature of the almost unique reality with which the story is infused. For critical readers the problem has been the definition of the evil, and the identification of the methods by which the awareness of evil is brought to disturbing intensity.

It is probably safe to say that the Freudian interpretation of the story, of which the best known exponent is Edmund Wilson, no longer enjoys wide critical acceptance.[1] If, then, we cannot account for the evil by treating the governess as pathological, we must seek elsewhere an explanation of the story's hold. I am convinced that, at the level of action, the story means exactly what it says: that at Bly there are apparitions which the governess sees, which Mrs. Grose does not see but comes to believe in because they are consistent with her own independent experience, and of which the children have a knowledge which they endeavor to conceal. These dramatic circumstances have a symbolic import which seems not too difficult to get hold of: the ghosts are evil, evil which comes subtly, conquering before it is wholly seen; the governess, Cassandra-like in the intuitions which are inaccessible to others, is the guardian whose function it is to detect and attempt to ward off evil; Mrs. Grose—whose name, like the narrator's title, has virtually allegorical significance—is the commonplace mortal, well intentioned, but perceiving only the obvious; the children are the victims of evil, victims who, ironically, practice concealment—who doubtless must conceal —when not to conceal is essential to salvation. If this reading of the symbolism be tenable, we can understand in part the imaginative power of the story, for, beneath the strange and startling action-surface, we have the oldest of themes—the struggle of evil to possess the human soul. And if this struggle appears to resolve itself into a Christian form, that impulse, as it were, of the materials need not be surprising.

[1] Philip Rahv calls attempts to explain away the ghosts "a fallacy of rationalism," and asserts, I think correctly, that the Freudian view narrows and conventionalizes the story in a way that contradicts both James's intentions and artistic habits, and, I might add, our own sense that large matters are at stake. In their symposium in *Invitation to Learning*, Katherine Anne Porter, Mark Van Doren, and Allen Tate have all specifically denied the validity of the Freudian reading of the story. I have attempted, in some detail, to show how Wilson's account of *The Turn* runs afoul of both the story and James's preface (*Modern Language Notes*, 1947, 433–445).

II

But the compelling theme and the extraordinary vivid plot form are not the entirety of *The Turn of the Screw;* there are other methods by which James extends and intensifies his meaning and strikes more deeply into the reader's consciousness. Chief of these is a highly suggestive and even symbolic language which permeates the entire story. After I had become aware of and begun to investigate this phenomenon, I found Mr. Matthiessen, in quite fortuitous corroboration of my own critical method, commenting on the same technical aspect of James's later works—his ability to "bind together his imaginative effects by subtly recurrent images of a thematic kind" and to "extend a metaphor into a symbol," and the fact that later in his career "realistic details had become merely the covering for a content that was far from realistic." In *The Turn* there is a great deal of recurrent imagery which powerfully influences the tone and the meaning of the story; the story becomes, indeed, a dramatic poem, and to read it properly one must assess the role of the language precisely as one would if the public form of the work were poetic. For by his iterative imagery and by the very unobtrusive management of symbols, which in the organic work cofunction with the language, James has severely qualified the bare narrative; and, if he has not defined the evil which, as he specified, was to come to the reader as something monstrous and unidentified, he has at least set forth the mode and the terms of its operation with unrecognized fullness.

For a mature reader it is hardly necessary to insist that the center of horror is not the apparitions themselves, though their appearances are worked out with fine uniqueness, but is the children, and our sense of what is happening to them. What is happening to them is Quint and Jessel; the governess's awareness of the apparitions is her awareness of a change within the children; the shock of ghostly appearances is the shock of evil perceived unexpectedly, suddenly, after it has secretly made inroads. Matthiessen and R. P. Blackmur both refer, as a matter of course, to the corruption of the children; E. M. W. Tillyard, in a volume on Shakespeare, remarks incidentally that James "owes so much of the power with which evil is conveyed to showing it in the minds of children; where it should least be found." Perhaps two modern phenomena, the sentimentalizing of children and the disinclination to concede to evil any status more profound than the melodramatic, account for a frequent unwillingness to accept what the story says. James is not disposed to make things easier; he emphasizes that it is the incorruptible who have taken on corruption. He introduces no mere pathos of childhood catastrophe; his are not ordinary children. He is at pains to give them a special quality—by repetition which in so careful an artist can hardly have been a clumsy accident. As the repeated words achieve a cumulative tonal force, we can see the working of the poetic imagination.

Flora has "extraordinary charm," is "most beautiful." Miles is "incredibly beautiful." Both have "the bloom of health and happiness." Miles is "too fine and fair" for the world; he is a "beautiful little boy." The governess is "dazzled by their loveliness." They are "most loveable" in their "helplessness." Touching their "fragrant faces" one could believe only "their incapacity and their beauty." Miles is a "prodigy of delightful, loveable goodness." In midstory Flora still emerges from concealment "rosily," and one is caught by "the golden glow of her curls," by her "loveliest, eagerest simplicity," by "the excess of something beautiful that shone out of the blue" of her eyes, by "the lovely little lighted face." In both, "beauty and amiability, happiness and cleverness" are still paramount. Miles has still the "wonderful smile" and the "beautiful eye" of "a little fairy prince." Both write letters "too beautiful to be posted." On the final Sunday the governess sees still Miles's "beautiful face" and talks of him as "beautiful and perfect"; he smiles at her "with the same loveliness" and spars verbally with "serenity" and "unimpeachable gaiety." Even after Flora is gone, Miles is "the beautiful little presence" as yet with "neither stain nor shadow"; his expression is "the most beautiful" the governess has ever known.

James devotes an almost prodigal care to creating an impression of special beauty in the children, an impression upon which depends the extraordinary effectiveness of the change which takes place in them. In such children the appearance of any imperfection is a shock. The shock is emphasized when the governess wonders whether she must "pronounce their loveliness a trick of premature cunning" and reflects upon the possibility that "the immediate charm . . . was studied"; when Miles's "sweet face" must be described as a "sweet ironic face"; when his "happy laugh" goes off into "incoherent, extravagant song"; and when, above all, the governess must declare with conviction that their "more than earthly beauty, their absolutely unnatural goodness [is] a game, . . . a policy and a fraud."

Is James, then, laboriously overusing the principle of contrast, clothing the children with an astonishing fascination merely to accentuate the shock of their being stripped bare? Obviously not. Beneath the superficial clash we can already sense a deeper paradox. When James speaks of Miles's "beautiful fevered face" and says that he "lives in a setting of beauty and misery," he puts into words what the reader has already come to feel—that his real subject is the dual nature of man, who is a little lower than the angels, and who yet can become a slave in the realm of evil. The children's beauty, we have come to feel, is a symbol of the spiritual perfection of which man is capable. Thus the battle between the governess and the demons becomes the old struggle of the morality play in new dress.

III

But that statement of the struggle is much more general and abstract than the formulation of it made by the story itself. When James speaks of "any clouding of their innocence," he reminds us again of a special quality in their beauty which he has quietly stressed with almost thematic fullness. The *clouding* suggests a *change* in a characteristic brightness of theirs, a brightness of which we are made aware by a recurrent imagery of light. Flora, at the start, "brightly" faces the new governess; hers is a "radiant" image; the children "dazzle" the governess; Flora has "a lovely little lighted face," and she considers "luminously"; in his "brightness" Miles "fairly glittered"; he speaks "radiantly"; at his "revolution" he speaks with "extraordinary brightness." This light-giving quality of theirs is more than a mere amplification of a charm shockingly to be destroyed; it is difficult not to read it as a symbol of their being, as it were, at the dawn of existence. For they are children, and their radiance suggests the primal and the universal. This provisional interpretation is supported by another verbal pattern which James uses to describe the children. Miles has a "great glow of freshness," a "positive fragrance of purity," a "sweetness of innocence"; the governess comments again on the "rose-flush of his innocence"; in him she finds something "extraordinarily happy, that, . . . struck me as beginning anew each day"; he could draw upon "reserves of goodness." Then, as things change, the governess remarks, on one occasion, that "He couldn't play any longer at innocence," and mentions, on another, his pathetic struggles to "play . . . a part of innocence." To the emphasis upon beauty, then, is added this emphasis upon brightness and freshness and innocence. What must come across to us, from such a context, is echoes of the Garden of Eden; we have the morality play story, as we have said, but altered, complemented, and given unique poignance by being told of mankind at its first radical crisis, in consequence of which all other morality stories are; Miles and Flora become the childhood of the race. They are symbolic children as the ghosts are symbolic ghosts. Even the names themselves have a representative quality as those of James's characters often do: Miles—the soldier, the archetypal male; Flora—the flower, the essential female. Man and woman are caught even before the first hint of maturity, dissected, and shown to have within them all the seeds—possible of full growth even now—of their own destruction.

James's management of the setting and of other ingredients in the drama deepens one's sense of a story at once primeval and eternal, lurking beneath the surface of the action. Bly itself is almost an Eden with its "lawn and bright flowers"; the governess comments, "The scene had a greatness . . ." Three times James writes of the "golden" sky, and one unconsciously recalls that Flora was a "rosy sprite" with "hair of gold." Miss Jessel first appears "in the garden," where "the old trees, the thick shrubbery, made a great and pleasant shade. . . ." Here, for a time, the three "lived in a cloud of music and love . . ."; the children are "extraordinarily at one" in "their quality of sweetness." Now it is significant that James uses even the seasons to heighten his drama: the pastoral idyl begins in June, when spring is at the full, and then is gradually altered until we reach the dark ending of a November whose coldness and deadness are unobtrusively but unmistakably stressed: ". . . the autumn had dropped . . . and blown out half our lights" (a variation of the light-pattern); the governess now notices "grey sky and withered garlands," "bared spaces and scattered dead leaves." What might elsewhere be Gothic trimming is here disciplined by the pattern. When, on the final Sunday night, the governess tries hard to "reach" Miles, there is "a great wind"; she hears "the lash of the rain and the batter of the gusts"; at the climax there is "an extraordinary blast and chill," and then darkness. The next afternoon is "damp and grey." After Flora's final escapade at the pond, James stresses the governess's feelings at the end of the day; the evening is "portentous" without precedent; she blows out the candles and feels a "mortal coldness." On the final day with Miles she notices "the stupid shrubs," "the dull things of November," "the dim day." So it is not merely the end of a year but the end of a cycle: the spring of gay, bright human innocence has given way to the dark autumn—or rather, as we might pun, to the dark *fall*.

And in the darkness of the latter end of things we might note the special development of the light which, to the sensitive governess, the children seem actually to give off. It is, I think, more than a coincidence that, when the governess mentions Miss Jessel, Flora's face shows a "quick, smitten glare," and that, in the final scene, Miles is twice said to be "glaring"—the same verb which has been used to describe Quint's look. All three characters, of course, look with malevolence; yet *glare* must suggest, also, a hard, powerful, ugly light—an especially effective transformation of the apparently benign luminousness of the spring.

The same movement of human experience James portrays in still another symbolic form. As the light changes and the season changes and the children's beauty becomes ambiguous, another alteration takes place in them. Their youth, of course, is the prime datum of the story, and of it we are ever conscious; and at the same time we are aware of a strange maturity in them—in, for instance, their poise, their controlled utilization of their unusual talents to give pleasure. Our sense of something that transcends their youth is first defined overtly late in the story when the governess speaks of her feeling that Miles is "accessible as an older person." Though she does not speak of change, there is subtly called forth in us a conviction that years have been added to Miles. So we are not surprised when the governess assures Mrs. Grose, and goes out of her way, a little later, to remind her of the assurance, that, at meetings with Miss Jessel, Flora is "not a child" but "an old, old woman"—an insight that receives a measure of authentication, perhaps, by its reminiscence of the Duessa motif. The suggestion that Flora has become older is skillfully conveyed, in the pond scene, by her silence (and silence itself has an almost symbolic value throughout the story), by her quick recovery of her poised gaiety, and especially by the picture of her peeping at the governess over the shoulder of Mrs. Grose, who is embracing her—the first intimation of a cold adult calculatingness which appears in all her remaining actions. The governess says, ". . . her incomparable childish beauty had suddenly failed, had quite vanished . . . she was literally . . . hideously, hard; she had turned common and almost ugly." Mrs. Grose sums up, "It has made her, every inch of her, quite old." More effective, however, than any of this direct presentation of vital change is a delicate symbol which may pass almost unnoticed: when she is discovered at the pond, Flora picks up, and drops a moment later, "a big, ugly spray of withered fern"—a quiet commentary on the passage of symbolic spring, on the spiritual withering that is the story's center. When, at the end of the scene, the governess looks "at the grey pool and its blank, haunted edge," we automatically recall, "The sedge has withered from the lake"—the imagery used by Keats in his account of an ailing knight-at-arms in another bitter autumn.

Besides the drying of foliage and the coming of storms and darkness there is one other set of elements, loosely working together and heavy with implications, which suggest that this is a story of the decay of Eden. At Quint's first appearance Bly "had been stricken with death." After Miles's nocturnal exploit the governess utters a cliché that, under the influence of the context, becomes vigorously meaningful: ". . . you . . . caught your death in the night air!" There are, further, some arresting details in the description of Quint: "His eyes are sharp, strange—awfully; . . . rather small and very fixed. His mouth's wide, and his lips are thin, . . ." These are unmistakably the characteristics of a snake. James is too fine an artist to allegorize the point, but, as he has shaped the story, the coming of Quint is the coming of the serpent into the little Eden that is Bly (both Miss Porter and Mr. Tate have noted other physical characteristics of Quint which traditionally belong to the devil). Quint's handsomeness and his borrowed finery, by which he apes the gentleman, suggest, perhaps, the specious plausibleness of the visitor in the Garden. As for the "fixed eyes": later we learn that Miss Jessel "only fixed the child" and that the apparition of Quint "fixed me exactly as it had fixed me from the tower and from the garden." Of Quint's position at Bly Mrs. Grose says, "The master believed in him and placed him here because he was supposed not to be well and the country air so good for him." The master, in other words, has nourished a viper in his bosom. The secret influence upon Miles the governess describes as "poison," and at the very end she says that the demonic presence "filled the room like the taste of poison." In the first passage the governess equates "poison" with "secret precocity"; toward the end she emphasizes Miles's freedom and sorrowfully gives up "the fiction that I had anything more to teach him." Why is it a fiction? Because he already knew too much, because he had eaten of the fruit of the tree of knowledge? We have already been told of the "dark prodigy" by which "the imagination of all evil *had* been opened up to him," and of his being "under some influence operating in his small intellectual life as a tremendous incitement."

IV

We should not press such analogies too hard, or construct inflexible parables. Our business is rather to trace all the imaginative emanations that enrich the narrative, the associations and intimations by which it transcends the mere horror story and achieves its own kind of greatness. But by now it must be clear from the antipodal emphases of the story that James has an almost religious sense of the duality of man, and, as if to manifest an intention, he makes that sense explicit in terms broadly religious and even Christian. The image of Flora's "angelic beauty" is "beatific"; she has "the deep, sweet serenity . . . of one of Raphael's holy infants"; she has "placid heavenly eyes." In Miles there is "something divine that I have never found to the same degree in any child." In a mildly humorous context the children are called "cherubs." Seeing no signs of suffering from his school experience, the governess regards Miles as an "angel." Mrs. Grose imputes to Flora a "blessed innocence," and the governess surrenders to the children's "extraordinary childish grace"—a noun which in this patterned structure can hardly help being ambivalent. In mid-story Flora has still a "divine smile"; both children remain "adorable." This verbal pattern, which is too consistent to be coincidental, irresistibly makes us think of the divine in man, of his capability of salvation. Now what is tragic and terrifying in man is that to be capable of salvation is to be capable also of damnation—an equivocal potentiality suggested early by the alternation of moods in the newly arrived governess, who senses immediately a kind of wavering, a waiting for determination, at Bly. And James, to present the spiritual decline of the children, finds terms which exactly balance those that connote their spiritual capabilities.

We are never permitted to see the apparitions except as moral realities. Miss Jessel is a figure of "unmistakeable horror and evil . . . in black, pale and dreadful." She is a "horror of horrors," with "awful eyes," "with a kind of fury of intention," and yet "with extraordinary beauty." Again she is described as "Dark as midnight in her black dress, her haggard beauty, and her unutterable woe. . . ." It is brilliant to give her beauty, which not only identifies her with Flora and thus underscores the dual possibilities that lie ahead of Flora, but also enriches the theme with its reminder of Milton's fallen angels who retain something of their original splendor—"the excess/Of glory obscured." So, with the repeated stress upon her woe, we almost expect the passage which tells us that she "suffers the torments . . . of the damned": she is both damned and an agent of damnation—another reminiscence of the Miltonic myth. She is called later a "pale and ravenous demon," not "an inch of whose evil . . . fell short"—which reminds us of James's prefatory insistence that the apparitions were to be thought of as demons. Again, she is "our infernal witness"; she and Quint are "those fiends"; "they were not angels," and they could be bringing "some yet more infernal message." "And to ply them with that evil still, to keep up the work of demons, is what brings the others back." They are "tempters," who work subtly by holding out fascinating "suggestions of danger." In the last scene Quint presents—the phrase is used twice—"his white face of damnation."

By this series of words, dispersed throughout the story yet combining in a general statement, James defines as diabolic the forces attacking the children of whose angelic part we are often reminded. Now these attacking forces, as often in Elizabethan drama, are seen in two aspects. Dr. Faustus has to meet an enemy which has an inner and an outer reality—his own thoughts, and Mephistopheles; James presents evil both as agent (the demons) and as effect (the transformation in the once fresh and beautiful and innocent children). The dualistic concept of reality appears most explicitly when Mrs. Grose asks, "And if he was so bad there as that comes to, how is he such an angel now?" and the governess replies, "Yes, indeed—and if he was a fiend at school!" By the *angel-fiend* antithesis James underscores what he sees as a central human contradiction, which he emphasizes throughout the book by his chosen verbal pattern. The governess speaks of the children's "love of evil" gained from Quint and Miss Jessel, of Miles's "wickedness" at school. In such a context the use of the word *revolution* to describe Miles's final taking matters up with the governess—a move by which, we should remember, he becomes completely "free"—cannot help calling to mind the Paradise and Eden revolutions of Judæo-Christian mythology. The revolutionary change in character is nicely set forth by the verbal counterpoint in one passage. "He found the most divine little way," the governess says, "to keep me quiet while she went off." " 'Divine'?" Mrs. Grose asks, and the governess replies, "Infernal then!" The divine has paradoxically passed into the infernal. Then we see rapidly the completed transition in Flora: she turns upon the governess an expression of "hard, fixed gravity" and ignores the "hideous plain presence" of Miss Jessel—"a stroke that somehow converted the little girl herself into the very presence that could make me quail." In Miles, by contrast, we see a protracted struggle, poignantly conveyed by a recurrent metaphor of illness. Early in the story Miles is in "the bloom of health and happiness," but near the end he seems like a "wistful patient in a children's hospital," "like a convalescent slightly fatigued." At the end he shows "bravery" while "flushing with pain"; he gives "a sick little headshake"; his is a "beautiful fevered face." But the beauty goes, the fever gains; Miles gives "a frantic little shake for air and light"; he is in a "white rage." The climax of his disease, the binding together of all the strands we have been tracing, is his malevolent cry to the governess—"you devil!" It is his final transvaluation of values: she who would be his savior has become for him a demon. His face gives a "convulsive supplication"—that is, actually, a prayer, for and to Quint, the demon who has become his total deity. But the god isn't there, and Miles despairs and dies. We need not labor the dependence of this brilliant climax upon the host of associations and evocations by which, as this outline endeavors to show, James prepares us for the ultimate resolution of the children's being.

There are glimmerings of other imaginative kinships, such as that already mentioned, the Faustian. Miles's "You devil!" is in one way almost identical with Faustus's savage attack, in Marlowe's play, upon the Old Man who has been trying to save him; indeed James's story, in its central combat, is not unlike the Faustus story as it might be told by the Good Angel. But whereas Dr. Faustus is a late intellectualist version of Everyman, James, as we have said, weaves in persuasive hints, one after another, of mankind undergoing, in his Golden Age, an elemental conflict: thus we have the morality play, but in a complicated, enriched, and intensified version. When the governess first sees Quint, she is aware of "some challenge between us"; the next time it seems "as if I had been looking at him for years and had known him always"; near the end she says, "I *was* . . . face to face with the elements," and, of the final scene, "It was like fighting with a demon for a human soul."

V

What, then, does the story say about the role of the governess, and how does this contribute to the complex of the impressions built up in part by James's language? From the start the words used by the governess suggest that James is attaching to her the quality of savior, not only in a general sense, but with certain Christian associations. She uses words like "atonement"; she speaks of herself as an "expiatory victim," of her "pure suffering," and at various times—twice in the final scene—of her "torment." Very early she plans to "shelter my pupils," to "absolutely save" them; she speaks variously of her "service," "to protect and defend the little creatures . . . bereaved . . . loveable." When she fears that she cannot "save or shield them" and that "they're lost," she is a "poor protectress." At another time she is a "sister of Charity" attempting to "cure" Miles. But by now what we cannot mistake is the relation of pastor and flock, a relationship which becomes overt when the governess tells Miles, "I just want you to help me to save you." It is in this sense that the governess "loves" Miles—a loving which must not be confused, as it is confused by some critics, with "making love to" or "being in love with" him. Without such pastoral love no guardian would consider his flock worth the sacrifice. The governess's priestly function is made still more explicit by the fact that she comes ultimately to act as confessor and to use every possible means to bring Miles to confession; the long final scene really takes place in the confessional, with the governess as priest endeavoring, by both word and gesture, to protect her charge against the evil force whose invasion has, with consummate irony, carried even there. In one sense the governess must elicit confession because, in her need for objective reassurance, she will not take the lead as accuser; but securing the confession is, more importantly, a mitigation of Miles's own pride, his self-will; it could soften him, make him accessible to grace. The experience has a clear sacramental quality: the governess says that Miles senses "the need of confession . . . he'll confess. If he confesses, he's saved." It is when he begins to break and confess that "the white face of damnation" becomes baffled and at a vital moment retreats; but it returns "as if to blight his confession," and it is in part through the ineptitude of the governess-confessor-savior, we are led to understand, that Miles is lost.

It is possible that there are even faint traces of theological speculation to give additional substance to the theme of salvation and damnation which finally achieves specific form in the sacramentalism of the closing scenes. Less than halfway through the story the governess refers to the children thus: "blameless and foredoomed as they were." By *blameless* she can only mean that she does not have direct, tangible evidence of voluntary evildoing on their part; they still look charming and beautiful; she does not have grounds for a positive placing of blame. Why, then, "foredoomed"? May this not be a suggestion of original sin (which Miss Porter has already seen as an ingredient in the story), an interpretation consistent with the view of Bly as a kind of Eden? Three-quarters of the way through the story the governess again turns to speculation: ". . . I constantly both attacked and renounced the enigma of what such a little gentleman could have done that deserved a penalty." *Enigma* is perhaps just the word to be applied to a situation, of which one technical explication is the doctrine of original sin, by an inquiring lay mind with a religious sense but without precise theological tools. What is significant is that the governess does not revolt against the penalty as if it betokened a cosmic injustice. And original sin, whether it be natural depravity or a revolt in a heavenly or earthly paradise, fits exactly into the machinery of this story of two beautiful children who in a lovely springtime of existence already suffer, not unwillingly, hidden injuries which will eventually destroy them.

VI

This summary of the imaginative overtones in *The Turn of the Screw* has taken us rather deeply into a view of the book as strongly religious in cast. Yet this very moving impression is produced by agencies that quietly penetrate the story, not by devices that stick out of it, so to speak, and become commanding guideposts. There are no old familiar signs announcing a religious orientation of experience. There is nothing of the Bible overtly; there are no texts, no clergymen; there are no conventional indices of religious feeling—no invocations or prayers or meditations; all there is is a certain amount of churchgoing of a very matter-of-fact sort, and otherwise the context is ostensibly secular. Thus the story becomes no bland preachment; it simply "has life"—to use James's criterion of excellence—and it is left to us to define the boundaries and extensions and reverberations of that life. Right where we might expect the most positive assistance, perhaps, in seeking that definition, we find least. Yet even in a few dry and casual ecclesiastical mementoes we sense some ever-so-mild symbolic pressures, as of a not-very-articulate wispish presence that quietly makes itself felt. These intimations of a presence would not be magnified into a solid "character" who demands our attention. But in their small way they collaborate with other intimations. The reading of the story, for instance, takes place during the Christmas season; the framework action begins on Christmas Eve. Quint appears for the second time on a Sunday, a grey, rainy Sunday, just before the governess is about to go to the late church service with Mrs. Grose; after that she is, she says, "not fit for church"; and their only service is then "a little service of tears and vows, of prayers and promises, . . ." This is the important occasion on which Mrs. Grose identifies the apparition with Quint. As the governess reflects on the situation, she speaks of the "inconceivable communion" of which she has learned—a Black Mass, as it were. The event next in importance to the identification of Quint also occurs on a Sunday—Miles's "revolution." Miles and the governess are "within sight of the church"; she thinks "with envy" of the "almost spiritual help of the hassock." After they enter the churchyard gate, Miles detains her "by a low, oblong, table-like tomb"—a reminder that Bly was "stricken with death" on the first appearance of Quint. Then Miles threatens to bring his uncle down, and it is he, with fine irony, who "marched off alone into the church," while the governess can only walk "round the church" and listen "to the sounds of worship." Here, for once, what we may call the Christian apparatus is out in the open, with a clear enough ironic function. From this we go on to the most tantalizing body of suggestion in the whole book, less a body than a wraith, indeed, and yet the more urgent for its not falling within the every-day commonplaces of fictional method. Miles's revolution introduces a straight-line action which continues with remarkably increasing tension to the end of the story. James allots 40 percent of his total space to this action, which—and here is the notable point—takes only three days. Thus he puts the heaviest emphasis on those three days—Sunday, Monday, and Tuesday. During those three days the governess, the clergyman's daughter, undertakes her quasi-priestly function with a new intensity and aggressiveness. On Sunday night she enters upon a newly determined, if still cautious, effort to bring Miles to confession; she openly asserts her role as savior. On Monday she tries to shock Flora into spiritual pliability—and fails. All her will to redeem, she now turns upon Miles; in the final scene she fights the adversary directly. She succeeds to an extent: Miles cannot see Quint. But the end of the climactic triduum of her ordeal as savior is failure: Quint comes again, as if to "blight" Miles's confession; Miles still cannot see him—and dies. The would-be redeemer of the living is called "devil"; in Quint we see one who has risen again to tempt the living to destruction—that is, the resurrection and the death. Here, Sunday does not triumphantly end a symbolic ordeal that had begun in apparent failure on Friday; rather it hopefully initiates a struggle which is to end, on the third day, in bitter loss. We have, then, a modern late-fall defeat patterned on the ancient springtide victory. To transmit its quality and to embrace all of its associations, may we not call it a Black Easter?

VII

If this interpretation will hold up, it will crown the remarkable associational edifice which is both a part of and an extension of the dramatic structure of the story, an edifice which figures forth man's quality, his living, so to speak, as a potentiality which may be fulfilled or may paradoxically be transformed into its radical opposite. This we are told, by implication, through the beauty which can become ugliness, the brightness which becomes darkness, the innocence which can become sophistication, the spring which becomes fall, the youth which becomes age, the Eden which can be stricken with death, the angelic which becomes diabolic; and through the pictured capacity, whether it be understood as original sin or otherwise, for revolt, for transvaluation of values, for denial of the agency of salvation. And this truth comes to us with peculiar shock because we see enacted, not that imperceptible movement by which man's advance in age and in corruption becomes endurable, but the transformation from one extreme to the other in pure state, in essence, in symbolic immediacy. In this poem about evil, youth is age.

James deliberately chose to omit certain matters from his narrative statement. But in his poetic statement he has elaborated upon his story and given adequate clues to the metaphysical foundations of his plot. The universality which has stimulated many critics is the Christian dualism of good and evil; this substance James has projected by poetic methods into numerous details of symbolic language and action of which the implications may, in their subtlety, almost be missed. For, like all poetic statements, James's is not direct; even in prose medium it eschews a conventional prose logic; it endows his tale with an atmosphere in which we sense the pressure of so much more imaginative force than meets the casual fiction-reading eye. In attempting to state schematically the origins of that pressure, we fall into much more blunt statements than we ought to make. We say, too forthrightly, that Bly "becomes" a Garden of Eden. As in studying all good poetry, we must resist the impulse to line up, on a secondary level of meaning, exact equivalents for the narrative elements, for such a procedure stems from the rude assumption that every part of the story is a precision-tooled cog in an allegorical machine. But we must be sensitive to parallels, analogies, intimations; thus, while preserving the fullness and flexibility of the work, we can investigate its extraordinarily moving tonal richness. And in accounting for tone we necessarily move toward a definition of structure. The verbal and imagistic patterns which have been described do not have the structural finality that they would have in lyric verse. Yet these patterns, which overlap and interfuse in a way badly obscured by the clumsy analytical process, are unquestionably important in the formation of the story and the qualifying of its meaning; they are one of the ways in which the esemplastic imagination, as Coleridge called it, works; and they collaborate closely with the larger structural units—the parts of the narrative as such—in defining this version of the struggle between good and evil.

Come Back to the Raft Ag'in, Huck Honey!

By Leslie Fiedler

It is perhaps to be expected that the Negro and the homosexual should become stock literary themes in a period when the exploration of responsibility and failure has become again a primary concern of our literature. It is the discrepancy they represent that haunts us, that moral discrepancy before which we are helpless, having no resources (no tradition of courtesy, no honored mode of cynicism) for dealing with a conflict of principle and practice. It used once to be fashionable to think of puritanism as a force in our lives encouraging hypocrisy; quite the contrary, its emphasis upon the singleness of belief and action, its turning of the most prosaic areas of life into arenas where one's state of grace is tested, confuse the outer and the inner and make hypocrisy among us, perhaps more strikingly than ever elsewhere, *visible,* visibly detestable, the cardinal sin. It is not without significance that the shrug of the shoulders (the acceptance of circumstance as a sufficient excuse, the sign of self-pardon before the inevitable lapse) seems in America an unfamiliar, an alien gesture.

And yet before the continued existence of physical homosexual love (our crudest epithets notoriously evoke the mechanics of such affairs), before the blatant ghettos in which the Negro conspicuously creates the gaudiness and stench that offend him, the white American must make a choice between coming to terms with institutionalized discrepancy or formulating radically new ideologies. There are, to be sure, stopgap devices, evasions of that final choice; not the least interesting is the special night club: the "queer" café, the black-and-tan joint, in which fairy or Negro exhibit their fairy-ness, their Negro-ness as if they were divertissements, gags thought up for the laughs and having no reality once the lights go out and the chairs are piled on the tables by the

303

cleaning women. In the earlier minstrel show, a Negro performer was required to put on with grease paint and burnt cork the formalized mask of blackness; while the queer must exaggerate flounce and flutter into the convention of his condition.

The situations of the Negro and the homosexual in our society pose quite opposite problems, or at least problems suggesting quite opposite solutions. Our laws on homosexuality and the context of prejudice they objectify must apparently be changed to accord with a stubborn social fact; whereas it is the social fact, our overt behavior toward the Negro, that must be modified to accord with our laws and the, at least official, morality they objectify. It is not, of course, quite so simple. There is another sense in which the fact of homosexual passion contradicts a national myth of masculine love, just as our real relationship with the Negro contradicts a myth of that relationship; and those two myths with their betrayals are, as we shall see, one.

The existence of overt homosexuality threatens to compromise an essential aspect of American sentimental life: the camaraderie of the locker room and ball park, the good fellowship of the poker game and fishing trip, a kind of passionless passion, at once gross and delicate, homoerotic in the boy's sense, possessing an innocence above suspicion. To doubt for a moment this innocence, which can survive only as *assumed,* would destroy our stubborn belief in a relationship simple, utterly satisfying, yet immune to lust; physical as the handshake is physical, this side of copulation. The nineteenth century myth of the Immaculate Young Girl has failed to survive in any *felt* way into our time. Rather, in the dirty jokes shared among men in the smoking car, the barracks, or the dormitory, there is a common male revenge against women for having flagrantly betrayed that myth; and under the revenge, the rather smug assumption of the chastity of the revenging group, in so far as it is a purely male society. From what other source could arise that unexpected air of good clean fun which overhangs such sessions? It is this self-congratulatory buddy-buddiness, its astonishing naïveté that breed at once endless opportunities for inversion and the terrible reluctance to admit its existence, to surrender the last believed-in-stronghold of love without passion.

It is, after all, what we know from a hundred other sources that is here verified: the regressiveness, in a technical sense, of American life, its implacable nostalgia for the infantile, at once wrongheaded and somehow admirable. The mythic America is boyhood—and who would dare be startled to realize that the two most popular, most *absorbed*, I am sure, of the handful of great books in our native heritage are customarily to be found, illustrated, on the shelves of the children's library. I am referring, of course, to *Moby-Dick* and *Huckleberry Finn*, so different in technique and language, but alike children's books or, more precisely, *boys'* books.

There are the Leatherstocking Tales of Cooper, too, as well as Dana's *Two Years Before the Mast* and a good deal of Stephen Crane, books whose continuing favor depends more and more on the taste of boys; and one begins to foresee a similar improbable fate for Ernest Hemingway. Among the most distinguished novelists of the American past, only Henry James completely escapes classification as a writer of juvenile classics; even Hawthorne, who did write sometimes for children, must in his most adult novels endure, though not as Mark Twain and Melville submit to, the child's perusal. A child's version of *The Scarlet Letter* would seem a rather farfetched joke if it were not a part of our common experience. Finding in the children's department of the local library what Hawthorne liked to call his "hell-fired book," and remembering that *Moby-Dick* itself has as its secret motto *"Ego te baptizo in nomine diaboli,"* one can only bow in awed silence before the mysteries of public morality, the American idea of "innocence." Everything goes except the frank description of adult heterosexual love. After all, boys will be boys!

What, then, do all these books have in common? As boys' books we should expect them shyly, guiltlessly as it were to proffer a chaste male love as the ultimate emotional experience —and this is spectacularly the case. In Dana, it is the narra-

tor's melancholy love for the *kanaka,* Hope; in Cooper, the
lifelong affection of Natty Bumppo and Chingachgook; in
Melville, Ishmael's love for Queequeg; in Twain, Huck's feeling for Nigger Jim. At the focus of emotion, where we are
accustomed to find in the world's great novels some heterosexual passion, be it "platonic" love or adultery, seduction,
rape, or long-drawn-out flirtation, we come instead on the
fugitive slave and the no-account boy lying side by side on a
raft borne by the endless river toward an impossible escape,
or the pariah sailor waking in the tattooed arms of the brown
harpooner on the verge of their impossible quest. *"Aloha,
aikane, aloha nui,"* Hope cries to the lover who prefers him
to all his fellow whites; and Ishmael in utter frankness tells
us: "I found Queequeg's arm thrown over me in the most
loving and affectionate manner. You had almost thought I
had been his wife . . . he still hugged me tightly, as though
naught but death should part us twain. . . . Thus, then, in
our heart's honeymoon, lay I and Queequeg—a cozy, loving
pair . . . he pressed his forehead against mine, clasped me
around the waist, and said that henceforth we were married."

In Melville, the ambiguous relationship is most explicitly
rendered; almost, indeed, openly explained. Not by a chance
phrase or camouflaged symbol (the dressing of Jim in a
woman's gown in *Huck Finn,* for instance, which can mean
anything or nothing at all), but in a step-by-step exposition,
the Pure Marriage of Ishmael and Queequeg is set before us:
the initial going to bed together and the first shyness overcome, that great hot tomahawk-pipe accepted in a familiarity
that dispels fear; next, the wedding ceremony itself (for in
this marriage like so many others the ceremonial follows the
deflowering), with the ritual touching of foreheads; then, the
queasiness and guilt the morning after the *official* First Night,
the suspicion that one has joined himself irrevocably to his
own worst nightmare; finally, a symbolic portrayal of the
continuing state of marriage through the image of the
"monkey rope" which binds the lovers fast waist to waist (for
the sake of this symbolism, Melville changes a *fact* of whaling
practice—the only time in the book), a permanent alliance

that provides mutual protection but also threatens mutual death.

Physical it all is, certainly, yet somehow ultimately innocent. There lies between the lovers no naked sword but a childlike ignorance, as if the possibility of a fall to the carnal had not yet been discovered. Even in the *Vita Nuova* of Dante, there is no vision of love less offensively, more unremittingly chaste; that it is not adult seems beside the point. Ishmael's sensations as he wakes under the pressure of Queequeg's arm, the tenderness of Huck's repeated loss and refinding of Jim, the role of almost Edenic helpmate played for Bumppo by the Indian—these shape us from childhood: we have no sense of first discovering them or of having been once without them.

Of the infantile, the homoerotic aspects of these stories we are, though vaguely, aware; but it is only with an effort that we can wake to a consciousness of how, among us who at the level of adulthood find a difference in color sufficient provocation for distrust and hatred, they celebrate, all of them, the mutual love of *a white man and a colored*. So buried at a level of acceptance which does not touch reason, so desperately repressed from overt recognition, so contrary to what is usually thought of as our ultimate level of taboo— the sense of that love can survive only in the obliquity of a symbol, persistent, obsessive, in short, an archetype: the boy's homoerotic crush, the love of the black fused at this level into a single thing.

I hope I have been using here a hopelessly abused word with some precision; by "archetype" I mean a coherent pattern of beliefs and feelings so widely shared at a level beneath consciousness that there exists no abstract vocabulary for representing it, and so "sacred" that unexamined, irrational restraints inhibit any explicit analysis. Such a complex finds a formula or pattern story, which serves both to embody it, and, at first at least, to conceal its full implications. Later, the secret may be revealed, the archetype "analyzed" or "allegorically" interpreted according to the language of the day.

I find the complex we have been examining genuinely mythic; certainly it has the invisible character of the true archetype, eluding the wary pounce of Howells or Mrs. Twain, who excised from *Huckleberry Finn* the cussing as unfit for children, but who left, unperceived, a conventionally abhorrent doctrine of ideal love. Even the writers in whom we find it attained it, in a sense, dreaming. The felt difference between *Huckleberry Finn* and Twain's other books must lie in part in the release from conscious restraint inherent in the author's assumption of the character of Huck; the passage in and out of darkness and river mist, the constant confusion of identities (Huck's ten or twelve names; the question of who is the real uncle, who the true Tom), the sudden intrusions into alien violences without past or future, give the whole work, for all its carefully observed detail, the texture of a dream. For *Moby-Dick* such a point need scarcely be made. Even Cooper, despite his insufferable gentlemanliness, his tedium, cannot conceal from the kids who continue to read him the secret behind his overconscious prose: the childish, impossible dream. D. H. Lawrence saw in him clearly the boy's Utopia: the absolute wilderness in which the stuffiness of home yields to the wigwan, and "My Wife" to Chingachgook.

I do not recall ever having seen in the commentaries of the social anthropologist or psychologist an awareness of the role of this profound child's dream of love in our relation to the Negro. (I say Negro, though the beloved in the books I have mentioned is variously Indian and Polynesian, because the Negro has become more and more exclusively for us *the* colored man, the colored man *par excellence*.) Trapped in what have by now become shackling clichés—the concept of the white man's sexual envy of the Negro male, the ambivalent horror of miscegenation—they do not sufficiently note the complementary factor of physical attraction, the archetypal love of white male and black. But either the horror or the attraction is meaningless alone; only together do they make sense. Just as the pure love of man and man is in general set off against the ignoble passion of man for woman,

so more specifically (and more vividly) the dark desire which
leads to miscegenation is contrasted with the ennobling love
of a white man and a colored one. James Fenimore Cooper
is our first poet of this ambivalence; indeed, miscegenation is
the secret theme of the Leatherstocking novels, especially of
The Last of the Mohicans. Natty Bumppo, the man who
boasts always of having "no cross" in *his* blood, flees by
nature from the defilement of all women, but never with so
absolute a revulsion as he displays toward the *squaw* with
whom at one point he seems at the point of being forced to
cohabit; and the threat of the dark-skinned rapist sends pale
woman after pale woman skittering through Cooper's imagined
wilderness. Even poor Cora, who already has a fatal drop of
alien blood that cuts her off from any marriage with a white
man, insofar as she is white cannot be mated with Uncas, the
noblest of redmen. Only in death can they be joined in an
embrace as chaste as that of males. There's no good woman
but a dead woman! Yet Chingachgook and the Deerslayer are
permitted to sit night after night over their campfire in the
purest domestic bliss. So long as there is no mingling of blood,
soul may couple with soul in God's undefiled forest.

Nature undefiled—this is the inevitable setting of the
Sacred Marriage of males. Ishmael and Queequeg, arm in
arm, about to ship out, Huck and Jim swimming beside the
raft in the peaceful flux of the Mississippi—here it is the
motion of water which completes the syndrome, the American
dream of isolation afloat. The notion of the Negro as the
unblemished bride blends with the myth of running away to
sea, of running the great river down to the sea. The immen-
sity of water defines a loneliness that demands love; its
strangeness symbolizes the disavowal of the conventional
that makes possible all versions of love. In *Two Years Before the Mast*, in *Moby-Dick*, in *Huckleberry Finn* the water
is there, is the very texture of the novel; the Leatherstocking
Tales propose another symbol for the same meaning: the
virgin forest. Notice the adjectives—the virgin forest and
the forever inviolable sea. It is well to remember, too, what
surely must be more than a coincidence, that Cooper, who

could dream this myth, also invented for us the novel of the sea, wrote for the first time in history the sea story proper.

The rude pederasty of the forecastle and the captain's cabin, celebrated in a thousand jokes, is the profanation of a dream; yet Melville, who must have known such blasphemies, refers to them only once and indirectly, for it was *his* dream that they threatened. And still the dream survives; in a recent book by Gore Vidal, an incipient homosexual, not yet aware of the implications of his feelings, indulges in the reveries of running off to sea with his dearest friend. The buggery sailors is taken for granted everywhere, yet is thought of usually as an inversion forced on men by their isolation from women; though the opposite case may well be true: the isolation sought more or less consciously as an occasion for male encounters. At any rate, there is a context in which the legend of the sea as escape and solace, the fixated sexuality of boys, the myth of the dark beloved, are one. In Melville and Twain at the center of our tradition, in the lesser writers at the periphery, the archetype is at once formalized and perpetuated. Nigger Jim and Queequeg make concrete for us what was without them a vague pressure on the threshold of our consciousness; the proper existence of the archetype is in the realized character, who waits, as it were, only to be asked his secret. Think of Oedipus biding in silence from Sophocles to Freud!

Unwittingly, we are possessed in childhood by these characters and their indiscriminated meaning, and it is difficult for us to dissociate them without a sense of belief. What—these household figures clues to our subtlest passions! The foreigner finds it easier to perceive the significances too deep within us to be brought into focus. D. H. Lawrence discovered in our classics a linked mythos of escape and immaculate male love; Lorca in *The Poet in New York* grasped instinctively (he could not even read English) the kinship of Harlem and Walt Whitman, the fairy as bard. But of course we do not have to be conscious of what possesses us; in every generation of our own writers the archetype reappears, refracted, half-understood, but *there*. In the gothic reverie of

Capote's *Other Voices, Other Rooms,* both elements of the syndrome are presented, though disjunctively: the boy moving between the love of a Negro maidservant and his inverted cousin. In Carson McCullers' *Member of the Wedding,* another variant is invented: a *female* homosexual romance between the boy-girl Frankie and a Negro cook. This time the Father-Slave-Beloved is converted into the figure of a Mother-Sweetheart-Servant, but remains still, of course, satisfactorily black. It is not strange, after all, to find this archetypal complex in latter-day writers of a frankly homosexual sensibility; but it recurs, too, in such resolutely masculine writers as Faulkner, who evokes the myth in the persons of the Negro and the boy of *Intruder in the Dust.*

In the myth, one notes finally, it is typically in the role of outcast, ragged woodsman, or despised sailor ("Call me Ishmael!"), or unregenerate boy (Huck before the prospect of being "sivilized" cries out, "I been there before!") that we turn to the love of a colored man. But how, we cannot help asking, does the vision of the white American as a pariah correspond with our long-held public status: the world's beloved, the success? It is perhaps only the artist's portrayal of *himself,* the notoriously alienated writer in America, at home with such images, child of the town drunk, the hapless survivor. But no, Ishmael is in all of us, our unconfessed universal fear objectified in the writer's status as in the outcast sailor's: that compelling anxiety, which every foreigner notes, that we may not be loved, that we are loved for our possessions and not our selves, that we are really—*alone.* It is that underlying terror which explains our incredulity in the face of adulation or favor, what is called (once more the happy adjective) our "boyish modesty."

Our dark-skinned beloved will take us in, we assure ourselves, when we have been cut off, or have cut ourselves off, from all others, without rancor or the insult of forgiveness. He will fold us in his arms saying, "Honey" or "Aikane"; he will comfort us, as if our offense against him were long ago remitted, were never truly *real.* And yet we cannot ever really forget our guilt; the stories that embody the myth dramatize as if compulsively the role of the colored man as the victim. Dana's Hope is shown dying of the white man's syphilis; Queequeg is portrayed as racked by fever, a pointless episode except in the light of this necessity; Crane's Negro is disfigured to the point of monstrosity; Cooper's Indian smolders to a hopeless old age conscious of the imminent disappearance of his race; Jim is shown loaded down with chains, weakened by the hundred torments dreamed up by Tom in the name of bulliness. The immense gulf of guilt must not be mitigated any more than the disparity of color (Queequeg is not merely brown but monstrously tattooed; Chingachgook is horrid with paint; Jim is portrayed as the sick A-rab dyed blue), so that the final reconciliation may seem more unbelievable and tender. The archetype makes no attempt to deny our outrage as fact; it portrays it as meaningless in the face of love.

There would be something insufferable, I think, in that final vision of remission if it were not for the presence of a motivating anxiety, the sense always of a last chance. Behind the white American's nightmare that someday, no longer tourist, inheritor, or liberator, he will be rejected, refused, he dreams of his acceptance at the breast he has most utterly offended. It is a dream so sentimental, so outrageous, so desperate, that it redeems our concept of boyhood from nostalgia to tragedy.

In each generation we *play out* the impossible mythos, and we live to see our children play it: the white boy and the black we can discover wrestling affectionately on any American sidewalk, along which they will walk in adulthood, eyes averted from each other, unwilling to touch even by accident. The dream recedes; the immacuate passion and the astonishing reconciliation become a memory, and less, a regret, at last the unrecognized motifs of a child's book. "It's too good to be true, Honey," Jim says to Huck. "It's too good to be true."

Synthesis

AN APPROACH NEED NOT, ought not become a rut. Although one or another of the five approaches helps to place most critics today, none serves fairly as a complete identification of any critic of stature. Yet since critics tend to emphasize a particular approach, there is always the danger of their excluding valuable points of view which lie outside the particular critical creed. Richard Blackmur, like others recently, argues against excessive faith in a single approach, against what has been called "critical monism," and in behalf of the provisional entertainment of any point of view that may send a reader to a work of literature with illumination.

A Critic's Job of Work

By R. P. Blackmur

CRITICISM, I take it, is the formal discourse of an amateur. When there is enough love and enough knowledge represented in the discourse it is a self-sufficient but by no means an isolated art. It witnesses constantly in its own life its interdependence with the other arts. It lays out the terms and parallels of appreciation from the outside in order to convict itself of internal intimacy; it names and arranges what it knows and loves, and searches endlessly with every fresh impulse or impression for better names and more orderly arrangements. It is only in this sense that poetry (or some other art) is a criticism of life; poetry names and arranges, and thus arrests and transfixes its subject in a form which has a life of its own forever separate but springing from the life which confronts it. Poetry is life at the remove of form and meaning; not life lived but life framed and identified. So the criticism of poetry is bound to be occupied at once with the terms and modes by which the remove was made and with the relation between—in the ambiguous stock phrase—content and form; which is to say with the establishment and appreciation of human or moral value. It will be the underlying effort of this essay to indicate approaches to criticism wherein these two problems—of form and value—will appear inextricable but not confused—like the stones in an arch or the timbers in a building.

These approaches—these we wish to eulogize—are not the only ones, nor the only good ones, nor are they complete. No approach opens on anything except from its own point of view and in terms of its own prepossessions. Let us set against each other for a time the facts of various approaches to see whether there is a residue, not of fact but of principle.

The approaches to—or the escapes from—the central work

315

of criticism are as various as the heresies of the Christian church, and like them testify to occasional needs, fanatic emphasis, special interest, or intellectual pride, all flowing from and even the worst of them enlightening the same body of insight. Every critic like every theologian and every philosopher is a casuist in spite of himself. To escape or surmount the discontinuity of knowledge, each resorts to a particular heresy and makes it predominant and even omnivorous.[1]

For most minds, once doctrine is sighted and is held to be the completion of insight, the doctrinal mode of thinking seems the only one possible. When doctrine totters it seems it can fall only into the gulf of bewilderment; few minds risk the fall; most seize the remnants and swear the edifice remains, when doctrine becomes intolerable dogma.[2] All fall notwithstanding; for as knowledge itself is a fall from the paradise of undifferentiated sensation, so equally every formula of knowledge must fall the moment too much weight is laid upon it—the moment it becomes omnivorous and pretends to be omnipotent—the moment, in short, it is taken literally. Literal knowledge is dead knowledge; and the worst bewilderment—which is always only comparative—is better than death. Yet no form, no formula, of knowledge ought to be surrendered merely because it runs the risk in bad or desperate hands of being used literally; and similarly, in our own thinking, whether it is carried to the point of formal discourse or not, we cannot only afford, we ought scrupulously to risk the use of any concept that seems propitious or helpful in getting over gaps. Only the use should be consciously provisional, speculative, and dramatic. The end-virtue of humility comes only after a long train of humiliations; and the chief labor of humbling is the constant, resourceful restoration of ignorance.

[1] The rashest heresy of our day and climate is that exemplified by T. S. Eliot when he postulates an orthodoxy which exists whether anyone knows it or not.
[2] Baudelaire's sonnet *Le Gouffre* dramatizes this sentiment at once as he saw it surmounted in Pascal and as it occurred insurmountably in himself.

The classic contemporary example of use and misuse is attached to the name of Freud. Freud himself has constantly emphasized the provisional, dramatic character of his speculations: they are employed as imaginative illumination, to be relied on no more and no less than the sailor relies upon his buoys and beacons.[3] But the impetus of Freud was so great that a school of literalists arose with all the mad consequence of schism and heresy and fundamentalism which have no more honorable place in the scientific than the artistic imagination. Elsewhere, from one point of view, Caesarism in Rome and Berlin is only the literalist conception of the need for a positive state. So, too, the economic insights of Marxism, merely by being taken literally in their own field, are held to affect the subject and value of the arts, where actually they offer only a limited field of interest and enliven an irrelevant purpose. It is an amusing exercise—as it refreshes the terms of bewilderment and provides a common clue to the secrets of all the modes of thinking—to restore the insights of Freud and Fascism and Marxism to the terms of the Church; when the sexual drama in Freud becomes the drama of original sin, and the politics of Hitler and Lenin becomes the politics of the City of God in the sense that theology provides both the sanctions of economics and the values of culture. Controversy is in terms absolutely held, when the problems argued are falsely conceived because necessarily abstracted from "real" experience. The vital· or fatal nexus is in interest and emotion and is established when the terms can be represented dramatically, almost, as it were for their own sakes alone and with only a pious or ritualistic regard for the doctrines in which they are clothed. The simple, and fatal, example is in the glory men attach to war; the vital, but precarious example, is in the intermittent conception of free institutions and the persistent reformulation of

[3] Santayana's essay "A Long Way Round to Nirvana" (in *Some Turns of Thought in Modern Philosophy*) illustrates the poetic-philosophic character of Freud's insight into death by setting up its analogue in Indian philosophy; and by his comparison only adds to the stimulus of Freud.

the myth of reason. Then the doctrines do not matter, since they are taken only for what they are worth (whatever rhetorical pretensions to the contrary) as guides and props, as aids to navigation. What does matter is the experience, the life represented and the value discovered, and both dramatized or enacted under the banner of doctrine. All banners are wrongheaded, but they make rallying points, free the impulse to cry out, and give meaning to the cry itself simply by making it seem appropriate.

It is on some analogue or parallel to these remarks alone that we understand and use the thought and art of those whose doctrines differ from our own. We either discount, absorb, or dominate the doctrine for the sake of the life that goes with it, for the sake of what is *formed* in the progressive act of thinking. When we do more—when we refine or elaborate the abstracted notion of form—we play a different game, which has merit of its own like chess, but which applied to the world we live in produces false dilemmas like solipsism and infant damnation. There is, taking solipsism for example, a fundamental distinction. Because of the logical doctrine prepare to support it, technical philosophers employ years[4] to get around the impasse in which it leaves them; whereas men of poetic imagination merely use it for the dramatic insight it contains—as Eliot uses it in the last section of the *Wasteland;* or as, say, everyone uses the residual mythology of the Greek religion—which its priests nevertheless used as literal sanctions for blood and power.

Fortunately, there exist archetypes of unindoctrinated thinking. Let us incline our minds like reflectors to catch the light of the early Plato and the whole Montaigne. Is not the inexhaustible stimulus and fertility of the Dialogues and the Essays due as much as anything to the absence of positive doctrine? Is it not that the early Plato always holds conflicting ideas in shifting balance, presenting them in contest and

[4] Santayana found it necessary to resort to his only sustained labor of dialectic, *Skepticism and Animal Faith,* which, though a beautiful monument of intellectual play, is ultimately valuable for its *incidental* moral wisdom.

evolution, with victory only the last shift? Is it not that Montaigne is always making room for another idea, and implying always a third for provisional, adjudicating irony? Are not the forms of both men themselves ironic, betraying in its most intimate recesses the duplicity of every thought, pointing it out, so to speak, in the act of self-incrimination, and showing it not paled on a pin but in the buff life? . . . Such an approach, such an attempt at vivid questing, borrowed and no doubt adulterated by our own needs, is the only rational approach to the multiplication of doctrines and arrogant technologies which fills out the body of critical thinking. Anything else is a succumbing, not an approach; and it is surely the commonest of ironies to observe a man altogether out of his depth do his cause fatal harm merely because, having once succumbed to an idea, he thinks it necessary to stick to it. Thought is a beacon not a life raft, and to confuse the functions is tragic. The tragic character of thought—as any perspective will show—is that it takes a rigid mold too soon; chooses destiny like a Calvinist, in infancy, instead of waiting slowly for old age, and hence for the most part works against the world, good sense, and its own object: as anyone may see by taking a perspective of any given idea of democracy, of justice, or the nature of the creative act.

Imaginative skepticism and dramatic irony—the modes of Montaigne and Plato—keep the mind athletic and the spirit on the stretch. Hence the juvenescence of the *Tempest,* and hence, too, perhaps, the air almost of precocity in *Back to Methuselah.* Hence, at any rate, the sustaining power of such varied works as *The Brothers Karamazoff, Cousine Bette,* and *The Magic Mountain.* Dante, whom the faithful might take to the contrary, is yet "the chief imagination of Christendom"; he took his doctrine once and for all from the Church and from St. Thomas and used it as a foil (in the painter's sense) to give recessiveness, background, and contrast. Virgil and Aristotle, Beatrice and Bertrans de Born, have in their way as much importance as St. Thomas and the Church. It was this security of reference that made Dante so much more a free spirit than were, say, Swift and Laurence Sterne. Dante had a habit (not a theory) of imagination which enabled him to dramatize with equal ardor and effect what his doctrine blessed, what it assailed, and what, at heart, it was indifferent to. Doctrine was the seed and structure of vision, and for his poems (at least to us) never more. The Divine Comedy no less than the Dialogues and the Essays is a true Speculum Mentis.

With lesser thinkers and lesser artists—and in the defective works of the greater—we have in reading, in criticizing, to supply the skepticism and the irony, or, as may be, the imagination and the drama, to the degree, which cannot be complete since then we should have had no prompts, that they are lacking. We have to rub the looking glass clear. With Hamlet, for example, we have to struggle and guess to bring the motive out of obscurity: a struggle which, aiming at the wrong end, the psychoanalysts have darkened with counsel. With Shelley we have to flesh out the Platonic Ideas, as with Blake we have to cut away, since it cannot be dramatized, all the excrescence of doctrine. With Baudelaire we have sometimes to struggle with and suppress the problem of belief, working out the irony implicit in either attitude. Similarly, with a writer like Pascal, in order to get the most out of him, in order to compose an artistic judgment, we must consider such an idea as that of the necessity of the wager, not solemnly as Pascal took it, but as a dramatized possibility, a savage, but provisional irony; and we need to show that the skepticisms of Montaigne and Pascal are not at all the same thing—that where one produced serenity the other produced excruciation.

Again, speaking of André Gide, we should remind ourselves not that he has been the apologist of homosexuality, not that he has become a communist, but that he is par excellence the French puritan chastened by the wisdom of the body, and that he has thus an acutely scrupulous ethical sensibility. It is by acknowledging the sensibility that we feel the impact of the apologetics and the political conversion. Another necessity in the apprehension of Gide might be put as the recognition of similarity in difference of the precocious small boys in Dostoevski and Gide, e.g. Kolya in *Karamazoff* and young George in *The Counterfeiters:* they are small, cruel engines, all naked sensibility and no scruple, demoniacally possessed, and used to keep things going. And these in turn may remind us of another writer who had a predilection for presenting the *terrible* quality of the young intelligence: of Henry James, of the children in *The Turn of the Screw,* of Maisie, and all the rest, all beautifully efficient agents of dramatic judgment and action, in that they take all things seriously for themselves, with the least prejudice of preparation, candidly, with an intelligence life has not yet violated.

Such feats of agility and attention as these remarks illustrate seem facile and even commonplace, and from facile points of view there is no need to take them otherwise. Taken superficially they provide escape from the whole labor of specific understanding; or, worse, they provide an easy vault from casual interpretation to an omnivorous world-view. We might take solemnly and as of universal application the two notions of demonic possession and inviolate intelligence in the children of Gide, Dostoevski, and James, and on that frail nexus build an unassailable theory of the sources of art, wisdom, and value; unassailable because affording only a stereotyped vision, like that of conservative capitalism, without reference in the real world. The maturity of Shakespeare and of Gertrude Stein would then be found on the same childish level.

But we need not go so far in order to draw back. The modes of Montaigne and Plato contain their own safety. Any single insight is good only at and up to a certain point of development and not beyond, which is to say that it is a provisional and tentative and highly selective approach to its field. Furthermore, no observation, no collection of observations, ever tells the whole story; there is always room for more, and at the hypothetical limit of attention and interest there will always remain, quite untouched, the thing itself. Thus the complex character—I say nothing of the value—of the remarks above reveals itself. They flow from a dramatic combination of all the skills and conventions of the thinking mind. They are commonplace only as criticism—as an end product of function. Like walking, criticism is a pretty nearly universal art; both require a constant intricate shifting and catching of balance; neither can be questioned much in process; and few perform either really well. For either a new terrain is fatiguing and awkward, and in our day most men prefer paved walks or some form of rapid transit—some easy theory or outmastering dogma. A good critic keeps his criticism from becoming either instinctive or vicarious, and the labor of his understanding is always specific, like the art which he examines; and he knows that the sum of his best work comes only to the pedagogy of elucidation and appreciation. He observes facts and he delights in discriminations. The object remains, and should remain, itself, only made more available and seen in a clearer light. The imagination of Dante is for us only equal to what we can know of it at a given time.

Which brings us to what, as T. S. Eliot would say,[5] I have been leading up to all the time, and what has indeed been said several times by the way. Any rational approach is valid to literature and may be properly called critical which fastens at any point upon the work itself. The utility of a given approach depends partly upon the strength of the mind making it and partly upon the recognition of the limits appropriate to it. Limits may be of scope, degree, or relevance, and may be either plainly laid out by the critic himself, or may be determined by his readers; and it is, by our argument, the latter case that commonly falls, since an active mind tends to overestimate the scope of its tools and to take as necessary those doctrinal considerations which habit has made seem instinctive. No critic is required to limit himself to a single ap-

[5] . . . that when "morals cease to be a matter of tradition and orthodoxy—that is, of the habits of the community formulated, corrected, and elevated by the continuous thought and direction of the Church—and when each man is to elaborate his own, then *personality* becomes a thing of alarming importance" (*After Strange Gods*). Thus Mr. Eliot becomes one of those viewers-with-alarm whose next step forward is the very hysteria of disorder they wish to escape. The hysteria of institutions is more dreadful than that of individuals.

proach, nor is he likely to be able to do so; facts cannot be exhibited without comment, and comment involves the generality of the mind. Furthermore, a consciously complex approach like that of Kenneth Burke or T. S. Eliot, by setting up parallels of reference, affords a more flexible, more available, more stimulating standard of judgment—though of course at a greater risk of prejudice—than a single approach. What produces the evil of stultification and the malice of controversy is the confused approach, when the limits are not seen because they tend to cancel each other out, and the driving power becomes emotional.

The worse evil of fanatic falsification—of arrogant irrationality and barbarism in all its forms—arises when a body of criticism is governed by an *idée fixe*, a really exaggerated heresy, when a notion of genuine but small scope is taken literally as of universal application. This is the body of tendentious criticism where, since something is assumed proved before the evidence is in, distortion, vitiation, and absolute assertion become supreme virtues. I cannot help feeling that such writers as Maritain and Massis—no less than Nordau before them—are tendentious in this sense. But even here, in this worst order of criticism, there is a taint of legitimacy. Once we reduce, in a man like Irving Babbitt, the magnitude of application of such notions as the inner check and the higher will, which were for Babbitt paramount—that is, when we determine the limits within which he really worked—then the massive erudition and acute observation with which his work is packed become permanently available.

And there is no good to be got in objecting to and disallowing those orders of criticism which have an ulterior purpose. Ulterior is not in itself a pejorative, but only so when applied to an enemy. Since criticism is not autonomous—not a light but a process of elucidation—it cannot avoid discovering constantly within itself a purpose or purposes ulterior in the good sense. The danger is in not knowing what is ulterior and what is not, which is much the same as the cognate danger in the arts themselves. The arts serve purposes beyond themselves; the purposes of what they dramatize or represent at that remove from the flux which gives them order and meaning and value; and to deny those purposes is like asserting that the function of a handsaw is to hang above a bench and that to cut wood is to belittle it. But the purposes are varied and so bound in his subject that the artist cannot always design for them. The critic, if that is his bent, may concern himself with those purposes or with some one among them which obsesses him; but he must be certain to distinguish between what is genuinely ulterior to the works he examines and what is merely irrelevant; and he must further not assume except within the realm of his special argument that other purposes either do not exist or are negligible or that the works may not be profitably discussed apart from ulterior purposes and as examples of dramatic possibility alone.

2

Three examples of contemporary criticism primarily concerned with the ulterior purposes of literature should, set side by side, exhibit both the defects and the unchastened virtues of that approach; though they must do so only tentatively and somewhat invidiously—with an exaggeration for effect. Each work is assumed to be a representative ornament of its kind, carrying within it the seeds of its own death and multiplication. Let us take then, with an eye sharpened by the dangers involved, Santayana's essay on Lucretius (in *Three Philosophical Poets*), Van Wyck Brooks's *Pilgrimage of Henry James,* and Granville Hicks's *The Great Tradition.* Though that of the third is more obvious in our predicament, the urgency in the approach is equal in all three.

Santayana's essay represents a conversion or transvaluation of an actually poetic ordering of nature to the terms of a moral philosophy which, whatever its own responsibilities, is free of the special responsibility of poetry. So ably and so persuasively is it composed, his picture seems complete and to contain so much of what was important in Lucretius that *De Rerum Natura* itself can be left behind. The philosophical nature of the insight, its moral scope and defect, the influence upon it of the Democritan atom, once grasped intellectually as Santayana shows us how to grasp them, seem a good substitute for the poem and far more available. But, what Santayana remembers but does not here emphasize since it was beyond his immediate interest, there is no vicar for poetry on earth. Poetry is idiom, a special and fresh saying, and cannot for its life be said otherwise; and there is, finally, as much difference between words used about a poem and the poem as there is between words used about a painting and the painting. The gap is absolute. Yet I do not mean to suggest that Santayana's essay—that any philosophical criticism—is beside the point. It is true that the essay may be taken as a venture in philosophy for its own sake, but it is also true that it reveals a body of facts about an ulterior purpose in Lucretius' poem—doubtless the very purpose Lucretius himself would have chosen to see enhanced. If we return to the poem it will be warmer as the facts come alive in verse. The reconversion comes naturally in this instance in that, through idioms differently construed but equally imaginative, philosophy and poetry both buttress and express moral value. The one enacts or represents in the flesh what the other reduces to principle or raises to the ideal. The only precaution the critic of poetry need take is negative: that neither poetry nor philosophy can ever fully satisfy the other's purposes, though each may seem to do so if taken in an ulterior fashion. The relationship is mutual but not equivalent.

When we turn deliberately from Santayana on Lucretius to Van Wyck Brooks on Henry James, we turn from the consideration of the rational ulterior purpose of art to the consideration of the irrational underlying predicament of the artist himself, not only as it predicts his art and is reflected in it, but also, and in effect predominantly, as it represents the conditioning of nineteenth century American culture. The consideration is sociological, the method of approach that of literary psychology, and the burden obsessive. The conversion is from literary to biographical values. Art is taken not as the objectification or mirroring of social experience but as a personal expression and escape-fantasy of the artist's personal life in dramatic extension. The point for emphasis is that the cultural situation of Henry James' America stultified the expression and made every escape ineffectual—even that of Europe. This theme—the private tragedy of the unsuccessful artist—was one of Henry James' own; but James saw it as typical or universal—as a characteristic tragedy of the human spirit—illustrated, as it happened for him, against the Anglo-American background. Brooks, taking the same theme, raises it to an obsession, an omnivorous concept, under which all other themes can be subsumed. Applied to American cultural history, such obsessive thinking is suggestive in the very exaggeration of its terms, and applied to the predicament of Henry James the man it dramatically emphasizes—uses for all and more than it is worth—an obvious conflict that tormented him. As history or as biography the book is a persuasive imaginative picture, although clearly not the only one to be seen. Used as a nexus between James the man and the novels themselves, the book has only possible relevance and cannot be held as material. *Hamlet,* by a similar argument, could be shown to be an unsuccessful expression of Shakespeare's personality. To remain useful in the field of literary criticism, Brooks' notions ought to be kept parallel to James' novels but never allowed to merge with them. The corrective, the proof of the gap, is perhaps in the great air of freedom and sway of mastery that pervades the Prefaces James wrote to his collected edition. For James art was enough because it molded and mirrored and valued all the life he knew. What Brooks' parallel strictures can do is to help us decide from another point of view whether to choose the values James dramatized. They cannot affect or elucidate but rather—if the gap is closed by will —obfuscate the values themselves.

In short, the order of criticism of which Brooks is a masterly exponent, and which we may call the psycho-sociological order, is primarily and in the end concerned less with the purposes, ulterior or not, of the arts than with some of the ulterior *uses* to which the arts can be appropriately put. Only what is said in the meantime, by the way—and does not depend upon the essence of argument but only accompanies it —can be applied to the arts themselves. There is nothing, it should be added, in Brooks' writings to show that he believes otherwise or would claim more; he is content with that scope and degree of value to which his method and the strength of his mind limit him; and his value is the greater and more urgent for that.

Such tacit humility, such implicit admission of contingency, are not immediate characteristics of Granville Hicks' *The Great Tradition,* though they may, so serious is his purpose, be merely virtues of which he deliberately, for the time being and in order to gain his point, deprives himself of the benefit. If that is so, however expedient his tactics may seem on the short view they will defeat him on the long. But let us examine the book on the ground of our present concern alone. Like Brooks, Hicks presents an interpretation of American literature since the Civil War, dealing with the whole body rather than single figures. Like Brooks he has a touchstone in an obsessive idea, but where we may say that Brooks *uses* his idea—as we think for more than it is worth—we must say that Hicks is victimised by his idea to the point where the travail of judgment is suspended and becomes the mere re-iteration of a formula. He judges literature as it expressed or failed to express the economic conflict of classes sharpened by the industrial revolution, and he judges individual writers as they used or did not use an ideology resembling the Marxist analysis as prime clue to the clear representation of social drama. Thus Howells comes off better than Henry James, and Frank Norris better than Mark Twain, and, in our own day, Dos Passos is stuck on a thin eminence that must alarm him.

Controversy is not here a profitable exercise, but it may be said for the sake of the record that although every period of history presents a class struggle, some far more acute than our own, the themes of great art have seldom lent themselves to propaganda for an economic insight, finding, as it happened, religious, moral, or psychological—that is to say, interpretative—insights more appropriate impulses. If *Piers Plowman* dealt with the class struggle, *The Canterbury Tales* did not, and Hicks would be hard put, if he looked sharp, to make out a better case of social implication in Dostoevski than in Henry James.

What vitiates *The Great Tradition* is its tendentiousness. Nothing could be more exciting, nothing more vital, than a book by Hicks which discovered and examined the facts of a literature whose major theme hung on an honest, dramatic view of the class struggle—and there is indeed such a literature now emerging from the depression. And on the other hand it would be worthwhile to have Hicks sharpen his teeth on all the fraudulent or pseudo art which actually slanders the terms of the class and every other struggle.

The book with which he presents us performs a very different operation. There is an initial hortatory assumption that American literature ought to represent the class struggle from a Marxist viewpoint, and that it ought thus to be the spur and guide to political action. Proceeding, the point is either proved or the literature dismissed and its authors slandered. Hicks is not disengaging for emphasis and contemporary need an ulterior purpose; he is not writing criticism at all; he is writing a fanatic's history and a casuist's polemic, with the probable result—which is what was meant by suggesting above that he had misconceived his tactics—that he will convert no one who retains the least love of literature or the least knowledge of the themes which engage the most of life. It should be emphasized that there is no more quarrel with Hicks' economic insight as such than there was with the insights of Santayana and Van Wyck Brooks. The quarrel is deeper. While it is true and good that the arts may be used to illustrate social propaganda—though it is not a great use—you can no more use an economic insight as your chief critical tool than you can make much out of the Mass by submitting the doctrine of transubstantiation to chemical analysis.

These three writers have one great formal fact in common, which they illustrate as differently as may be. They are concerned with the separable content of literature, with what may be said without consideration of its specific setting and apparition in a form; which is why, perhaps, all three leave literature so soon behind. The quantity of what can be said directly about the content alone of a given work of art is seldom great, but the least saying may be the innervation of an infinite intellectual structure, which however valuable in itself, has for the most part only an asserted relation with the works from which it springs. The sense of continuous relationship, of sustained contact, with the works nominally in hand is rare and when found uncommonly exhilarating; it is the fine object of criticism: as it seems to put us in direct possession of the principles whereby the works move without injuring or disintegrating the body of the works themselves. This sense of intimacy by inner contact cannot arise from methods of approach which hinge on seized separable content. We have constantly—if our interest is really in literature— to prod ourselves back, to remind ourselves that there was a poem, a play, or a novel of some initial and we hope terminal concern, or we have to falsify facts and set up fictions[6] to the effect that no matter what we are saying we are really talking about art after all. The question must often be whether the prodding and reminding is worth the labor, whether we might not better assign the works that require it to a different category than that of criticism.

3

Similar strictures and identical precautions are necessary in thinking of other, quite different approaches to criticism,

[6] Such a fiction, if not consciously so contrived, is the fiction of the organic continuity of all literature as expounded by T. S. Eliot in his essay, "Tradition and the Individual Talent." The locus is famous and represents that each new work of art slightly alters the relationships among the whole order of existing works. The notion has truth, but it is a mathematical truth and has little relevance to the arts. Used as Eliot uses it, it is an experimental conceit and pushes the mind forward. Taken seriously it is bad constitutional law, in the sense that it would provoke numberless artificial and insoluble problems.

where if there are no ulterior purposes to allow for there are other no less limiting features—there are certainly such, for example, for me in thinking of my own. The ulterior motive, or the limiting feature, which ever it is, is a variable constant. One does not always know what it is, nor what nor how much work it does; but one always knows it is there—for strength or weakness. It may be only the strength of emphasis—which is necessarily distortion; or it may be the worse strength of a simplifying formula, which skeletonizes and transforms what we want to recognize in the flesh. It may be only the weakness of what is unfinished, undeveloped, or unseen—the weakness that follows on emphasis; or it may be the weakness that shows when pertinent things are deliberately dismissed or ignored, which is the corresponding weakness of the mind strong in formula. No mind can avoid distortion and formula altogether, nor would wish to; but most minds rush to the defense of qualities they think cannot be avoided, and that, in itself, is an ulterior motive, a limiting feature of the mind that rushes. I say nothing of one's personal prepossessions, of the damage of one's private experience, of the malice and false tolerance they inculcate into judgment. I know that my own essays suffer variously, but I cannot bring myself to specify the indulgences I would ask; mostly, I hope, that general indulgence which consists in the task of bringing my distortions and emphases and opinions into balance with other distortions, other emphases, and better opinions.

But rather than myself, let us examine briefly, because of their differences from each other and from the three critics already handled, the modes of approach to the act of criticism and habits of critical work of I. A. Richards, Kenneth Burke, and S. Foster Damon. It is to characterize them and to judge the *character* of their work—its typical scope and value—that we want to examine them. With the objective validity of their varying theories we are not much here concerned. Objective standards of criticism, as we hope them to exist at all, must have an existence anterior and superior to the practice of particular critics. The personal element in a given critic—what he happens to know and happens to be able to understand——is strong or obstinate enough to reach into his aesthetic theories; and as most critics do not have the coherence of philosophers it seems doubtful if any outsider could ever reach the same conclusions as the critic did by adopting his aesthetics. Aesthetics sometimes seems only as implicit in the practice of criticism as the atomic physics is present in sunlight when you feel it.

But some critics deliberately expand the theoretic phase of every practical problem. There is a tendency to urge the scientific principle and the statistical method, and in doing so to bring in the whole assorted world of thought. That Mr. Richards, who is an admirable critic and whose love and knowledge of poetry are incontestable, is a victim of the expansiveness of his mind in these directions, is what characterizes, and reduces, the scope of his work as literary criticism. It is possible that he ought not to be called a literary critic at all. If we list the titles of his books we are in a quandary: *The Foundations of Aesthetics, The Meaning of Meaning* (these with C. K. Ogden), *The Principles of Literary Criticism, Science and Poetry, Practical Criticism, Mencius on the Mind,* and *Coleridge on Imagination.* The apparatus is so vast, so labyrinthine, so inclusive——and the amount of actual literary criticism is so small that it seems almost a by-product instead of the central target. The slightest volume, physically, *Science and Poetry,* contains proportionally the most literary criticism, and contains, curiously, his one obvious failure in appreciation——since amply redressed—— his misjudgment of the nature of Yeats's poetry. His work is for the most part *about* a department of the mind which includes the pedagogy of sensibility and the practice of literary criticism. The matters he investigates are the problems of belief, of meaning, of communication, of the nature of controversy, and of poetic language as the supreme mode of imagination. The discussion of these problems is made to focus for the most part on poetry because poetry provides the only great monuments of imagination available to verbal imagination. His bottom contention might I think be put as this: that words have a synergical power, in the realms of feeling, emotion, and value, to create a reality, or the sense of it, not contained in the words separately; and that the power and the reality as experienced in great poetry make the chief source of meaning and value for the life we live. This contention I share; except that I should wish to put on the same level, as sources of meaning and value, modes of imagination that have no medium in words—though words may call on them—and are not susceptible of verbal reformulation: the modes of great acting, architecture, music, and painting. Thus I can assent to Mr. Richards' positive statement of the task of criticism, because I can add to it positive tasks in analogous fields: "To recall that poetry is the supreme use of language, man's chief coordinating instrument, in the service of the most integral purposes of life; and to explore, with thoroughness, the intricacies of the modes of language as working modes of the mind." But I want this criticism, engaged in this task, constantly to be confronted with examples of poetry, and I want it so for the very practical purpose of assisting in pretty immediate appreciation of the use, meaning, and value of the language in that particular poetry. I want it to assist in doing for me what it actually assists Mr. Richards in doing, whatever that is, when he is reading poetry for its own sake.

Mr. Richards wants it to do that, too, but he wants it to do a great deal else first. Before it gets to actual poetry (from which it is said to spring) he wants literary criticism to become something else and much more: he wants it to become, indeed, the master department of the mind. As we become aware of the scope of poetry, we see, according to Mr. Richards, that "the study of the modes of language becomes, as it attempts to be thorough, the most fundamental and extensive of all inquiries. It is no preliminary or preparation for other profounder studies. . . . The very formation of the objects which these studies propose to examine takes place through the processes (of which imagination and fancy are modes) by which the words they use acquire their meanings. Criticism is the science of these meanings. . . . Critics in the future must have a theoretical equipment which has not been

felt to be necessary in the past. . . . But the critical equipment
will not be *primarily* philosophical. It will be rather a command *of the methods of general linguistic analysis.*" [7] I think
we may take it that *Mencius on the Mind* is an example of
the kind of excursion on which Mr. Richards would lead us.
It is an excursion into multiple definition, and it is a good one
if that is where you want to go and are in no hurry to come
back: you learn the enormous variety and complexity of the
operations possible in the process of verbally describing and
defining brief passages of imaginative language and the equal
variety and complexity of the result; you learn the practical
impossibility of verbally ascertaining what an author means
—and you hear nothing of the other ways of apprehending
meaning at all. The instance is in the translation of Mencius,
because Mr. Richards happens to be interested in Mencius,
and because it is easily to see the difficulties of translating
Chinese; but the principles and method of application would
work as well on passages from Milton or Rudyard Kipling.
The real point of Mr. Richards' book is the impossibility of
understanding, short of a lifetime's analysis and compensation, the mechanism of meaning in even a small body of
work. There is no question of the exemplary value and
stimulus of Mr. Richards' work; but there is no question
either that few would care to emulate him for any purpose
of literary criticism. In the first place it would take too long,
and in the second he does not answer the questions literary
criticism would put. The literal adoption of Mr. Richards'
approach to literary criticism would stultify the very power
it was aimed to enhance—the power of imaginative apprehension, of imaginative coordination of varied and separate
elements. Mr. Richards' work is something to be aware of,
but deep awareness is the limit of use. It is notable that in
his admirable incidental criticism of such poets as Eliot,
Lawrence, Yeats, and Hopkins, Mr. Richards does not himself find it necessary to be more than aware of his own doc-

[7] All quoted material is from the last four pages of *Coleridge on
Imagination.*

trines of linguistic analysis. As philosophy from Descartes to Bradley transformed itself into a study of the modes of knowing, Mr. Richards would transform literary criticism into the science of linguistics. Epistemology is a great subject, and so is linguistics; but they come neither in first nor final places; the one is only a fragment of wisdom and the other only a fraction of the means of understanding. Literary criticism is not a science—though it may be the object of one; and to try to make it one is to turn it upside down. Right side up, Mr. Richards' contribution shrinks in weight and dominion but remains intact and preserves its importance. We may conclude that it was the newness of his view that led him to exaggerate it, and we ought to add the probability that had he not exaggerated it we should never have seen either that it was new or valuable at all.

From another point of view than that of literary criticism, and as a contribution to a psychological theory of knowledge, Mr. Richards' work is not heretical, but is integral and integrating, and especially when it incorporates poetry into its procedure; but from our point of view the heresy is profound —and is far more distorting than the heresies of Santayana, Brooks, and Hicks, which carry with them obviously the impetus for their correction. Because it is possible to apply scientific methods to the language of poetry, and because scientific methods engross their subject matter, Mr. Richards places the whole burden of criticism in the application of a scientific approach, and asserts it to be an implement for the judgment of poetry. Actually, it can handle only the language and its words and cannot touch—except by assertion—the imaginative product of the words which is poetry: which is the object revealed or elucidated by criticism. Criticism must be concerned, first and last—whatever comes between—with the poem as it is read and as what it represents is felt. As no amount of physics and physiology can explain the *feeling* of things seen as green or even certify their existence, so no amount of linguistic analysis can explain the *feeling* or existence of a poem. Yet the physics in the one case and the linguistics in the other may be useful both to the poet and the reader. It may be useful, for example, in extracting the facts of meaning from a poem, to show that, whether the poet was aware of it or not, the semantic history of a word was so and so; but only if the semantics can be resolved into the ambiguities and precisions created by the poem. Similarly with any branch of linguistics; and similarly with the applications of psychology—Mr. Richards' other emphasis. No statistical description can either explain or demean a poem unless the description is translated back to the imaginative apprehension or feeling which must have taken place without it. The light of science is parallel or in the background where feeling or meaning is concerned. The Oedipus complex does not explain *Oedipus Rex;* not that Mr. Richards would think it did. Otherwise he could not believe that "poetry is the supreme use of language" and more, could not convey in his comments on T. S. Eliot's *Ash Wednesday* the actuality of his belief that poetry is the supreme use.

It is the interest and fascination of Mr. Richards' work in reference to different levels of sensibility, including the poetic, that has given him both a wide and a penetrating influence. No literary critic can escape his influence; an influence that stimulates the mind as much as anything by showing the sheer excitement as well as the profundity of the problems of language—many of which he has himself made genuine problems, at least for readers of poetry: an influence, obviously, worth deliberately incorporating by reducing it to one's own size and needs. In T. S. Eliot the influence is conspicuous if slight. Mr. Kenneth Burke is considerably indebted, partly directly to Mr. Richards, partly to the influences which acted upon Mr. Richards (as Bentham's theory of Fictions) and partly to the frame of mind which helped mold them both. But Mr. Burke is clearly a different person—and different from anyone writing today; and the virtues, the defects, and the élan of his criticism are his own.

Some years ago, when Mr. Burke was an animating influence on the staff of *The Dial,* Miss Marianne Moore published a poem in that magazine called "Picking and Choosing" which contained the following lines.

and Burke is a
psychologist—of acute and raccoon-
like curiosity. *Summa diligentia;*
to the humbug, whose name is so very amusing—very young
and ve-
ry rushed, Caesar crossed the Alps on the 'top of a
diligence.' We are not daft about the meaning but this
familiarity
with wrong meanings puzzles one.

In the index of Miss Moore's *Observations,* we find under Burke that the reference is to Edmund, but it is really to Kenneth just the same. There is no acuter curiosity than Mr. Burke's engaged in associating the meanings, right and wrong, of the business of literature with the business of life and vice versa. No one has a greater awareness—not even Mr. Richards—of the important part wrong meanings play in establishing the consistency of right ones. The writer of whom he reminds us, for the buoyancy and sheer remarkableness of his speculations, is Charles Santiago Saunders Peirce; one is enlivened by them without any *necessary* reference to their truth; hence they have truth for their own purposes, that is, for their own uses. Into what these purposes or uses are it is our present business to inquire.

As Mr. Richards in fact uses literature as a springboard or source for a scientific method of a philosophy of value, Mr. Burke uses literature, not only as a springboard but also as a resort or home, for a philosophy or psychology of moral possibility. Literature is the hold-all and the persuasive form for the patterns of possibility. In literature we see unique possibilities enacted, actualized, and in the moral and psychological philosophies we see the types of possibility generalized, see their abstracted, convertible forms. In some literature, and in some aspects of most literature of either great magnitude or great possibility, we see, so to speak, the enactment or dramatic representation of the type or patterns. Thus Mr. Burke can make a thrilling intellectual pursuit of the subintelligent writing of Erskine Caldwell: where he shows that Caldwell gains a great effect of humanity by putting in *none himself,* appealing to the reader's common stock: that is, what is called for so desperately by the pattern of the story must needs be generously supplied. Exactly as thrilling is his demonstration of the great emotional role of the outsider as played in the supremely intelligent works of Thomas Mann and André Gide. His common illustrations of the pervasive spread of symbolic pattern are drawn from Shakespeare and from the type of the popular or pulp press. I think that on the whole his method could be applied with equal fruitfulness either to Shakespeare, Dashiell Hammett, or Marie Corelli; as indeed he does apply it with equal force both to the field of anarchic private morals and to the outline of a secular conversion to Communism—as in, respectively, *Toward a Better Life* and *Permanence* and *Change.*

The real harvest that we barn from Mr. Burke's writings is his presentation of the types of ways the mind works in the written word. He is more interested in the psychological means of the meaning, and how it might mean (and often really does) something else, than in the meaning itself. Like Mr. Richards, but for another purpose, he is engaged largely in the meaning of meaning, and is therefore much bound up with considerations of language, but on the plane of emotional and intellectual patterns rather than on the emotional plane; which is why his essays deal with literature (or other writings) as it dramatizes or unfolds character (a character is a pattern of emotions and notions) rather than with lyric or meditative poetry which is Mr. Richards' field. So we find language containing felt character as well as felt coordination. The representation of character, and of aspiration and symbol, must always be rhetorical; and therefore we find that for Mr. Burke the rightly rhetorical is the profoundly hortatory. Thus literature may be seen as an inexhaustible reservoir of moral or character philosophies in action.

It is the technique of such philosophies that Mr. Burke explores, as he pursues it through curiosities of development and conversion and duplicity; it is the technique of the notions that may be put into or taken out of literature, but it is only a part of the technique of literature itself. The final reference is to the psychological and moral possibilities of the mind, and these certainly do not exhaust the technique or the reality of literature. The reality in literature is an object of contemplation and of feeling, like the reality of a picture or a cathedral, not a route of speculation. If we remember this and make the appropriate reductions here as elsewhere, Mr. Burke's essays become as pertinent to literary criticism as they are to the general ethical play of the mind. Otherwise they become too much a methodology for its own sake on the one hand, and too much a philosophy at one remove on the other. A man writes as he can; but those who use his writings have the further responsibility of redefining their scope, an operation (of which Mr. Burke is a master) which alone uses them to the full.

It is in relation to these examples which I have so unjustly held up of the philosophical, the sociological or historical, the tendentious, the semasiological, and the psychological approaches to criticism that I wish to examine an example of what composes, after all, the great bulk of serious writings about literature: a work of literary scholarship. Upon scholarship all other forms of literary criticism depend, so long as they are criticism, in much the same way that architecture depends on engineering. The great editors of the last century —men such as Dyce and Skeat and Gifford and Furness— performed work as valuable to the use of literature, and with far less complement of harm, as men like Hazlitt and Arnold and Pater. Scholarship, being bent on the collection, arrangement, and scrutiny of facts, has the positive advantage over other forms of criticism that it is a cooperative labor, and may be completed and corrected by subsequent scholars; and it has the negative advantage that it is not bound to investigate the mysteries of meaning or to connect literature with other departments of life—it has only to furnish the factual materials for such investigations and connections. It is not surprising to find that the great scholars are sometimes good critics, though usually in restricted fields; and it is a fact, on the other hand, that the great critics are themselves either good scholars or know how to take great advantage of scholarship. Perhaps we may put it that for the most part dead critics remain alive in us to the extent that they form part of our scholarship. It is Dr. Johnson's statements of fact that we preserve of him as a critic; his opinions have long since become a part of that imaginative structure, his personality. A last fact about scholarship is this, that so far as its conclusions are sound they are subject to use and digestion, not debate, by those outside the fold. And of bad scholarship as of bad criticism we have only to find means to minimize what we cannot destroy.

It is difficult to find an example of scholarship pure and simple, of high character, which can be made to seem relevant to the discussion in hand. What I want is to bring into the discussion the omnipresence of scholarship as a background and its immediate and necessary availability to every other mode of approach. What I want is almost anonymous. Failing that, I choose S. Foster Damon's *William Blake* (as I might have taken J. L. Lowe's *Road to Xanadu*) which, because of its special subject matter, brings its scholarship a little nearer the terms of discussion than a Shakespeare commentary would have done. The scholar's major problem with Blake happened to be one which many scholars could not handle, some refused to see, and some fumbled. A great part of Blake's meaning is not open to ordinarily well instructed readers, but must be brought out by the detailed solution of something very like an enormous and enormously complicated acrostic puzzle. Not only earnest scrutiny of the poems as printed, but also a study of Blake's reading, a reconstruction of habits of thought, and an industrious piecing together into a consistent key of thousands of clues throughout the work, were necessary before many even of the simplest appearing poems could be explained. It is one thing to explain a mystical poet, like Crashaw, who was attached to a recognised church, and difficult enough; but it is a far more difficult thing to explain a mystical poet like Blake, who was so much an eclectic in his sources that his mystery as well as his apprehension of it was practically his own. All Mr. Damon had to go on besides the texts, and the small body of previous scholarship that was pertinent, were the general outlines of insight to which all mystics apparently adhere. The only explanation would be in the facts of what Blake meant to mean when he habitually said one thing in order to hide and enhance another; and in order to be convincing—poetry being what it is—the facts adduced had to be self-evident. It is not a question here whether the mystery enlightened was worth it. The result for emphasis is that Mr. Damon made Blake exactly what he seemed least to be, perhaps the most intellectually consistent of the greater poets in English. Since the chief weapons used are the extended facts of scholarship, the picture Mr. Damon produced cannot be destroyed even though later and other scholarship modifies, re-arranges, or adds to it with different or other facts. The only suspicion that might attach is that the picture is too consistent and that the facts are made to tell too much, and direct, but instructed, apprehension not enough.

My point about Mr. Damon's work is typical and double. First, that the same sort of work, the adduction of ultimately self-evident facts, can be done and must be done in other kinds of poetry than Blake's. Blake is merely an extreme and obvious example of an unusually difficult poet who hid his facts on purpose. The work must be done to the appropriate degree of digging out the facts in all orders of poetry—and especially perhaps in contemporary poetry, where we tend to let the work go either because it seems too easy or because it seems supererogatory. Self-evident facts are paradoxically the hardest to come by; they are not evident till they are seen; yet the meaning of a poem—the part of it which is intellectually formulable— must invariably depend on this order of facts, the facts about the meanings of the elements aside from their final meaning in combination. The rest of the poem, what it is, what it shows, its final value as a created emotion, its meanings, if you like, *as* a poem, cannot in the more serious orders of poetry develop itself to the full without this factual or intellectual meaning to show the way. The other point is already made, and has been made before in this essay, but it may still be emphasized. Although the scholarly account is indispensible it does not tell the whole story. It is only the basis and perhaps ultimately the residue of all the other stories. But it must be seen to first.

My own approach, such as it is, and if it can be named, does not tell the whole story either; the reader is conscientiously left with the poem with the real work yet to do; and I wish to advance it—as indeed I have been advancing it *seriatim*—only in connection with the reduced and compensated approaches I have laid out; and I expect, too, that if my approach is used at all it will require its own reduction as well as its compensations. Which is why this essay has taken its present form, preferring for once, in the realm of theory and apologetics, the implicit to the explicit statement. It is, I suppose, an approach to literary criticism—to the discourse of an amateur—primarily through the technique, in the widest sense of that word, of the examples handled; technique on the plane of words and even of linguistics in Mr. Richards' sense, but also technique on the plane of intellectual and emotional patterns in Mr. Burke's sense, and technique, too, in that there is a technique of securing and arranging and representing a fundamental view of life. The advantage of the technical approach is I think double. It readily admits other approaches and is anxious to be complemented by them. Furthermore, in a sense, it is able to incorporate the technical aspect, which always exists, of what is secured by other approaches—as I have argued elsewhere that so unpromising a matter as T. S. Eliot's religious convictions may be profitably considered as a dominant element in his technique of revealing the actual. The second advantage of the technical approach is a consequence of the first; it treats of nothing in literature except in its capacity of reduction to literary fact, which is where it resembles scholarship, only passing beyond it in that its facts are usually further into the heart of the literature than the facts of most scholarship. Aristotle, curiously, is here the type and master; as the *Poetics* is nothing but a collection and explanation of the facts of Greek poetry, it is the factual aspect that is invariably produced. The rest of the labor is in the effort to find understandable terms to fit the composition of the facts. After all, it is only the facts about a poem, a play, a novel, that can be reduced to tractable form, talked about, and examined; the rest is the product of the facts, from the technical point of view, and not a product but the thing itself from its own point of view. The rest, whatever it is, can only be known, not talked about.

But facts are not simple or easy to come at; not all the facts will appear to one mind, and the same facts appear differently in the light of different minds. No attention is undivided, no single approach sufficient, no predilection guaranteed, when facts or what their arrangements create are in question. In short, for the arts, *mere* technical scrutiny of any order is not enough without the direct apprehension—which may come first or last—to which all scrutinies that show facts contribute.

It may be that there are principles that cover both the direct apprehension and the labor of providing modes for the understanding of the expressive arts. If so, they are Socratic and found within, and subject to the fundamental skepticism as in Montaigne. There must be seeds, let us say—seeds, germs, beginning forms upon which I can rely and to which I resort. When I use a word, an image, a notion, there must be in its small nodular apparent form, as in the peas I am testing on my desk, at least prophetically, the whole future growth, the whole harvested life; and not rhetorically nor in a formula, but stubbornly, pervasively, heart-hidden, materially, in both the anterior and the eventual prospect as well as in the small handled form of the nub. What is it, what are they, these seeds of understanding? And if I know, are they logical? Do they take the processional form of the words I use? Or do they take a form like that of the silver backing a glass, a dark that enholds all brightness? Is every metaphor—and the assertion of understanding is our great metaphor—mixed by the necessity of its intention? What is the mixture of a word, an image, a notion?

The mixture, if I may start a hare so late, the mixture, even in the fresh use of an old word, is made in the preconscious, and is by hypothesis unascertainable. But let us not use hypotheses, let us not desire to ascertain. By intuition we adventure in the preconscious; and there, where the adventure is, there is no need or suspicion of certainty or meaning; there is the living, expanding, *prescient* substance without the tags and handles of conscious form. Art is the looking-glass of the preconscious, and when it is deepest seems to participate in it sensibly. Or, better, for purposes of criticism, our sensibility resumes the division of the senses and faculties at the same time that it preens itself into conscious form. Criticism may have as an object the establishment and evaluation (comparison and analysis) of the modes of making the preconscious *consciously* available.

But this emphasis upon the preconscious need not be insisted on; once recognized it may be tacitly assumed, and the effort of the mind will be, as it were, restored to its own plane—only a little sensitive to the taproots below. On its own plane—that is the plane where almost everything is taken for granted in order to assume adequate implementation in handling what is taken for granted by others; where because you can list the items of your bewilderment and can move from one to another you assert that the achievement of motion is the experience of order—where, therefore, you must adopt always an attitude of provisional skepticism; where, imperatively, you must scrutinize until you have revealed, if it is there, the inscrutable divination, or, if it is not, the void of personal ambition; where, finally, you must stop short only when you have, with all the facts you can muster, indicated, surrounded, detached, somehow found the way demonstrably to get at, in pretty conscious terms which others may use, the substance of your chosen case.

Index